PLAY PRODUCTION

*the text of this book is printed
on 100% recycled paper*

ABOUT THE AUTHOR

Henning Nelms is well qualified to acquaint the reader with the varied problems faced by the people of the theater in bringing a play to life on the stage. He is a graduate of the Yale Drama School—where he studied under its distinguished founder, the late George P. Baker—and also holds degrees from George Washington University and the University of Virginia. He has been director of three major civic theaters, has taught and directed at the Pennsylvania State University, and has headed the Department of Speech and Drama at Middlebury College in Vermont. During this time he has directed seventy-two full-length plays, ranging from *My Sister Eileen* to *Peer Gynt* and *Julius Caesar*. He is a member of The National Theatre Conference. He has written plays which have received over a thousand performances and include the burlesque melodrama *Only an Orphan Girl*—a favorite with amateurs wherever English is spoken. Among his other works are *A Primer of Stagecraft,* and *Thinking with a Pencil,* published in 1964 by Barnes & Noble.

PLAY PRODUCTION

BY

HENNING NELMS

BARNES & NOBLE BOOKS

A DIVISION OF HARPER & ROW, PUBLISHERS

New York, Evanston, San Francisco, London

©

L.C. catalog card number: 56-10914
Dewey Decimal number: 792

SBN 389 00096 5

Arabic edition, 1962
Portuguese edition, 1964

75 76 77 78 79 80   12 11 10 9 8 7 6 5

Printed in the United States of America

To my teachers

DeWitt Clinton Croissant
of George Washington University
and
Alexander Dean, of Yale

PREFACE

This book covers in a single volume the entire field of play production. It should prove useful as the text for a regular course in the subject, as a handbook of reference for those interested in some special phase of play production, or as a guide for amateur theatrical groups. In addition, to anyone who ever goes to the theater or reads a play for his own entertainment, the book offers excellent material for sharpening appreciation and deepening critical insight and vocabulary.

Students of dramatic literature need a background in the practical workings of the theater in order to appreciate fully the plays they read. The author is fully qualified to enlighten them by virtue of his extensive experience with actual stage productions, and his book will acquaint them with the practical problems faced by the people of the theater in bringing a play to life on the stage.

No aspect of play production is here overlooked, from the organization of personnel and finances and the choice of a script to the best method for taking curtain calls. The chapters on Scenery, Lighting, Costumes, and Make-up are adequate to serve as a text for general courses in stagecraft or play production, although they are not sufficiently detailed to be used as texts for courses devoted to the separate subjects. The sections on scene designing present information not assembled elsewhere in a single volume.

The bibliography is small but select: the author recommends no book which he himself has not found useful in his own teaching and directing experience.

The book may be readily used in conjunction with other textbooks on play production, or on special divisions of the subject such as Acting, Directing, Lighting, Scenery, etc., because its organization in topical form and its full index make it easy to locate pertinent passages.

THE PUBLISHERS

Preface to the Second Edition

The late Alexander Dean's chief contributions to the theory and practice of play production were his discovery of the significance of areas (p. 85) and his insistence on the basic importance of style (p. 36).

As the significance of areas can be easily demonstrated in rehearsal or in the class room, it is now well understood and generally accepted.

Dean's theory of style, however, could be grasped only by those who were lucky enough to enjoy long training in practical theater work under a competent teacher. Hence, it has been largely overlooked. For more than twenty-five years, I have tried to find some approach which would bring at least an elementary appreciation of style within reach of the beginner in the theater. I now believe that I have found this approach in the idea that style and spirit together control the viewpoint from which the audience will regard the production. The approach is explained on pp. 33-40 of this second edition. I hope that this will provide at least one step toward winning Alexander Dean's theory of style the recognition it so richly deserves.

Several reviewers of the first edition felt that the bibliography should have been fuller. My judgment is far from infallible, and I have no doubt omitted many excellent books. Nevertheless, I do not believe that the reader will benefit if I list books which, for one reason or another, I am not prepared to endorse. I have therefore clung to my original policy of including only books with which I am thoroughly familiar and which I can heartily recommend.

My thanks are due to my old friend John Knapp for reminding me that scene builders need to be warned against using cloth measuring tapes for stage carpentry and also against using melted glue for canvasing unless the glue is first mixed with paste and whiting.

HENNING NELMS

AUTHOR'S ACKNOWLEDGMENTS

I have learned something about the theater from everyone with whom I ever worked. Each of them had a share in writing this book.

Specific thanks are due to the Dramatists Play Service and to Barrett H. Clark for permission to reprint material from my earlier work, *A Primer of Stagecraft,* and also for much sound advice extended over many years.

The photographs of productions in the Yale University Theater were obtained through the kindness of my friends Boyd Smith, Frank Bevan, Edward C. Cole, and Mabel Hastings. All of these photographs are the work of the Commercial Photo Service of New Haven, Conn. I am also indebted to Frank Bevan for much of the material in the chapter on stage costuming.

The photograph of *Jim Dandy* was made by the Jordan Studio of Washington, D.C. Permission to use it was graciously granted by the Catholic University Theater.

Jean Rosenthal, of Theater Production Service, Frederic Stover, and Raymond Wardell all helped with the photographs, and I wish to express my appreciation.

Almost every worth-while idea in modern stage lighting is based on principles originated by Stanley McCandless of Yale. Mr. McCandless has been kind enough to read, and correct, my chapter on lighting. His experience and mine have run along different lines, so we are not in complete agreement on all points. However, I believe that the matters on which we differ concern details rather than principles, and presentation rather than technique. I also wish to thank Frederick Wolff, Mr. McCandless's assistant, for many courtesies.

Finally, I take pleasure in acknowledging my indebtedness to my publishers for much kindness, of which their generosity in allowing me so many illustrations is the most obvious example. I especially wish to thank Gladys Walterhouse and Lawrence Cohen for their editorial assistance, and to express the pleasure I have found in working with them.

HENNING NELMS

Contents

LIST OF ILLUSTRATIONS

Photographs

Drawings, Charts, and Diagrams

Illustrations xvii

CORONATION, Setting by Roger Sherman

All the details of a production should harmonize
completely. In this illustration the scenery, the costumes, and the arrangement of the figures are all in
exactly the same key.

Chapter I

ORGANIZATION

A person who works backstage for the first time is almost sure to remark, "I didn't realize there was so much to it!" If you have not already suffered—and enjoyed—your own initiation on the magic side of the footlights, this book, too, may make you feel that play production is an unexpectedly complicated business. Well, so it is, but fortunately that need not worry you. The theater is the one art in the world in which it is possible to take part effectively without years of practice. This is because the beginner is not left alone but always has some more experienced person to guide him. Moreover, he does not have to learn everything for his first play, but only those things which apply to his own part in that particular production. Under these circumstances, the novice often does amazingly well.

Furthermore, the rewards are enormous. The successful practice of any art is one of the deepest of all satisfactions. The theater is nearer to life than any other art and has the advantage of evoking an immediate response. When you do well, the spectators let you know it. They may laugh, or applaud, or they may sit in that tense, electric silence which is the highest tribute of all, and which is as plainly felt backstage as the most noisy ovation.

There are other satisfactions, too, quite apart from the money that may be earned by those who make the stage their profession. The more you understand the stage, the more enjoyment you will find in the plays and films you see. The best way to understand an art is to participate in it yourself. Even a small part in a well-produced play will teach you many things that most professional critics never learn. Furthermore, the theater not only is an art in its own right but combines all the other arts as well. This makes it an ideal introduction to practical art appreciation. If you are interested in improving yourself, the theater is a training school in which a number of desirable qualities may be acquired. Designers increase their taste and knowledge, actors acquire poise and vividness, backstage workers develop executive ability and a wide variety of craft skills. Finally, an amateur theater usually attracts the most interesting people in your college or community. By taking part in production activities, you will have an opportunity to meet and associate with these people.

Your Relation to the Audience. No matter what you hope to gain from the theater, you will find that you cannot seek it directly, but must strive to improve the quality of the production. In this way you will learn most and enjoy the greatest sense of achievement and the greatest pleasure from your backstage social contacts. Groups which stage plays merely for fun never get so much fun out of it as those which put the play first and the fun second.

Occasionally some actor tries to gratify his vanity by calling attention to himself at the expense of the production. Even from the most selfish viewpoint, this cheap method of attracting notice brings no real satisfaction. Such a person always knows (though he may never admit it even to himself) that he is not acting but merely showing off, and that a pig brought on stage would attract more attention and be at least as worthy of praise.

The true patron saint of the theater is not Thespis—the first playwright-producer-actor—but that personification of the audience, 'The Deaf Old Lady in the Back Row.' It is for her that we produce our plays. Her interest and her financial support make our whole theater possible. Of course, this mythical personage is not always old and is not always a lady—though it is always safe to assume that she is a little deaf. There are few theatrical problems which you cannot solve if you will ask yourself, *"How should I handle this so that it may be most easily heard, seen, and appreciated by the Deaf Old Lady in the Back Row?"*

THE SCIENCE OF THE THEATER

Underlying the art of the theater there is a science. Everything that happens on stage is both an experiment and a demonstration in applied psychology, with the audience acting as guinea pigs. For at least three thousand years men have been producing plays and observing, more or less consciously, the effect on the audience of each pose, action, and inflection. What they learned they passed on to their successors by precept and example. They also used their knowledge as a guide in writing plays, by choosing and arranging their material in a way to offer the actor the greatest opportunities. During periods of decadence in the practical theater, armchair theorists have laid down 'rules' made up out of their own heads. Sometimes, as in the French classical theater of Racine and Corneille, practical playwrights and actors have been forced to abide by these 'rules,' and contemporary critics judged their work not by its effectiveness but by whether or not it was 'correct.'

Artificial rules are always bad, and a reaction against them is inevitable. Unfortunately, those who condemn the bad rules often go further and insist that the drama follows no laws whatever, which is nonsense. Scientifically, the theater is a branch of psychology and, like every other science, it obeys definite laws. We may fail to understand those laws, we may misunderstand them, or we may apply them incorrectly, but any given stimulus will invariably produce the same audience reaction under the same conditions.

Whether your scientific knowledge of audience psychology is conscious or subconscious, you must apply it, and that is where the art comes in. The science can be taught; the art cannot. Rules followed blindly, simply because they are rules, produce only stiff and inartistic results, though even so the results may be better than if you follow no rule at all. The best plan is to eliminate the ideas of 'rule' and 'law' from your thinking. Treat each bit of audience psychology that you find in a book, or discover from your own practice, as a principle—a guide to the solution of theatrical problems. For example, actors for three thousand years have found that when they spoke with their backs to the audience the reaction was normally unsatisfactory. Therefore, in choosing a position in which to speak, you should start out with one somewhere between full face and profile. On some particular occasion you may decide to turn your back because you wish to create an unusual effect. On another occasion you may turn your back because you feel that it will give an impression of greater naturalism. Whether you are right or wrong, you are not denying the principle about speaking with the back to the audience; you are merely saying that in these special cases the principle is overcome by something stronger. Airplanes and balloons do not repeal the law of gravitation; they find ways to turn it to their use.

This book is made up of the findings in practical mechanics and psychology which theater people have made during the past three thousand years. I have taken nothing on the authority of earlier writers. Instead, I have repeated their observations and experiments in my own work, and everything you will find here has been tested both in rehearsal and before an audience. This does not mean that all my opinions are correct. Theatrical phenomena are often complicated, and it is easy to assign effects to the wrong cause. Before accepting what I say you should test it for yourself. In that way you will acquire the all-important theatrical habit of doing your own thinking, and when you do reach conclusions you will have every reason to have confidence in them.

DIFFICULTIES

There are certain difficulties which you will encounter in reading this book and about which you should be warned in advance. The first is the outline form. It has the great advantage of giving you a bird's-eye view of the whole subject, but on the other hand it overcompresses and oversimplifies everything. A book this size could easily be written on the material in each chapter. I do not believe I have omitted anything of basic importance, but the brevity of the explanations and examples may demand closer reading on your part than would be necessary if I had more space. To compensate for this difficulty, I have tried to make the diagrams particularly clear.

Technical Terms. No craft has a less satisfactory technical vocabulary than the theater. Many of our terms are awkward, many are inappropriate, some are flatly ridiculous. They are not used consistently by different writers or in different parts of the country. Most of the useful terms are included in this book. I have tried to make the meaning of each clear where it is first used. Do not try to memorize them. Those which you see and hear many times, you will learn automatically. The rest you can safely forget.

Abstractions. You will find many abstract ideas in this book. They may confuse you at first because they are undoubtedly difficult to grasp, but although they are abstract they are far from theoretical. In fact, abstract ideas are of as much practical value as anything else in the whole craft of the theater. Remember that nothing is more abstract than the multiplication table and nothing has greater everyday utility. Similarly, the abstract geometrical path along which an actor moves has a real and practical effect on the emotions of the audience. You may have difficulty in grasping these abstract ideas because their effects seem so out of proportion to the means that they appear magical, so magical that they are hard to believe. Well, they *are* magical—a fundamental part of that magic of the theater which turns a group of painted actors moving before a background of flimsy screens into characters in a drama which, to the audience, is as real as life and far more vivid.

ORGANIZATION FUNCTIONS

The theater is a group art. Even the simplest production requires the intelligent collaboration of many people.

Occasionally attempts have been made to elevate one person to the role of puppet-master and to reduce the rest to marionettes. Such attempts have always ended by proving again that when actors become marionettes they turn to wood. Furthermore, no such attempt could be complete in practice. Every production requires an enormous number of decisions, ranging from the place to drive an individual nail or the way to inflect a particular syllable, to the interpretation of the play as a whole. Even if a genius controlling a troupe of super-robots could supply all the ideas and make all the decisions, he would lose far more by the inefficiency of his method than he would gain by making his production the creation of a single mind.

The other extreme, where each person follows his own ideas, is equally hopeless. Without intelligent direction there can be no collaboration, and the result is not a single production but a collec-

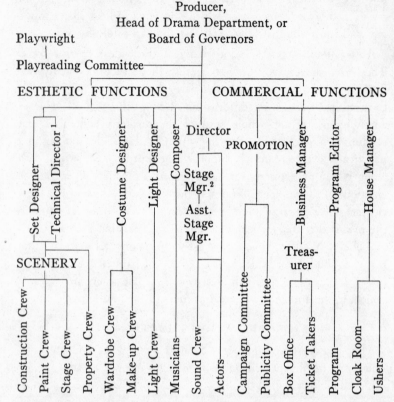

[1] The Technical Director does technical design of scenery, properties, lights, and sound; organizes the scene, property, and light shifts. He also supervises the work of the construction, paint, stage, property, light, and sound crews.

[2] During performances the Stage Manager supervises all crews.

tion of parts from many productions. This is no more satisfying to an audience than trying to assemble pieces taken from different jig-saw puzzles.

Organization Chart. You can avoid both extremes by following a wise form of organization. The chart on this page shows an organization suited to colleges and community theaters. Smaller groups may follow the same plan by assigning several duties to one person. Actually, no theater follows the strictly logical procedure of allotting a single function to each individual. This is particularly true in amateur work, where a person may act, design part of the scenery, and help with the publicity—all for the same play. Furthermore, the titles of the various offices are often misused, either through ignorance or through a desire to flatter someone. Thus the 'business manager' may be merely the box-office clerk or he may be a full-time professional who supervises all of the financial and many of the executive functions of the theater.

ORGANIZATION—A. EXECUTIVE FUNCTIONS

Some person, or a clearly defined group, should bear the responsibility for success or failure. This should involve the ultimate power to make (or overrule) all decisions. It should also include the major executive functions which are necessary to carry out this power. Such a combination of responsibility and authority is best illustrated by small professional organizations in which one man, the 'producer,' has complete charge of both the executive and the business aspects of the production. He may delegate many of his duties, but no important step is taken without his approval. In larger professional organizations the authority is held jointly by the members of a partnership or by the officers of a corporation.

In colleges the head of the department of drama usually bears the responsibility, though his decisions may be subject to interference by other officials. In community theaters the authority is in the hands of the officers and the board of governors. In both college and community groups, the director usually is given so much authority and responsibility, particularly in esthetic matters, that he becomes co-producer in fact though not in name.

The director rarely delegates his authority, though he may delegate many of his executive duties. He will find it particularly helpful to appoint an executive assistant for each play and put him (or more often her) in charge of recruiting and organizing the technical workers (called collectively the 'staff'). This executive assistant also sees that the staff functions smoothly and keeps its work up to schedule. Such executives are frequently called 'producers.' Although the title is not technically correct, it pleases them and adds to their authority in the eyes of the staff members.

Another executive assistant to the director is the 'stage manager,' who relieves the director of much of the detail of rehearsal by warning actors of their entrance cues, arranging rehearsal furniture, answering the telephone, greeting strangers, etc. During perform- ance the stage manager is in complete charge backstage. Men usually make better stage managers than women.

A third assistant keeps notes during rehearsals in the director's copy of the play (called the 'prompt book'). See Pl. VI, p. 26. Women do this better than men. The same person does the prompt- ing and is sometimes called the 'prompter.' However, 'assistant stage manager' is a more satisfactory title, as prompting is not a subject to which we wish to call attention in the program.

ORGANIZATION—B. ESTHETIC FUNCTIONS

Play selection is one of the most important producer-functions. In college work it is usually carried out jointly by the department head and the director. In community theaters it is done by a 'playreading committee' of three or four people including the di- rector. Play interpretation is also a producer-function, as every- thing else is based on it. The interpretation of a play theoretically involves the selection of the director, designers, and cast best fitted to express the interpretation. In practice some of these people may be under contract and work on any play selected. In this case the director usually helps to choose the play, interprets it himself, and selects the cast, all in his capacity as co-producer. This is always true in amateur work.

Production Elements. Every production is made up of the fol- lowing elements:

GROUPINGS. These are arrangements of the actors on the stage.

MOVEMENTS. These include both the movements of the actors from place to place, and the 'gestures,' which are abstract move- ments of the actor's limbs and body.

BUSINESS. When a movement—or a series of movements—is intended to convey an idea which the audience will recognize con- sciously, it is called 'business.' Thus, when Romeo says, "O, I am fortune's fool!" (III–1), he undoubtedly emphasizes it by a gesture, but as the audience will sense this rather than notice it consciously, we do not ordinarily call it 'business.' However, the movements in the duel scene are understood consciously as a whole, and therefore the term 'business' is appropriate. 'Movement' and 'gesture' always apply to single things, whereas 'business' often, in fact usually, applies to a series. The distinctions between 'movement,' 'gesture,' and 'business' are not important except that we often use movements and gestures to convey an emotion, whereas business always conveys an idea.

FACIAL EXPRESSIONS. These are of great importance on the screen, but are limited in stage work, where only the broadest expressions are visible.

SOUNDS. This covers speech inflections, music, and 'sound effects.'

TIMING. This involves: (1) 'setting cues,' or choosing the exact moment when any particular movement or piece of business is to be carried out or any particular line is to be spoken; (2) the synchronization of two or more things which are to occur simultaneously; (3) 'pacing,' which is determining the speed at which the various passages of the play are to be performed.

SCENERY. This is the background, or backgrounds, against which the play is acted. Such backgrounds are individually referred to as 'settings' or 'sets.'

PROPERTIES OR PROPS. These terms take in: (1) the furniture; (2) the 'trim,' which includes all objects used to decorate a set; (3) the 'hand props,' which are articles handled by the actors. In professional work, union rules make anything within the walls of a set (such as a tree trunk in an exterior scene) a prop. This arbitrary and sometimes awkward regulation is rarely observed by amateurs.

COSTUMES. These include everything worn by the actors. Union rules count a pistol as part of a costume if an actor wears it in a holster when he enters. On the other hand, a costume which happens to be lying on a chair at the rise of the curtain is considered a prop. With amateurs such distinctions are a matter of convenience.

MAKE-UP. This comprises face and body paint, false hair, and body padding. However, amateurs ordinarily treat padding as part of the costume.

LIGHTING. This is usually thought of in terms of electricity, but matches, candles, and even cigars and cigarettes may play a definite part.

Design. Every production element must be designed or selected. The design of groupings, of large movements, and of the broader aspects of timing is primarily the concern of the director, whereas gestures and speech inflections are usually designed by the actor using them. The design of business is conducted jointly by the director and the actors. One of the director's most important duties is to sit 'out front' at rehearsal and note how each effect will appear to the audience. This is a matter which an actor cannot judge accurately for himself, so any contributions made by the actors must be subject to comment—and, if necessary, correction—by the director. However, the director should never forget that it is no more his function to act the play than it is the actor's function to direct it.

Scenery and properties are usually designed or selected by the same person, though there may be a separate 'scene designer' for each set. In any case the director must approve the designs and selections, because groupings and movements are dependent upon the size, shape, and other physical characteristics of the settings and furniture. Often the director works out the general arrangement of each set, while the designer adds the coloring and decoration. The scene designer may also design or select costumes and make-up, or a separate 'costume designer' may be appointed. The 'technical director' is responsible for the technical work of design, such as the structure of scenery and properties, the method of scene shifting, the location of lighting apparatus, etc.

Music is usually selected by the director. In special cases the music may be composed by a 'composer' or prepared for particular instruments by an 'arranger.' Sound effects are generally worked out by the joint effort of the director, the technical director, and the stage manager. If the effects are elaborate, a special 'sound-effects designer' may be appointed.

The lighting may be designed by the scene designer or the director, or by a special 'lighting designer.'

Execution. Groupings, movements, business, speech, and timing are, of course, executed by the actors. Properties, costumes, and lighting are in the hands of groups which in professional work are called 'departments,' but which amateurs call 'crews.' Each crew is in charge of a 'chief' or 'head.' Usually the same crews assemble the various articles and equipment and handle them during the performance. Sometimes costumes are made or assembled by a 'costume crew' and handled by a 'wardrobe crew' in charge of a 'wardrobe mistress.' Members of the wardrobe crew who help actors to change their costumes are called 'dressers.' The head of the 'light crew' is called the 'chief electrician.' The head of the 'prop crew' is the 'prop master.' One of the traditional duties of the prop crew is to keep the stage clean. This includes the duty (and privilege) of preventing actors and members of other crews from sitting on prop furniture.

Scenery is built by the 'building crew,' headed by the 'building carpenter,' and painted by the 'paint crew.' On stage it is set up and shifted by the 'stage crew' under the direction of the 'stage carpenter.' The members of the stage crew are called collectively 'stagehands.' (Professionally this term includes prop men and electricians.) Stagehands who shift scenery on the stage floor are called 'grips.' Those who lift scenery into the air on 'lines' (ropes or cables, Pl. II, p. 14) are called 'flymen.' The curtain is controlled by the 'curtain man.' The technical director usually supervises the work of the construction, stage, prop, sound, and light crews. He may also supervise the work of the paint crew if the designer does not do that himself.

When an orchestra is provided, the person in charge is called the 'conductor' if he wields a baton, or the 'leader' if he actually plays an instrument himself. Simple sound effects, such as bells, are normally handled by the stage manager or the assistant stage manager. More complicated effects are operated by the prop crew. Unusually elaborate effects may require a special 'sound-effects crew.'

Organization—C. Commercial Functions

The main commercial functions are indicated in the chart (p. 6). Their relative importance differs widely with different organizations. One group may be content with a single-page, mimeographed program whereas another may publish a sizable pamphlet and make the advertising an important source of revenue. Again, the campaign to sell season tickets (usually called 'subscriptions' or 'memberships') is the chief resource of most community theaters. However, campaigns are less common with college groups, and are comparatively rare in the professional field.

The significance of the titles also varies. Thus, in amateur work the 'treasurer' is the man who does the bookkeeping and pays the bills. In the professional theater he is merely the head box-office clerk.

Chapter II

THE STAGE

No matter what your interest in the theater is, you will need an intimate knowledge of the place in which plays are produced. The large room of which the stage is the floor is called the 'stage house.' The opening through which the audience views the play is the 'proscenium opening.' This is framed by the 'proscenium' itself. The wall opposite the proscenium is the 'back wall' of the stage house (see Pl. II, p. 14). To right and left are the 'side walls.' The corresponding walls of sets are also known as back and side walls.

PERMANENT EQUIPMENT

A stage is primarily a large empty space in which temporary structures may be quickly and easily erected. Some equipment is essential, but the more elaborate devices, such as revolving and elevator stages, are usually more trouble than they are worth.

Curtains. These may either 'fly' (i.e., be raised and lowered) or 'draw' as shown in the diagram. Draw curtains run on tracks which should overlap 2'0" or 2'6" (read "two feet or two feet six inches") in the center. The curtains should hang from little rollers, not the wooden balls sometimes sold.

The Inner Proscenium. The real frame of the stage picture is located immediately behind the curtain. As it must be adjusted to fit scenes of different sizes, it is made in three parts. The horizontal member at the top is the 'teaser.' This is usually a wooden framework, covered with canvas and heavily painted to keep the stage lights from shining through it when the auditorium is dark. Sometimes a valance is draped on the audience side of the teaser for ornamental purposes. The sides of the inner proscenium are called

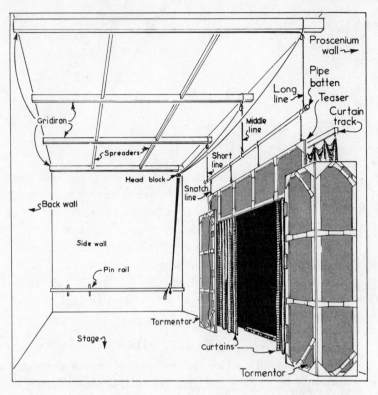

'tormentors.' Each tormentor usually consists of two canvas-covered frames hinged together like a screen. Such tormentors provide a rigid support to which the edges of the scenery are attached. The drapery tormentors often found in high schools are useless for this purpose.

Rigging. Flown scenery is attached by ropes called 'snatch lines' to pieces of pipe called 'pipe battens.' These battens are raised and lowered by 'lines.' To simplify the diagram, only the lines that control the teaser are shown, but in practice from six to thirty battens with their accompanying lines will be needed. Each line has its own pulley, or 'loft block,' and all three lines lead over the 'head block,' which has three wheels called 'sheaves.' The lines are then brought down to the 'pin rail' where they are 'tied off.' If the lines are of ordinary rope, the pin rail is a heavy beam or pipe placed about 4'0" from the floor and fitted with belaying pins like those used on sailing ships. In elaborate systems employing counter-weights, the lines are of steel cable, and the pin rail is equipped with patented locking devices. The total weight of the flown scenery pulls *up* on the pin rail, so it must be well anchored.

The rigging system is supported by the 'gridiron' or 'grid.' A simple type is shown in Pl. II. Such a grid should be capable of carrying a total safe load of at least 1000 lbs. The four main beams bear the weight of the load in unequal proportions. If a pipe batten and its attached scenery weigh 40 pounds, the head-block beam must bear the whole 40 pounds; the beams supporting the 'short' and 'long' lines (see diagram) will take only 10 lbs. each, while the 'middle' beam carries 20 lbs. The weight tends to pull the beams together, so 'spreaders' must be installed to prevent this.

Background. If the back wall of the stage house is plastered and then painted a pale gray-blue, it will serve either as a sky or as a screen on which lighting effects can be projected. Sometimes this plastered wall is elaborated into a quarter-sphere called a 'dome.' Spectacular lighting effects are possible with domes, but for the ordinary play they often interfere with the scene shifting. Some-times a 'sky cyclorama,' which is a half-cylinder of light blue canvas, takes the place of a dome. A sky cyclorama is less of a nuisance than a dome, as it can be moved out of the way. Nevertheless, it is not worth the trouble it causes unless the theater specializes in spectacu-lar or experimental plays. Do not confuse the sky cyclorama with the drapery cycloramas with which most high-school stages are equipped, and which serve as a substitute for ordinary scenery.

Traps. Openings in the stage floor are occasionally desirable. Unfortunately, the 'traps' which cover them are a source of endless annoyance, as they squeak when walked on and make the stage floor uneven. For most theaters, openings in the stage are more trouble than they are worth. On the rare occasions when such an opening is essential, you can build a platform and cut a hole in that rather than in the stage floor.

STAGE GEOGRAPHY

The principal terms used in giving stage directions are shown in Pls. III and IV, pp. 16 and 17. If you are not already familiar

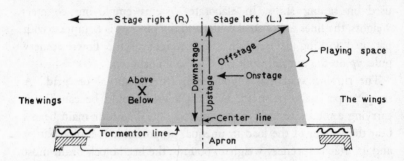

STAGE GEOGRAPHY

Directions

The four points of the stage compass are: (1) 'Stage right,' abbreviated 'R.' (i.e., toward the actor's right as he faces the audience). (2) 'Stage left,' abbreviated 'L.' (i.e., toward the actor's left). (3) 'Downstage' (i.e., toward the audience). (4) 'Upstage' (i.e., away from the audience). The sides of the stage are sometimes called 'prompt' and 'OP' (opposite prompt) instead of R. and L. However, there is no fixed rule as to which is which. Anything upstage of an object is said to be 'above' it, as the word 'above' is above the cross in the diagram. Anything between an object and the audience is 'below' the object. When anything is vertically above or below an object we use the terms 'over' and 'under.' 'Offstage' is an adjective and adverb meaning 'away from the center of the stage.' 'Onstage' is the corresponding adjective and adverb meaning 'toward the center of the stage.' We also use the phrases 'on stage' (i.e., 'on the stage') and 'off stage' (i.e., 'not on the stage'). That part of the stage used by the actors when they are visible to the audience is called the 'playing space.' The hidden portion on either side is 'the wings.' The hidden space overhead is called 'the flies.' The imaginary line on the floor joining the tormentors is the 'tormentor line.' Another imaginary line on the floor, perpendicular to the tormentor line at its center, is called the 'center line.' The intersection of the tormentor line and the center line is an important point, as all measurements for scenery are made from it. The exact spot should be permanently marked by driving a nail there, so that its head is flush with the floor. That part of the stage which is downstage of the tormentor line is called the 'apron.' All the floor plans in this book are drawn with the footlights at the bottom. Working drawings made for the use of the building crew often show the footlights at the top.

You cannot hope to carry out any activity in the theater effectively until you are thoroughly familiar with the stage itself. A bare stage has only three real landmarks, the footlights and the two tormentors. However, the imaginary landmarks are just as important as the real ones, and you should be able to locate them and to follow any path on the stage without giving it a moment's thought. If you cannot find a stage to practice on, let one side of your room represent the footlights and make sure you understand all the terms that are mentioned on this page and the next.

Plate IV 17

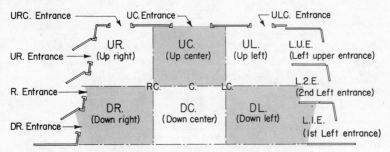

STAGE GEOGRAPHY

Areas

The playing space is conveniently divided into six areas. These are referred to constantly, so both their names and the abbreviations (UC., DL., etc.) should be thoroughly familiar. RC., C., and LC. are points, not areas. The points URC., DRC., ULC., and DLC. are also used occasionally. URC., of course, means 'up right center,' i.e., above RC. on the line between UR. and UC. The other abbreviations may be interpreted on the same principle.

As the small sketch indicates, an area is not something permanent which can be bounded by lines painted on the floor, but should be thought of as a natural space made by the furniture and the walls. The exact dividing lines between areas are never either clear-cut or important.

Although the limits of the areas are vague, the areas themselves are of great practical use. They are the basis on which the designer plans his sets, the electrician works out his lighting, and the director arranges his groupings and movements. Actors and staff workers must be able to think in terms of areas in order to carry out directions easily and without hesitation.

The modern names of the various openings in the set (exits and entrances) are shown on the R. of the plan. Terms for openings in the back wall follow the same system. Note that UR. is in the side wall whereas URC. is in the back wall.

In the old-fashioned type of scenery, still used for musical comedies and formal settings, the sides consist of a number of separate units, as shown on the L. of the plan. Each unit is called a 'wing.' Do not confuse these with 'the wings,' which is the space hidden by the scenery wings. Openings between the scenery wings are called 'wing entrances.' The one behind the L. tormentor is 'L.1.E.' (or '1.L.E.' or 'L.E.1.'), meaning the first or downstage entrance L. Succeeding entrances are numbered 'L.2.E.,' 'L.3.E.,' etc. The one farthest upstage is called 'L.U.E.'

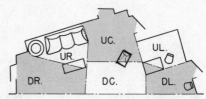

For front view of this set, see p. 147 and also A, Fig. 4, Pl. XXIV, p. 170.

Plate V

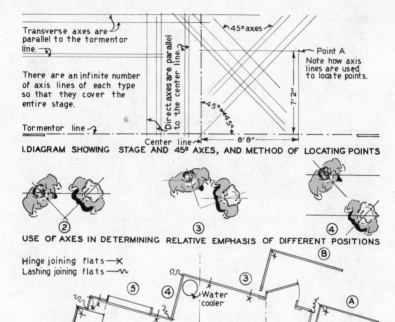

Transverse axes are parallel to the tormentor line.

Direct axes are parallel to the center line.

45° axes

Point A
Note how axis lines are used to locate points.

There are an infinite number of axis lines of each type so that they cover the entire stage.

45°
45°

7'2"

Tormentor line

45°

8'8"

Center line

I. DIAGRAM SHOWING STAGE AND 45° AXES, AND METHOD OF LOCATING POINTS

USE OF AXES IN DETERMINING RELATIVE EMPHASIS OF DIFFERENT POSITIONS

② ③ ④

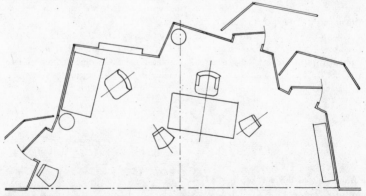

Hinge joining flats — ✕
Lashing joining flats — ∿

⑤ ④ ③ ② ① ⑥ Ⓐ Ⓑ Ⓒ

Water cooler

Scrap basket

Bookcase

p q r

5. SET DESIGNED ON ITS OWN AXES — METHOD OF FIXING ACTORS' POSITIONS

6. CONFUSED EFFECT WHEN SAME SET IS DESIGNED WITHOUT REGARD TO AXES

with these, you should study them until their use becomes second nature. No matter what else you learn, you will never feel really at home in the theater until you can find your way around the stage without thinking.

STAGE GEOGRAPHY—AXES

Points on a map are located by the intersection of the lines of latitude and longitude. There are an infinite number of such lines, but only the important ones are marked. Imaginary lines used for the same purpose in the theater are called 'axes.' The two sets of 'stage axes' are mutually perpendicular—that is, they meet each other at right angles (Fig. 1, Pl. V, p. 18). The 'transverse axes' run across stage, parallel to the tormentor line. The 'direct axes' run up- and down-stage, parallel to the center line.

Suppose the designer's floor plan shows a floor lamp at point A, which is 8'8" L. and 7'2" upstage. To locate it, draw the center and tormentor lines on the stage floor with chalk or paint. Then measure 8'8" along the tormentor line and 7'2" upstage, parallel to the center line.

The stage axes are also useful guides for the actor and director. A character's relative importance is to a large extent governed by his distance from the tormentor line. This is why a haughty person is said to be 'upstage.' When two characters are of equal importance, they normally stand on the same transverse axis (Fig. 2). If one character is more important, he usually stands upstage (Fig. 3). In either case the transverse axes serve as reference lines. Until a young actor develops an awareness of the stage axes, he will continually make mistakes in his position. The floor boards of the stage will be on either the transverse or the direct axis, and the young actor will find this helpful in locating himself until he develops a feel for the axes. The floor boards are useful only in rehearsal, as the actor cannot afford to locate himself by glancing surreptitiously at the floor during performance.

Angles. The angle that the actor makes with the audience is also of basic importance (Figs. 2 and 3, Pl. V, and Fig. 2, Pl. XXI, p. 150). An actor who faces along a transverse axis relates himself primarily to the play. One who faces downstage along a direct axis relates himself primarily to the audience. Usually, of course, an actor faces at an angle between these extremes, and the axes are used as base lines from which the angle is gauged.

45° Axes.　The actor and director will find it convenient to recognize a second system of mutually perpendicular axes placed at 45° to the stage axes (Fig. 1, Pl. V). An actor who faces downstage along a 45° axis is relating himself equally to the play and the audience. As both relationships are usually important, it follows that the 45° position is by far the most common. The experienced actor adopts the 45° position as normal during the first few rehearsals and then modifies it as occasion demands. Until an actor acquires this habit he has an unfortunate tendency either to turn his back on the audience or to face downstage along a direct axis. Neither angle is much used in practice, so the director must waste valuable time turning the neophyte around.

Movement along a 45° axis seems more forceful than movement along a stage axis and is therefore appropriate to dramatic and emotional scenes.

Set Axes.　When the back wall of a set is on a transverse axis, the set is said to be 'placed parallel' (i.e., parallel to the tormentor line). When the principal walls of the set are at an angle to the stage axes, the set is said to be 'raked' (Fig. 5, Pl. V). The positions and movements of the actors in a raked set differ in many respects from those used in a set which is placed parallel. Furthermore, the two types of sets differ in the emotional effect they have on the audience. Raked sets are 'dynamic'; they suggest movement and lend themselves to scenes of action. Sets placed parallel are 'static' and are appropriate to plays dominated by the intellect, including comedies where the laughter is aroused by the lines rather than the action.

Fig. 5 shows how a raked set is given a sense of order and arrangement by placing the walls at right angles to each other. Compare the lack of vividness in Fig. 6, which is the same set but with the walls allowed to sprawl every which way. Even a glance is enough to make you realize instinctively that a scene played in Fig. 5 would be more effective and forceful than the same scene played in Fig. 6. The difference is not due to the fact that the walls of a real room normally meet at right angles, but to the fact that the set in Fig. 5

follows a definite order or pattern, whereas the walls in Fig. 6 are placed at random and give a haphazard effect.

When the walls of a setting meet at right angles, they establish a new set of mutually perpendicular axes, as shown in Fig. 5. The most important of these axes are those which pass through the centers of things or along their edges. Props may be located by using such axes. The two desks, the swivel chair R., and the bookcase L. are all on the same axis. The chair downstage of the desk C. has its back in line with the R. edge of that desk, and its center in line with the downstage edge of the desk R. Fig. 5 represents an efficient office. To convey an impression of efficiency all the props have been placed on the set axes except the chair, L., which is on the stage axes. Usually a more casual effect is desired, as in Fig. 2, Pl. XXV, p. 174, where the L. wall and the chairs near it are on the stage axes, and the chair by the piano is deliberately placed off axis.

When an actor moves or faces along one of the set axes, he definitely relates himself to the set. Many subtle effects can be based upon this fact. If one character tends to move or face along the stage axes while the others usually move or face along the set axes, the audience will feel instinctively that the first character is an outsider and that the others are at home. In a raked set, the set axes supply the need for diagonal axes, so the 45° axes cease to be of importance.

Locating the Actor. Each actor's exact position is important at every moment of the play. An actor cannot remember a particular spot on the floor, so he locates himself by means of axis lines. Either stage or set axes, or a combination of the two, may be used. The actor at p in Fig. 5, Pl. V uses the set axes of the wall and the upstage edge of the desk C. The actor at q uses the stage axes from the R. jamb of the door C. and the corner of the wall. The actor at r finds his place at the intersection of the transverse axis through the chair L. and the set axis through the center of the door L. The choice of axes is largely a matter of convenience, though relationships do play some part; e.g., the actor at p is related to the set, whereas the actor at q is not.

Chapter III

THE SCRIPT

Under normal conditions a play is originated by a playwright. He is the 'original artist,' while the producer, director, designers, and actors are 'interpretive artists.' This does not mean that they are less important or contribute less; often they contribute a great deal more. It does mean that the script is the foundation on which they build. Competent interpretive artists can mold a script amazingly. I have known of a case in which the character who was the hero in one production was made the villain in another without changing a word of the text. However, both these interpretations were inherent in the script. If they had not been, such a shift in point of view would have been impossible.

The first function of a script is to inspire the interpretive artists—to make them say, "There are wonderful opportunities here!" If the script fails to do this, nothing happens. This may not be the fault of the script. I have been left unmoved by scripts which inspired other directors to splendid productions. If the interpretive artist is not inspired by the script, he is like a carpenter following a blueprint that he does not understand.

The second function of the script is to supply the words the actors will speak; in fact, a script is often called 'the book of the words.' Sometimes these words may be cut or changed deliberately, but there is no excuse for changing them at random. The actor who 'gets the idea,' and then paraphrases his speeches, assumes that he can make up better words offhand than the playwright could after long thought. This assumption is rarely justified.

Printed scripts often contain much more than the words. Many of them have elaborate stage directions as well. Occasionally these explain the meaning of some line which would otherwise be obscure, but usually they are more confusing than helpful. The printed directions are either from an imaginary production in the play-wright's mind or from the Broadway production. Your production will differ from both. You will have a different audience, different scenery, different actors, and to some extent at least a different in-terpretation. A few of the printed directions will fit your production; the rest will lead you astray. You probably cannot tell which is which. Even if you decide to read all the directions, do not follow them blindly.

PLAY SELECTION

A play should be chosen for the audience, and *not* because it offers opportunities for the director and actors to display their talents. The standard of excellence should be the best your spectators can appreciate. Do not give them the lowest trash they will accept and do not try to elevate their taste by offering something 'too good for them.' No audience can be bored and improved at the same time.

Many young directors go through a stage where they believe that vagueness and an unhappy ending make a play Art. No audience will agree with this. A few plays are great in spite of being vague, but no play is great because it is vague. As for tragedy, remember that if a play is to succeed it must end satisfactorily for the audience, whether or not it ends tragically for the characters.

Tests. Once you are sure that the play suits your audience, ask yourself the following questions:

Can your director direct it? If a director does not understand a play, or has a personal dislike for it, he cannot do it justice. Either find another director or choose another play.

Can you cast it from the actors available? This is always guess-work to some extent, but if you cannot think of at least one poten-tial actor for each role, the odds against success are too heavy. When even one important role is seriously miscast, the play is almost certain to fail.

Can you stage it? You will be foolish to attempt a play that depends on scenery or costumes which you are unable to provide. If you must shift a number of scenes quickly, or make a ghost disappear, be sure you know how you can do these things *before* you select the play. Also ask yourself whether the play is worth the trouble. A number of weak plays exist which may be satisfactory if supported by elaborate staging, but with the same money and effort you could stage a really fine play and produce twice the effect.

Planning a Season. Most amateur productions are not isolated events but parts of a season, and their relationship to each other must be considered as well as their individual worth and practicability. The first rule is to vary your program as much as possible. Choose plays of contrasting type—a melodrama, a comedy, a drama, a spectacle, a farce. Have the size of the cast vary from play to play. Also have the setting vary—a succession of living-room plays will be a little dull even if the plays are all good; include plays which call for exteriors, or something fantastic.

After your plays have been selected, the order in which they are arranged is also important. The play most likely to be popular should end the season, to leave your patrons in a good mood for the following year. The second most popular play should come first. Serious plays do best in winter; February is a good time for your lavish spectacle, or for some novelty.

PLAY CUTTING

Some directors boast that they never cut a line for profanity or salaciousness, but give the play "just as it was done on Broadway." Unfortunately, Broadway lines require Broadway actors and a Broadway audience. Amateur actors, no matter how lurid their own language may be, have trouble with stage profanity. They either swallow the words or shout them. In either case the Broadway lines do not give the Broadway effect. Also, New York audiences have grown callous to profanity and vulgarity. The theater deals in effects. If you want the Broadway effect you cannot get it by the Broadway words any more than a glass of whiskey would have the same effect on a teetotaler that it has on a drunkard. In cutting profanity, the first step is to eliminate all the words which add nothing to the meaning of the sentences in which they appear. You will find that nine out of ten can be cut on this basis. Next, note those cases where some expletive is necessary but where milder words

Middlebury College

THE MAN WHO CAME TO DINNER
Setting by Henning Nelms

This set is crowded into a stage only 22' 7" wide. Such a restricted stage makes the work of the designer and the director much more difficult. Even a small setting like this should be thought of as containing the usual six areas. However, in this case the areas would overlap. For example, the standing figure is considered UL. in this grouping; if he formed a group with a figure in the large chair, the group would be thought of as being DL. The stair landing adds an extra area.

can be substituted. If 'God damn' appears in the text, 'damn' alone will usually suffice. In other cases an adequate substitute can be found, such as 'Lord' for 'God,' 'confounded' for damned,' etc. In a few cases no softening is possible; then you must either use the original or choose another play.

WORKING SCRIPTS

Professionals use 'sides,' which contain only the actor's own lines and cues. The actor cannot use them to study the play as a whole or to work out his reactions to the speeches of the other characters. Amateurs prefer printed copies of the script, or if these are not available, hektographed or mimeographed copies on 8½" × 11" paper, clipped together at the top with round-headed fasteners (Pl. VII, p. 27). Carbon copies on thin paper are possible but unsatisfactory. Scripts should be double-spaced with a 1" margin all around. Type the characters' names in capitals. Omit all stage directions not essential to an understanding of the lines. Pages should be

III-2

Chrysanthemums
Lap robe
Pennant on stick
Badge
Thermos jug

Paper

ALL THE WAY HOME

MRS. TAYLOR. But Bubbles didn't know you'd be able to take her to the game, Teddy. How could she have found out you weren't going to play yourself?

TEDDY (*incredulously*). My gosh, it was in all the papers! (*To Bubbles.*) My gosh, don't you ever read anything? Don't you even read the sports page?

BUBBLES (*defensively*). But Teddy, Cuthbert said . . .

TEDDY. Cuthbert, Cuthbert—all I ever hear around here is Cuthbert.

MERIWEATHER (*drily*). The rest of us hear you now and then.

TEDDY (*turning to Meriweather*). Well, my gosh, I guess a person's got an occasional right to open his mouth, occasionally.

MERIWEATHER (*amused*). Have another piece of fudge?

TEDDY. Thanks. (*Takes piece of fudge and sits.*) As for you, Mr. Meriweather, when a person is trying to explain to a person how he feels about another person, it is extremely—to say the least—exasperating, to be continuously interrupted by an altogether different person. (*DOOR BELL. Teddy and Bubbles jump to their feet.*)

MRS. TAYLOR. Oh dear, that must be Cuthbert.

BUBBLES. I'll go. (*Starts across to door, R.*)

TEDDY (*crossing DRC. to stop her*). Do you mean to let him into this house right before my face?

MRS. TAYLOR. She can't leave the boy standing on the doorstep. (*Bubbles sneaks around Teddy and opens door.*)

TEDDY. He doesn't have to stand there. He can go away.

BUBBLES (*offstage*). Oh Cuthbert, how beautiful! (*Teddy turns with a jerk. Enter Cuthbert. He has a plaid robe over his left arm and carries a bunch of chrysanthemums.*) These are for you.

CUTHBERT. ① How do you do, Mrs. Taylor. ② Mr. Meriweather. Hello, Ted. Too bad they wouldn't let you play. (*He offers the chrysanthemums to Bubbles.*) These are for you.

TEDDY. Chrysanthemums! This is the last straw. (*He marches out in high dudgeon, slamming the door behind him.*)

CUTHBERT (*staring after Teddy*). What's the matter with him?

BUBBLES (*furiously*). You and your old chrysanthemums.

T. takes plate automatically, then decides that eating fudge at such a moment would not be dignified.

Begin build

Absentmindedly takes piece of fudge.

Each speech tops one before it.

Puts plate on table.

CUTHBERT COMES
TRANSITION
C, T, B, F, M.

C DOESN'T UNDERSTAND WOMEN
CONFLICT
C, B, M, F.

Climax of build. Look for costume touches: pennant, badge, etc.

At this point T. reaches back for fudge.

Beginning of B's attack on C.

Long, silent X. Make T's indignation comic. C moves on T's 4th step after T. takes fudge.

At this point T. pops fudge into his mouth.

PROMPT BOOK WITH DIRECTOR'S NOTES

Printed stage directions fit set in Fig.5, Pl.XXIV. For the meanings of the symbols, see Pl.VII.

Spread paste on margin.

Cut opening to fit type area.

Cut leaves of printed play apart and paste over openings in 8½"X 11" notebook paper.

Rear view, showing leaf of play pasted over opening in notebook sheet.

Main illustration, above, is front view showing text through opening.

METHOD OF PREPARING PROMPT BOOK FROM PRINTED PLAY

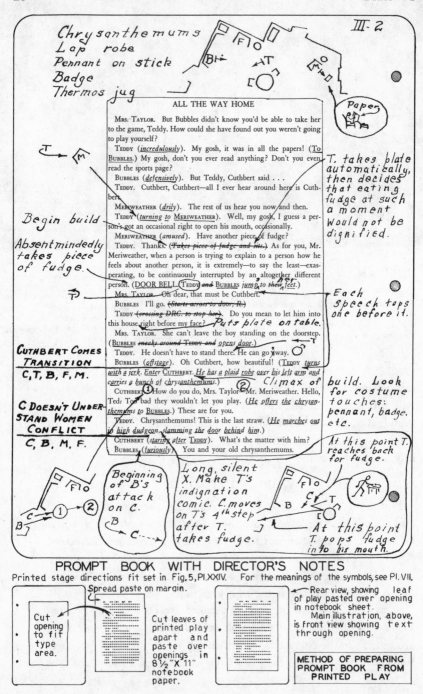

Plate VII   27

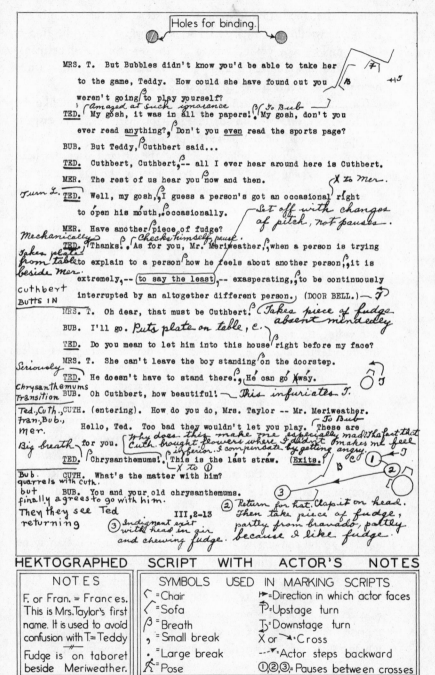

Holes for binding.

MRS. T. But Bubbles didn't know you'd be able to take her to the game, Teddy. How could she have found out you weren't going to play yourself?

Amazed at such ignorance

TED. *To Bub* My gosh, it was in all the papers! My gosh, don't you ever read anything? Don't you even read the sports page?

BUB. But Teddy, Cuthbert said...

TED. Cuthbert, Cuthbert -- all I ever hear around here is Cuthbert.

MER. The rest of us hear you now and then. *X to Mer.*

Turn L. TED. Well, my gosh, I guess a person's got an occasional right to open his mouth, occasionally.

Set off with changes of pitch, not pauses.

Mechanically MER. Have another piece of fudge?

Takes plate from table beside Mer. TED. Thanks. *Checks himself, pause* As for you, Mr. Meriweather, when a person is trying to explain to a person how he feels about another person, it is extremely, -- (to say the least) -- exasperating, to be continuously

Cuthbert Butts IN interrupted by an altogether different person. (DOOR BELL.)

MRS. T. Oh dear, that must be Cuthbert. *(Takes piece of fudge absent mindedly)*

BUB. I'll go. *Puts plate on table, e.*

TED. Do you mean to let him into this house right before my face?

Seriously MRS. T. She can't leave the boy standing on the doorstep.

TED. He doesn't have to stand there. He can go away.

Chrysanthemums Transition BUB. Oh Cuthbert, how beautiful! *This infuriates T.*

Ted., Cuth., Fran., Bub., mer. CUTH. (entering). How do you do, Mrs. Taylor -- Mr. Meriweather.

Hello, Ted. Too bad they wouldn't let you play. *To Bub* These are especially for you. *Why does this make me especially mad? The fact that Cuth. brought flowers where I didn't makes me feel inferior. I compensate by getting angry.*

Big breath TED. Chrysanthemums! This is the last straw. Exits.

Bub. quarrels with Cuth. but finally agrees to go with him. CUTH. What's the matter with him? *X to ①*

BUB. You and your old chrysanthemums.

They they see Ted returning

III, 2-13

② Return for hat. Clap it on head. Then take piece of fudge, partly from bravado, partly because I like fudge.

③ Indignant exit with head in air and chewing fudge.

HEKTOGRAPHED SCRIPT WITH ACTOR'S NOTES

NOTES

F. or Fran. = Frances. This is Mrs. Taylor's first name. It is used to avoid confusion with T = Teddy

Fudge is on taboret beside Meriweather.

SYMBOLS USED IN MARKING SCRIPTS

⌒ = Chair
⌐ = Sofa
β = Breath
, = Small break
. = Large break
⅄ = Pose

⊢ = Direction in which actor faces
P = Upstage turn
J = Downstage turn
X or ↘ = Cross
---↖ = Actor steps backward
①②③ = Pauses between crosses

numbered at the bottom. Number each scene separately. Thus Act I, page 25 would be I–25; Act II, Scene 2, page 6 would be II, 2–6. One complete copy will be needed for the director, the stage manager, each important actor, and each technical crew. Minor actors need only the scenes in which they appear.

If the director uses a printed copy, he should prepare it like the one in Pl. VI, p. 26, to provide margins for his notes. The script is cut apart and each leaf is pasted upon a sheet of $8\frac{1}{2}'' \times 11''$ notebook paper in which a hole the size of the printed page has been cut. This makes it possible to read both sides of the page. If the act and scene number are not printed on each page, they should be marked.

Preliminary Markings. Before the actor begins to study his script he should underscore his character name, preferably in red pencil (Pl. VII, p. 27). Never underscore the whole speech. It serves no purpose, and fills the space between the lines which will be needed for other markings.

Another preliminary, valuable to both actor and director, consists in dividing the text into 'sequences.' A sequence begins whenever an important character enters or exits. They are sometimes called 'French scenes,' because plays in French are divided in this way by the printer. The entrance or exit of a character always requires some technical readjustment in the grouping, etc., and usually introduces a new topic or a change in mood. Mark the beginning of each sequence with a red line extending from the text into the left-hand margin. Under the line, list the characters who appear in the sequence. Later, when the meaning of the sequence is understood, it should be given a title which is then written above the line (see Pls. VI and VII, pp. 26 and 27). This title merely serves to clarify your own thinking. The scene is not called by it in rehearsal. If the topic or mood changes within the sequence, sub-sequences may be indicated in blue pencil. Marking sequences makes it easy for you to find your way around in the script and also gives you a grasp of the basic plan of the play. The actor need not mark sequences in which his character does not appear, but should summarize them in the margin so that he can think of the play as a whole rather than as a series of disconnected bits. He should not use the director's sequence titles but should find titles of his own which express the significance of the various sequences from the standpoint of his character.

Notes. Both directors and actors should make frequent notes of ideas, groupings, movements, problems, interpretations, etc. (Pls. VI and VII). Diagrams are better than written notes. They can be read more quickly, are far more exact, and can be found at a glance. *Never mark a script in ink. Many of your notes will have to be erased and changed.*

The director's notes will often be of a general character, and many of them will deal with technical matters, such as light and sound cues. Props should be noted in the upper left-hand corner of the page on which they first appear. The actors' notes are largely limited to matters which concern him or his character but are correspondingly more detailed.

Stage Manager's Script. The stage manager's script notes deal primarily with entrance cues and cues for lights, sound effects, and curtains. All cues should be marked in red pencil. 'Warnings' should also be marked, so that the stage manager may check to see that the actor or stagehand is ready. Warnings are normally placed half a page before the cue, but there are many cases in which an earlier warning is desirable. Blue pencil should be used to mark warnings.

Chapter IV

PLAY INTERPRETATION

In the 19th century each actor interpreted his own role. As this involved interpreting the play as a whole, there were sometimes as many interpretations as there were actors. In competent modern productions, the basic interpretation is done by the producer or the director, and only the details are left to the actor. However, the actor must know how a play is interpreted in order to understand the interpretation given him by the director.

MATERIALS AND VALUES

We begin the study of a play by taking a rough inventory of its 'dramatic material.' Everything in the script, or suggested by it, is dramatic material—speeches, characters, scenery, ideas, business—everything. Next we begin to group this material in terms of 'values' for the audience, just as a manufacturer estimates the 'customer appeals' of his goods. A dress may offer 'utility appeals' in warmth and durability, 'eye appeals' in color, cut, etc. Similarly a play offers its audience emotional values that move them to laughter or tears, intellectual values that present new ideas or express old ones in a more impressive form, and abstract values that give pleasure through beauty, smoothness of execution, or other esthetic means. Dramatic values are made out of dramatic materials much as dress appeals are made out of design, workmanship, dress goods, etc. For example, in *Macbeth* we find the witches, the cauldron, the incantation, and the prophecies. From these materials we make the supernatural values of the play. A material is something that we use; a value is something the audience receives. However, the term 'values' is often employed to cover potential values as well as actual ones.

Intellectual values must be understood to be appreciated, and must be presented with the maximum clarity and simplicity. This calls for bold strokes—so bold that they often seem crude when their secrets are explained. On the other hand, emotional and abstract values are not understood but felt, and may be expressed through details which are so subtle that the layman finds difficulty in believing they can affect an audience at all.

Intellectual Values. (1) The ideas behind a play are called 'philosophical values.' A moral, such as 'Crime does not pay,' is one type of idea. Often an idea is not a statement but a question—'Does crime pay?' Other ideas are character studies: 'How will this type of person react to a situation chosen to bring out his fundamental characteristics?' Do not be disappointed if the ideas you find in a play are trite. Profundity is largely a matter of language. When a thought is expressed briefly and clearly, the profundity disappears. A play almost never says anything new. What it does is to state old ideas in a more vivid form.

(2) Besides its philosophical values, a play has educational values. Education in the theater must be heavily sugar-coated, but that does not diminish its effectiveness. *Lady in the Dark* is an excellent popularization of psychoanalysis. *Destination Tokyo, Objective Burma,* and other war films gave welcome information about conditions in various branches of the service.

Emotional Values. (1) In many plays the experiences of the characters (or at least those of the principals) are shared in imagination by the audience. This 'vicarious experience' produces emotions, and is one of the chief attractions of the theater.

(2) Emotional values also exist in which the spectator is emotionally detached from the character. Laughter is the best example of this. We laugh *at* the character who is the butt of a jest, not *with* the one who makes it.

Abstract Values. These include: (1) appeals to the eye—beauty, spectacle, etc.; (2) appeals to the ear—poetry, fine voices, music, etc.; (3) abstract appeals to the mind through pattern, rhythm, etc.

THEME

The main philosophical idea of a play is its 'theme,' and this theme is the basis on which the unity of the play is founded. This is true even of plays which depend almost entirely upon emotional values. The fruit of a grapevine is edible and the leaves are decorative, but it is the vine itself that supports them and makes them one.

Choosing the Theme. Most plays contain a number of ideas, but only those which underlie the play as a whole can be considered as possible themes. Even so, there may be several from which to choose. Possible themes for *Macbeth* are: (1) Character study of Macbeth. (2) 'Crime does not pay.' (3) 'Exaggerated ambition is evil.' (4) 'Traffic with the supernatural is dangerous.' Only one of these can be used as the theme of any particular production. In every field the effect is greatest when all the available forces are directed toward a single goal. If your play shifts from theme to theme, it will not raise strong emotions any more than a shifting wind will raise large waves. The theme chosen will govern everything in the production. If you choose 'ambition' as your theme, the supernatural material will become relatively unimportant and you should minimize it. Another director might choose 'traffic with the supernatural' as his theme, and would then stress the witch scenes and the prophecies. You should always choose that theme which you feel will do most to unify your production and bring out its values. *In the discussions which follow, some particular theme, usually the most obvious one, is always assumed.* Do not say, "I don't think Macbeth (or Romeo) was like that." Under a different interpretation you may be right, but you must tentatively accept my interpretation in order to follow the examples I give. However, this should not cause much difficulty, as modern plays rarely contain more than one really practical theme.

Selection of a theme does not mean that the other ideas must be abandoned. They are still useful as long as they are not permitted to become too prominent. Of course, when two ideas conflict, both cannot be used. If you use 'Crime does not pay' in *Macbeth*, you could not at the same time use 'The satisfaction of being a king is worth whatever it costs.'

TREATMENT

The theme holds the play together, but the theme itself may receive little stress. The stress should be placed on the most important values. Many of the educational war pictures used the theme: 'Devotion to duty is the soldier's highest virtue,' but camp life and battle tactics took up most of the film, and this was as it should be. Sometimes the theme must even be deliberately suppressed. The theme of *The Doughgirls* was that our Washington bureaucracy ran the war inefficiently and selfishly. However, if such a serious and unpleasant idea had been emphasized, the audience would have become despondent, instead of laughing at the farce values, which were the play's chief reason for existence. The theme governed the selection of the farce values, tied them together, and gave the play point, but otherwise it was submerged.

Determining Treatment. Selecting the proper values to stress, and finding the best way of expressing them, is called 'treatment.' It is the most important element in the whole production. All types of values are potentially present in every script, but only a few types can be exploited profitably in a single production. Thus, in *Romeo and Juliet,* we would probably bring out: (1) abstract values of beauty, spectacle, fine voices, music, etc.; (2) vicarious-experience values of love and adventure; (3) certain comic values. However, we would ignore the chance to educate our audiences in Italian history and customs, and would suppress certain comic values. (How would you treat the sequence in IV, 5 between Peter and the musicians when Juliet is thought to be dead?)

TREATMENT—A. VIEWPOINT

The significance of a play depends as much on the attitude of the audience as it does on the words of the script. A spectator rarely has much idea of what attitude to adopt until the curtain rises. He then makes up his mind quickly. Once his viewpoint is established, he tries to fit everything he sees and hears into a pattern which makes sense from that viewpoint. When any detail refuses to fit, he becomes confused and irritated. For example, the early scenes of *Peer Gynt* could be staged in such a way that an audience might mistake them for a serious picture of Norwegian life. Then Peer suddenly throws the bride over his shoulder and runs up the mountainside so fast that no one can catch him. From a realistic standpoint, this is simply silly. A little later, Peer encounters a series of imaginary creatures. That forces the spectators to abandon any idea that the play represents real life and leaves them completely bewildered.

This sort of confusion can be avoided only if the spectators regard the performance from a viewpoint which makes it consistent throughout. They must know from the start in what spirit they are to take the play, and whether they are to judge it by the standards of everyday life or by some set of theatrical conventions.

<h3 style="text-align:center">Treatment—B. Spirit</h3>

The spirit in which the audience will take the performance is governed by the spirit of the production, which, in turn, depends on the spirit of the script. You can determine the spirit of a script by listing adjectives which seem appropriate to it. Thus, "light," "frothy," "comic," "satirical," suit *The Mikado* (p. 239), and "gloomy," "rugged," "baleful," "doomed," "eldritch," "tortured," apply to *Macbeth*. In either case, the spirit of the script combines the qualities described by the appropriate adjectives.

If the adjectives seem contradictory, this does not indicate a mistake. Maxwell Anderson's *Winterset* is both "romantic" and "sordid," and its ability to reconcile these apparently conflicting qualities accounts for much of its interest.

Weight. If you find yourself selecting adjectives like "frothy," "cheerful," "brisk," the play has little spiritual weight and is said to be 'light.' If your list contains such words as "strong," "brave," "somber," "harsh," the spirit is 'heavy.' Normally, light plays deal with trifles, whereas heavy plays concern themselves with strong emotions and profound ideas, but exceptions occur.

Ending. The ending of a play strongly influences its spirit. A happy ending requires a hopeful spirit, even though the early scenes appear gloomy. An unhappy ending, on the other hand, does not indicate a spirit of despair but one of completeness; the spirit should say, "This was inevitable," or "It was a good life while it lasted."

Viewpoint and Spirit. The spirit of the play and the spirit in which the audience views it should ordinarily correspond. There are, however, important exceptions. For example, old-fashioned melodramas like *Perils of a Great City* (p. 109) succeed today because they take themselves with a seriousness which the audience regards as absurd.

Unity of Spirit. Audiences attend the theater for pleasure. They may take greater pleasure in tragedy and drama than they do in comedy, but even so they want their emotions exercised, not harrowed. Above all, they demand emotional security. To insure this, the spirit of a play must be consistent throughout, without emotional shocks or surprises. In Alfred Hitchcock's early picture, *The Woman Alone,* the heroine's young brother carried a time bomb without knowing it. As the moment for the explosion arrived, he stopped to talk to a charming old lady with an equally charming puppy. The audience accepted this as proof that the bomb would be rendered harmless in the proverbial nick of time. Instead it exploded, killing boy, lady, and dog. It also killed the emotional security of the spectators. They did not dare let their feelings become involved again, so the remaining reels were simply wasted.

An audience is like a child; never surprise it without first saying in some fashion, "Now I am going to surprise you." Usually this takes the form of warning the audience that something is to happen without saying what that something is. Even in such a pseudo surprise, what happens must be at least as pleasant as what was expected. In tragedy, the future is always heavily foreshadowed to prevent unpleasant audience surprise. In farce, the audience constantly expects some pleasant 'surprise.'

The need for unity of spirit does not mean that drama and comedy should not be mixed; in fact, current American taste almost demands such a mixture. However, the mixture must be uniform throughout, just as the ingredients are mixed in a good pudding. Make sure that the proportion of comedy to drama is roughly the same in every act and that the transition from one to the other is not unpleasantly sudden. Variations of the spirit are called 'moods.'

The emotions of the characters are constantly changing, and may either harmonize or contrast with the spirit of the play or with each other. The emotional tone of the background is called 'atmos-

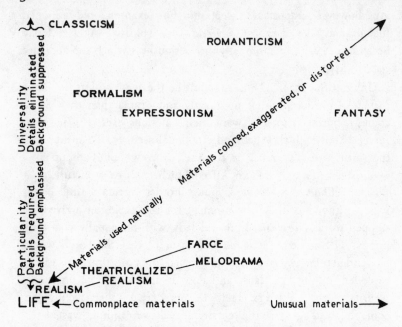

phere.' It also may change, and may harmonize or contrast with the spirit of the play.

Once established, the spirit of the production serves as a guide. Macbeth's death has been played in every possible way, from a quiet announcement by Macduff, to a swashbuckling sword fight. Which is right? No answer is possible until the spirit of the production is determined, but once that is settled, it is easy to devise a scene with the appropriate restraint or melodrama.

TREATMENT—C. STYLE

Style, which is the relation of the play to reality, is the second factor that controls the viewpoint of the audience. A play like *The Lower Depths* (p. 139), which is close to actual life, demands a very different viewpoint from a play like *Jim Dandy* (p. 46) or one like *Chanticleer* (p. 226).

The chart in Pl. VIII, p. 36, shows the theoretical types of style. But the style of a real play never matches one of these categories exactly, and no two plays have quite the same style.

The Realistic Styles. When a play is intended to be judged from the viewpoint of ordinary life, it is roughly classified as 'realistic.' This does not imply a complete imitation of nature, which is impossible on the stage and would be deadly dull. A play is realistic if it avoids anything which is *noticeably* unnatural. Sometimes, a realistic style is adopted to lull the spectators into a frame of mind where they are willing to overlook impossibilities. *Arsenic and Old Lace* would be pointless if the audience refused to accept it as something that might actually take place.

Four realistic styles are generally recognized. Plays like *The Lower Depths* (p. 139), which imitate reality as closely as possible and make only the essential concessions to the theater, are classed as 'realism' or 'naturalism.' Such plays as *No More Frontier* (p. 45), which are plausible without attempting to reproduce every detail of nature whether or not it affects the plot, belong to the style known as 'theatricalized realism.' When a play is superficially realistic but uses technical devices to heighten its effects at the expense of plausibility, its style is 'farce' if the spirit is comic, and 'melodrama' if the spirit is dramatic.

The Nonrealistic Styles. If a play cannot be judged by the standards of everyday life, it must be given a nonrealistic style so that the audience can adopt the proper viewpoint. Any departure from realism is usually revealed by some intentional artificiality in the dialog, such as verse, unnatural phraseology, or marked rhythm. The characters often declaim rather than converse. Also, they may employ asides and soliloquies or make remarks which are clearly intended for the audience rather than for the other characters.

There are several reasons for deliberately avoiding realism. The playwright may wish to say, "This is not an event in the lives of individuals; it is a universal truth, valid for all times and places." The Greek tragedies written by Aeschylus and Sophocles did this, and the style which they used is known as 'classicism.' It concentrates on essentials, eliminates all unnecessary details, and has a strong tendency to symmetry.

Plays like *The Yellow Jacket* (p. 79) which are frankly theatrical performances adopt the style known as 'formalism.' This employs

Yale University Theater

UNCLE HARRY   Setting by Henry C. Pearson

This illustrates a type of realism known as 'impressionism.' The setting occupies only a portion of the stage and blends into darkness at the top and sides. However, such portions as are visible are complete in every detail. This style is especially adapted to plays of many scenes.

the methods of classicism, but uses them as practical conveniences to simplify staging rather than as devices to achieve universality. It is also freer and less exalted.

'Romanticisim' provides the audience with magic spectacles which make everything more vivid and colorful than it is in real life. Like *The Warrior's Husband* (p. 180), plays in this style usually deal with love and adventure.

Such plays as *Chanticleer* (p. 226) employ the style of 'fantasy' to warn the audience that the action takes place in a completely unreal world. Fantasy usually implies distortion in the forms and colors of the scenery and costumes.

A few plays try to combine the best features of all styles. They use realistic costumes and business but follow formalism in ignoring any inconvenient demands of realism. They omit unessential details as classicism does and distort essential details in the manner of fantasy. Usually, the result is simply a hodgepodge, but when a production succeeds in blending such diverse elements into a single, harmonious style, the emotional effect on the audience is tremendous. *Jim Dandy* (p. 46) and *Divine Comedy* (p. 258) illustrate the possibilities of this style, which is called 'expressionism.'

Interpreting Style. To determine the style of a script, start by deciding whether it is definitely realistic, definitely nonrealistic, or

YALE UNIVERSITY THEATER

Setting by Roger Sherman

Structurally, this set is much like the one on the opposite page. The only important difference is the lack of detail, but this can be accepted as realistic in a bare prison cell. Nevertheless, the lighting and treatment produce an entirely different effect. They emphasize the edges of the set and permit the characters to be seen as they walk from the wings to the set proper. These changes are enough to destroy the feeling of realism and to make the setting expressionistic.

one of the rare plays like Barrie's *Dear Brutus* which falls on the borderline. At the same time, you can decide on the exact degree of realism. Unrealistic plays differ widely in this respect; compare *One Shall Be* (p. 118) with *Chanticleer* (p. 226).

Next, note the nonrealistic influences. All plays have them. Even *The Lower Depths* is touched with classicism because it implies that its bums, thieves, and prostitutes can be viewed as a cross section of all humanity. It is also romantic in leading us to look at these unsavory creatures through glasses with a decidedly rosy tint.

You should now be able to name both the basic style and the minor style influences. Thus, *Candlelight* (p. 147) is theatricalized realism tending toward farce, with a strong element of romanticism and a touch of fantasy. *Aren't We All* (p. 160) is theatricalized realism with undertones of classicism. *Perils of a Great City* (p. 109) is formalism masquerading as pseudorealistic melodrama.

A few plays permit more than one interpretation, and any change in interpretation will affect the style. The basic style of *Macbeth* is romanticism. However, if we interpret the play as a character study, its style will seem slightly more realistic. If we give prominence to the witches, the element of fantasy is increased. If we stress the melodramatic values, the style becomes more theatrical. Such variations are never great, because the dialog remains fixed and confines the style within narrow limits. The dialog in the ordinary play is much less flexible than Shakespeare's and allows almost no variation in style.

When you have decided on the style, ask yourself what viewpoint it suggests. Then read the script from this viewpoint and see if everything fits. Thus, if you assume that *Peer Gynt* is romantic fantasy, you will be prepared for improbable happenings, color, beauty, and perhaps a kind of mad logic. But as you study the play, you will find a large element of philosophy which is neither romantic nor fantastic. Philosophy is universal; you must therefore reinterpret the style and introduce a strong note of classicism.

Style as a Guide. The spirit of the production may, on rare occasions, differ from that of the script. This is never true of style. If we try to make the production force a style on the script, the true style is bound to show through at inconvenient moments; the total effect will be as unconvincing as a fat soprano playing Carmen. *The style of the script should always be the style of the production.*

This does not mean that every element of the production must be in the same style; *Jim Dandy* combines realistic costumes with fantastic scenery. But every stage picture, as a whole, should reveal a harmonious style—and this style should be the same throughout

In order to achieve consistency of style in a production, you must first form a clear idea of the style required and of the viewpoint which this will indicate to the audience. Then look at everything from this viewpoint yourself. Whenever something seems meaningless or out of key, change it until it becomes appropriate to the viewpoint you have adopted.

SEQUENCE INTERPRETATION

So far we have dealt with the contents of a play rather than with its structure, but the latter is equally important.

Plot. To understand the structure of a play, we must know its 'plot.' *The plot is an anecdote told to illustrate the theme.* Thus, if the theme of *Macbeth* is 'Crime does not pay,' the plot will be: 'Macbeth gains the throne of Scotland by murdering the king, but thereby loses his own security and peace of mind. His attempts to strengthen his position by more murders cause his enemies to unite against him, and he is surrounded and killed.' If a play has several possible themes, it will have several different possible plots, so it is important to see that the plot you use is the one which corresponds to the theme you have selected. The plot is the bare bones of the action and therefore the key to the structure of the play. This is true even in plays where other values, such as character, comedy, etc., seem to overshadow the plot. Without a firm grasp of the plot, you cannot really understand the play, and the only way to be sure you understand the plot is to write it out. This is not as easy as it may seem. If you need more than three or four sentences, you are not down to the bare plot but have added other values. Do not expect the plot to sound interesting. The most thrilling play in the world seems dull when reduced to the bare plot.

Continuity. Once you see the plot clearly, the structure of the play will begin to take on meaning. A play rarely tells its story in strict logical order. Instead, the sequences are arranged to make the action flow smoothly, and the plot material is introduced in whatever way seems most convenient. When you have given titles to all your sequences and sub-sequences in the script (see pp. 26 and 27), make a list of these titles on a separate sheet of paper. This makes the structure clear and shows how the parts fit together.

Sequence Functions. In titling a sequence, the technical function which it serves should be taken into account. There are five main types: (1) Sequences of 'conflict' (usually mental), which provide the main plot interest of the play. (2) 'Parallel' sequences, in which the characters agree throughout, e.g., love scenes and scenes of exposition. (3) 'Background' sequences, in which the environment is presented but the plot does not move forward. (4) 'Transition' sequences, during which characters enter or exit. (5) 'Relief' sequences, in which the audience tension is permitted to relax after being stretched near the breaking point. The Porter's sequence in *Macbeth* is the stock example of relief. Sequences of pure relief are rare in modern plays.

CHARACTER INTERPRETATION

Even the leading characters are not important in themselves but must be interpreted for the play as a whole.

Functions. In a well-written play each character serves several functions, but one usually dominates. An understanding of the chief function or functions of a character is the first step toward interpreting that character. The more common functions are listed below. Do not expect to find all of them in any one play.

PRINCIPAL. The character whose story is told in the plot is often the key to the interpretation. He is known either as the 'principal' or as the 'protagonist.' Sometimes, as in *Romeo and Juliet,* there will be two characters of equal importance, and a few plays like *The Lower Depths* distribute their emphasis so evenly that no character can be called the principal. Usually the principal is the most prominent character and also the one with the most lines, but this is not necessarily true. The Stage Manager in *Our Town* is the leading actor but *not* the principal character. If the play has any principals, they are the girl and boy.

ANTAGONIST. This is the chief opponent of the principal.

SUBJECT OF CONTROVERSY. In *Cyrano de Bergerac,* Cyrano is the principal, De Guiche and Chrétien are his antagonists, and Roxane is the subject of controversy.

CONFIDANT. In modern plays most thoughts are spoken aloud to someone, and a character may be introduced to serve as the recipient of such statements.

UTILITY CHARACTER. Most plays contain a character, often a servant, who answers the door and the telephone, takes messages, etc. Such characters may have little to do with the plot or values, but their technical importance is considerable.

RAISONNEUR. This is a character who is the mouthpiece for the playwright. The Waiter and the Barrister in Shaw's *You Never Can Tell* both serve this function. The Waiter is also a utility character.

CHARACTERS REPRESENTING GROUPS OR FORCES. Macduff in *Macbeth* is, of course, the antagonist, but he has almost no individuality and really is a symbol for the Scottish resistance movement. Characters symbolizing groups are very common. In *Abe Lincoln in Illinois,* Stephen A. Douglas represents all Lincoln's political opponents. In *The Man Who Came to Dinner,* Banjo and Beverly Carleton stand for all Whiteside's famous friends.

CHARACTERS WHO SERVE SPECIAL VALUES. The Gravediggers in

Hamlet serve comic purposes, and the courtiers lend realism (as there must be courtiers even in a romantic court) and also wear colorful costumes and make beautiful groupings possible.

Distribution of Sympathy. Here 'sympathy' is a technical term and means the audience's liking for and interest in the character. Distribution of sympathy is often a vital and difficult problem. In *The Merchant of Venice,* modern custom plays Shylock as sympathetic. However, he has too small a part to be the principal character, and the fact that the play is a comedy makes it impossible to interpret the other characters as 'unsympathetic' in spite of their heartless treatment of Shylock. A nice balance of sympathy, changing from moment to moment, is required if the play is to be successful. A character is made more sympathetic by adding to his likable qualities, or by giving him business which displays such qualities. Reversing the procedure decreases his sympathy. Hollywood directors are often very skillful at this and are worth studying for examples.

An excellent way to make a character sympathetic is to make him comic, as was done with Whiteside in *The Man Who Came to Dinner.* It may be a sad commentary on human nature, but no audience ever really disapproves of a character who makes it laugh. This is the secret of making an audience like a character who is fundamentally dishonest, immoral, or vicious. It also represents a danger in some plays because no serious hero, however charming and virtuous, can ever take the sympathy of an audience from a comic villain.

Characterization. Once a character's function and degree of sympathy are established, we can interpret his nature. Aristotle said, "Make no character unnecessarily bad." This is one of the few laws of the theater which admit of no exceptions. 'Bad' means undesirable in any way, without troubling about fine-spun ethical theories unless they are clearly brought out by the play. To be cowardly, or stingy, or ugly, or stupid, is 'bad,' and such characteristics are to be avoided wherever they are unnecessary. Of course there are many necessary reasons for making a character bad in some way. The villain in a melodrama is 'bad' so that the audience may hate him; the confidant of the heroine must be made less attractive than the

heroine herself; plot reasons may compel us to interpret one character as dishonest and another as vicious. The point is that if these
characteristics are unnecessary, they should not be used.

The mistake is fatally easy to make. Mary (Mrs. Lincoln), in
Robert Sherwood's *Abe Lincoln in Illinois,* is a case in point. It is
tempting to play her as an overambitious, selfish, nagging shrew
(which she seems to have been in real life), because this gives the
actress more scope for melodramatic emotionalism. However, such
an interpretation would obscure the subtler dramatic values and
also give Mary an emphasis above her real importance in the play.
On the other hand, it would be equally wrong to go to the other
extreme and show her as a completely admirable character, although
that could easily be done. It is dramatically necessary to make Mary
a little 'bad' because, according to the play, one of the Lincolns
treated the other unfairly and the more the spectators sympathize
with Mary and respect her, the less they can sympathize with and
respect Abe. As he is the principal, his character must be preserved
even at the expense of lowering hers.

Whenever two characters are balanced in this way, decide on the
sympathy for the more important one first, and then degrade
the other character in proportion. Remember, however, that 'bad-
ness' and lack of sympathy are not the same thing. We can rob
Mary Lincoln of sympathy either by making her motives selfish or
by having her nag Abe. There is no need to do both, or to give her
any other bad qualities.

When a character is bad for no reason, he tends to approach the
melodramatic villain. Shylock is a perfect example of this. At one
time he was played as a spiteful usurer. As a result he was so mon-
strous that he was comic, and stood below Launcelot Gobbo in
importance. Now he is played with all possible faults removed, and
he ranks as one of the greatest of Shakespeare's creations in spite of
the fact that he has only some three hundred lines.

DYNAMIC CHARACTERS. Important characters should be interpreted in a way that will make them 'dynamic' rather than 'static.'
In this sense 'dynamic' means that the character changes, whereas
'static' means that he remains the same. Macbeth can be interpreted
statically as a gangster type who bullies when he is strong and

NO MORE FRONTIER

Setting by Isaac Benesch

This represents the extreme degree of realism that is possible with an exterior setting. Difficulties of masking, lighting, and simulating foliage make a closer approach to nature impractical. Any attempt to go farther will only call attention to the difference between realism and reality. Compare this setting with the interiors on pp. 139 and 222. Interiors permit much greater realism.

blusters when he is beaten. Obviously, he will be far more interesting if he is interpreted dynamically. Make him a hero at the start; show him slowly yield to temptation, then disintegrate morally because of his conscience and the insecurity of his position; and finally have him rally and defy his fate. Few characters can show as much change as this, but the principle can be applied except in the lightest comedies.

Consistency. *All inconsistencies must be eliminated or explained.* Seeming inconsistencies may be due to a misinterpretation of some speech or action. In *Romeo and Juliet,* III, 1, Mercutio has three speeches in which he accuses Benvolio of being quarrelsome. If these speeches are delivered seriously, they are inconsistent with the facts, because Benvolio is a level-headed peacemaker and Mercutio knows it. The difficulty vanishes if Mercutio makes it clear that he is teasing his friend—that he is saying to Benvolio the things that Benvolio should really be saying to him.

What appears as an inconsistency may be really a change in opinion or purpose. Hamlet will seem inconsistent unless the

JIM DANDY

Setting by Ralph Brown

Pure expressionism. This example is surrealistic, **but** many forms of expressionism exist. Successful **expressionism** has the effect of a diagram. It con-

veys ideas and emotions directly, without suggesting that the action is taking place in a real world. The characters may be either real or fanciful.

audience realizes his vacillating nature. In *Richard II,* Richard seems at first to be guided by mere whim. In the last three acts he becomes solemn and steadfast. The spectators will be completely mystified unless they are shown that in the early acts Richard behaves arbitrarily in order to display his power, and that in the later acts he has been sobered by adversity.

Character Interpretation as Guide. Once you have worked out a characterization, it will solve many problems for you. Ask yourself, "What would this character think under these circumstances? What would he mean by these words? How would he react to this situation?"

LINE INTERPRETATION

When an Arab says, "Peace be unto you," he expresses the same thought that we express by the completely different words, "How are you?" and this in turn has the same significance as "Hello!" The meaning is not in the form of the words but in the thought behind them. Not only can one thought be expressed by different phrases, but one phrase can express different thoughts. Thus:

"How are you?" (I've been worried about you.)
"How are you!" (My, I'm glad to see you!)
"How are you?" (I'll condescend to notice you, but that's all.)

In these cases the meaning is conveyed chiefly by the situation and inflection, and only slightly by the words.

If the meaning of a line in a play can shift in this fashion, how can you know which is the right meaning? The answer is that the meaning depends upon the interpretation of the play as a whole, of the character who speaks the line, and of the scene in which it appears. The exact meaning could only be determined by considering the whole interpretation of the production, but the following examples from *Macbeth* show the general principle.

INTERPRETED ON THE THEME THAT 'TRAFFIC WITH THE SUPERNATURAL IS DANGEROUS.'	INTERPRETED ON THE THEME THAT 'CRIME DOES NOT PAY.'

Act V, Scene 3

MACBETH. Bring me no more reports; let them [*i.e., Macbeth's nobles*] fly all; (*I have sure prophecies that I shall win this battle.*)	MACBETH. Bring me no more reports; let them fly all; (*My crimes have found me out; my only hope is to make my soldiers believe the prophecies that I am invulnerable.*)
Till Birnam wood remove to Dunsinane I cannot taint with fear. What's the boy Malcolm? Was he not born of woman?	Till Birnam wood remove to Dunsinane I cannot taint with fear. What's the boy Malcolm? Was he not born of woman?

Act V, Scene 8

MACBETH. (*To Macduff*) Of all men else I have avoided thee (*because the prophecy told me to beware of you*). But get thee back; my soul is too much charg'd With blood of thine already. . . . (*If we fight I shall kill you because:*)	MACBETH. (*To Macduff*) Of all men else I have avoided thee. But get thee back; (*I don't want to hurt you*) my soul is too much charg'd With blood of thine already. . . . (*Nor do I want you to kill me, so if you insist on fighting, I'll try to frighten you by saying that:*)
. . . I bear a charmed life, which must not yield To one of woman born.	. . . I bear a charmed life, which must not yield To one of woman born.

Emphasis. The proper location of the emphasis is an important step in line interpretation. Do not emphasize more than one word in a sentence, or a long clause, without a strong reason for doing so. Occasionally, two words may be emphasized to contrast them (e.g., "Not *mine* but *yours*."), but this is rarely necessary. The other occasions for emphasizing more than one word are so rare that you can practically ignore them.

Any experimentation with emphasis by stressing one word and then another will only confuse you. Interpret the line to determine the important word; then emphasize that word.

Mark emphasized words in your script by underscoring them (Pl. VII, p. 27).

Breaks. An actor who learns each speech as a unit tends to speak it as a unit, without any interruptions. However, most speeches contain several thoughts, and unless they are separated by breaks of some sort (e.g., a pause or a sudden change in loudness) the audience will not follow the meaning. There are three distinct types of breaks:

(1) A complete change in thought. These are rare, and so obvious that they do not give much trouble.

(2) A change to a different but related thought.

(3) A change to another part of the same thought.

Types (2) and (3) correspond roughly to the changes marked in print by periods and commas respectively. However, the analogy is not exact because punctuation follows arbitrary laws, whereas breaks represent real changes in thought.

A change to a different thought—type (2)—may be marked in the script with a large dot (Pl. VII). A change to another part of the same thought—type (3)—may be marked with a comma-shaped dot. (Do not confuse these with printed commas, although they often come in the same places.)

A careful consideration of breaks, both in interpretation and in speaking your lines, will do much to improve your effectiveness as an actor.

Chapter V

CONVEYING VALUES

A script contains many potential values. Interpretation selects those on which your particular production is to be based. Potential values, however, are worthless unless they can be converted into real values in the minds of the audience.

In expressing values, the director, the actors, and the designers should each try to be as self-sufficient as possible. It is the function of the director to convey the values by groupings, movements, and pacing; of the actors to convey the values through business, gestures, and inflection; and of the designers to convey the values through their respective mediums. When the hero says, "I love you," in words, the same intellectual and emotional values are being conveyed by the groupings, business, and inflections, and also to some extent by the scenery, costumes, and lighting. If the hero stands like a stick ten feet from his sweetheart, or if the lighting and costumes are too garish for the mood, the spectators will certainly miss part of the 'love' values and may even be so confused that they will not understand what is said. The playwright has already done everything that can be accomplished by the words. The director, designers, and actors must proceed as if the Deaf Old Lady in the Back Row spoke very little English.

Although everyone should do what he can to express every value, certain values cannot be conveyed by some mediums. Beauty of speech is an important esthetic value in a verse play, but it is not one which can be effectively conveyed by the scene designer. On the other hand, do not assume too readily that a value lies outside your province. 'Night' is an intellectual value that can be conveyed most vividly by the lighting, but movements, business, inflections, etc. can also express 'night,' so there is no excuse for the director and actors to leave this value entirely to the light designer's handling.

An idea is never adequately expressed by printing it in the program, any more than a picture is made more lifelike by writing under it, "This is a cow."

INTELLECTUAL VALUES

Intellectual values include not only ideas but facts. 'Courage is the supreme virtue,' 'John loves Mary,' and 'This bottle contains whiskey' may differ widely in importance but they are all intellectual values. The difference between intellectual and emotional values does not depend on the attitude of the character but on that of the audience. A character's emotional reaction to a situation often conveys an intellectual value; e.g., the King's reaction to the inner play in *Hamlet* tells the audience that he is guilty of murder.

The chief requirement of an intellectual value is that it shall be made clear to the spectators. On rare occasions you may puzzle them temporarily to create a mystery which will ultimately be explained. On still rarer occasions you may be vague when clarity would be unpleasant. However, you must *never* confuse your spectators by calling their attention to problems which they cannot solve or which are not worth solving.

Understand everything yourself. Unless an idea is clear to you, you cannot hope to express it. This is especially important when you plan to be intentionally vague. When an idea is not clear in your mind, you cannot even know how vague to be in stating it.

Intellectual Values—A. Emphasis

When you read in a book that "John's hand stole around Mary's waist, and their lips met," your mind goes from 'John's hand' to 'Mary's waist,' to 'they,' to 'lips,' to 'kiss.' The writer makes one point at a time and the reader follows automatically. The points of a play must also be made in order, but on stage a number of things exist simultaneously. If a spectator gives his attention to 'John's hand' or 'the door on the other side of the set' when he should be watching 'their lips,' he will miss a point. If many spectators miss many points, the play will fail.

Theoretically there are two types of attention: (1) voluntary attention, such as a student gives his books when he concentrates, and (2) involuntary attention, which is automatically aroused by any strong outside stimulus such as a bright light or a loud noise. Spectators rarely contribute much voluntary attention. We must supply the stimuli necessary to hold their involuntary attention and direct it to the right thing at the right time, so that the points of the play may be made in the proper order.

When something attracts attention it is said to be in some degree 'emphatic.' We cannot control attention directly, but we can control emphasis to a large extent. Many shades of emphasis exist at the same time. Much of our work in the theater consists in determining the relative importance of the various elements and giving the appropriate emphasis to each. This relative importance varies from moment to moment. When the words are important (and they usually are) the most important person is the speaker, even though he has only a minor role and all the principal characters in the play are on stage.

Contrast. Anything which contrasts with its surroundings is emphatic, but certain contrasts are more emphatic than others. Movement is more emphatic than rest. Dynamic emotions and poses are more emphatic than relaxed ones. In Pl. XI, p. 71, compare Figs. 17 and 24, with Figs. 4 and 5. A character in bright colors stands out from a crowd dressed in grays and browns. However, these effects can be reversed; Hamlet in black is made emphatic by contrast with the brilliant costumes of the court.

Increasing Emphasis. The new is always interesting by contrast with the old, so no form of emphasis can be effective for long. To give a character the maximum emphasis, do not put him in the most emphatic position and keep him there. Instead, deliberately make him unemphatic and then add emphasis bit by bit until the available means of emphasis are exhausted. When the peak is reached, make no attempt to hold it, but drop back and start over.

Blending. I cannot stress too strongly that emphasis is not desirable in itself. The emphasis on any character or thing should coincide with his or its importance at the moment. Acquiring emphasis is usually easy. Avoiding undesirable emphasis is much more difficult. It is called 'blending,' because it helps the actor to

RELATIONSHIPS · TELLING STORY THROUGH GROUPINGS · VARIETY IN TRIANGULAR GROUPINGS

1. A enters behind B and C and finds them together.

2. B stands back of C while C confronts A.

3. C knocks A down and triumphs over him.

4. B takes A's side.

5. C turns his back on A and B.

blend in rather than stand out. Emphasis is avoided by: (1) decreasing contrasts and eliminating sharp contrasts entirely; (2) having the less important actors look at the main center of interest.

Distraction. When the attention of the audience goes to the wrong thing, we say it is 'distracted.' Thus, attention may be distracted by the leading man when another character is more important. Still more serious distractions occur when an actor falls out of character, an electrician misses a light cue, or a fire engine screams down the street. In such cases the attention of the spectators is carried completely out of the play. They remember that they are sitting in a theater looking at actors, and several minutes may be lost before the illusion can be rewoven. All distractions cannot be avoided, but any effort that will eliminate, or even minimize, one of them is worth taking.

INTENTIONAL DISTRACTION. Occasionally the director uses intentional distraction. For example, death scenes sometimes have a moment of horror which can hardly be omitted without loss of reality, yet which no spectator will want to watch. Such cases are handled by giving some emphatic piece of business to an actor on the far side of the stage. All eyes go to him for a moment, and when they come back to the dying man, the moment of unpleasantness is over.

INTELLECTUAL VALUES—B. RELATIONSHIPS

We must not only show the relative importance of the characters, but we must show the various ways in which they are related to each other. Every grouping, every movement should be thought of as a kind of diagram intended to picture the relationships in the scene.

Focusing. Pl. IX, opposite, shows a series of such diagrams, and the way in which they are translated almost literally into groupings. Notice that the arrows in the diagrams are represented in the groupings by having the actor actually point with some part of his body. Indicating a relationship by pointing is called 'focusing.' The most obvious methods are to turn the face toward the person focused (as *A* is doing in Fig. 1), or actually to point with a hand or finger (*C* in Fig. 4). Other ways are more subtle but equally effective. In Fig. 1, *A* is not pointing, but is merely raising his hands in surprise. Nevertheless, the lines of his hands lead the eyes of the audience to *B* and *C* and so help to indicate the relationship between *A* and the others. In Fig. 3, the same sort of effect is created by *A*'s foot, which points toward *B* and helps to tie her into the picture. Even a figure's back may serve as a means of focusing. In Fig. 5, *C* has turned his back on the others and this makes his relationship to them plain to the audience. Note that the backs of *B* and *C* in Fig. 1 do not indicate relationships to *A* because they are unaware of his presence, and the back of a figure is not a sufficiently obvious focusing indicator to create a relationship unless it is used deliberately as in Fig. 5.

Subtle effects can be created by having a figure focus on two objects at once. Thus in Fig. 4 the girl's arms show a relationship to *A* while she shows another relationship to *C* by looking at him. Similarly in Fig. 5 she looks at *A,* but her toes point toward *C.* The toes provide a strong effect of focus, and inexperienced actors often create a false appearance of relationship by letting their toes accidentally point toward some unimportant object.

Relationship may also be expressed in other ways. Nearness is a powerful means of representing relationship. The usual way of showing that two inanimate objects are related is to put them close together. Any similarity between objects tends to relate them. Color is frequently used for this purpose. Thus, in *Romeo and Juliet,* we might well dress all the Montagues in shades of red and brown and all the Capulets in greens and blues.

Symbols.   We often need to express the relationship between the characters on stage and an absent character or some abstract idea. For this we must symbolize the absent character or the idea. When Macbeth thinks about kingship, we can symbolize it by a throne. When he thinks of the advantages of kingship, he moves toward the throne; when he thinks of the disadvantages, he turns his back on the throne. Even the dullest spectator will grasp the idea at once. A person whose arrival is expected may be symbolized by the door, and a character who looks toward the door will be understood to be thinking of the absent one. An aviator may be symbolized by a model airplane, time by a clock or calendar, murder by a weapon, etc. Set out in print, such ideas may seem trite, but they are not trite to an audience. Never forget that a theatrical symbol is the means of conveying an idea. Its significance must be *instantly* clear to the audience, or it ceases to be a symbol and becomes a source of confusion.

Significance of Position. The relative positions of the figures on stage will be interpreted symbolically (and subconsciously) by the audience. Strength or superiority is indicated by:

(1) Greater relative distance upstage.

(2) Relative nearness to stage R. The actor R. is definitely stronger. This surprising fact has been accounted for by our custom of reading from left to right (stage R. to stage L.). Whatever the reason may be, the difference in strength between the two sides of the stage is certainly real and of vital importance to the director, actor, and designer. An advancing army, a line waiting for tickets at a window, and in general anything which is thought of as overcoming resistance (literal or figurative) moves from L. to R. A retreating army, or anything thought of as yielding to a superior force, moves from R. to L.

(3) Greater relative height above the stage floor; the stronger man stands while the weaker one sits. When a seated master addresses a standing servant, the master's lack of height must be compensated for; e.g., he might be placed R.

Intellectual Values—C. Repetition

Variety is the rule in the theater, and we should never repeat anything without a purpose. There are three legitimate purposes for repetition: (1) Number—whenever we wish to say 'more than one,' repetition is forced upon us; thus a crowd is to some extent a repetition of the individual. (2) Emphasis—a thing done several times is obviously more emphatic than a thing done only once; it may also be more boring. (3) Relationship—the connection between two things may be shown by repetition.

Triplets. Another curious psychological fact is that in the theater 'several' normally means 'exactly three.' There are three witches in *Macbeth* and three acts in most modern plays. Any mechanical action, such as pounding with a hammer, normally calls for three strokes. If many strokes are required, try to divide them into three groups. However, groupings and large movements are rarely repeated three times.

Echo Scenes. When the playwright has intentionally made one scene echo another, this fact should be emphasized by at least a partial duplication in grouping and business. In *The Iceman Cometh,* for example, most of the characters end in the state from which they started. This can best be shown by having the final grouping nearly duplicate the one used for the opening scene. Often the repetition is in reverse. In *The Merchant of Venice,* IV, 1, Shylock triumphs on lines like "O wise and upright judge!" Then, when Portia's judgment reverses the situation and Gratiano mocks him with lines like "An upright judge, a learned judge!" the reversal of the situation should be expressed by reversing the positions of the characters.

Running Gags. When a piece of comic business is repeated many times, it is called a 'running gag.' There are two examples in *Arsenic and Old Lace:* Teddy's charge up the stairs, and Jonathan's anger when his resemblance to Boris Karloff is mentioned. Each is repeated six times. Running gags are used only in farce or the farcial scenes of a melodrama.

EMOTIONAL VALUES

The emotional values of a production are by far the most important. Even a drama of ideas relies on its emotional values to make its ideas vivid and interesting. The ideas may be the only thing the spectators carry away with them, but as long as they are in their seats the emotional values dominate.

Emotional Values—A. Creating Emotion through Intellectual Values

Although intellectual values are less important in themselves than emotional values, they may create emotional values in the minds of the audience. Once the spectators have adopted a definite attitude toward a character, every fact or idea (intellectual value) which affects the fortune of that character has an emotional effect on the audience. In *Arsenic and Old Lace* the audience learns that the wine has been poisoned. Considered separately, this is merely a fact, with no emotional overtones. When the hero starts to drink the wine (the drinking, considered separately, is another fact) an emotion of fear for the hero's safety is created. Later, when the villain starts to drink (another fact) it causes a feeling of hope, because if the villain accidentally poisons himself, the sympathetic characters will be saved. Finally, when the head of the asylum starts to drink (still another fact) the audience finds it funny. No emotion is attached to the bare idea of drinking poisoned wine, but three widely different emotions are created when this idea is associated with particular characters.

Emotional Values—B. Empathy

We need to know what makes an audience feel with our characters. However, we cannot get much help from the idea of sympathy, partly because the word 'sympathy' has a separate technical meaning (see p. 43), and partly because in its everyday use it is too vague—a label rather than an explanation. The term 'empathy' covers much the same idea but refers to a definite psychological process, which relies on the imitative impulse and the James-Lange effect.

The Imitative Impulse. When Houdini did his underwater tricks, he breathed deeply before being submerged. No doubt this was necessary, but it was also superb showmanship. After the first few breaths, the audience breathed with him—a thousand people breathing in unison, a perfect example of the effect of the imitative impulse on an audience.

James-Lange Effect. When we are afraid, we run away. It is equally true, though less obvious, that when we run away we become afraid. Actual running is not required; what some psychologists call a 'muscle set' is sufficient. When we hear a loud noise, our muscles set themselves for flight. Although the actual running may wait on our conscious will, a muscle set is enough to create in us an emotion of fear. This is known as the 'James-Lange effect,' after the psychologists who have given it the most attention.

Empathy. Whenever an imitative impulse is strong enough to cause a muscle set in a spectator, the appropriate James-Lange effect is created. When a character on stage assumes an attitude of, say, grief, the spectators tend to assume a muscle set in imitation of the character's attitude. This in turn produces in them the emotion appropriate to that attitude, i.e., grief. Empathy does not communicate the actor's emotion directly to the spectators. Instead it recreates, or induces, the emotion in them much as an electric current in one coil of a transformer is induced in the other coil.

Using Empathy. Some actors create stronger empathies than others. Normally, a director needs actors who arouse strong empathies, at least for the leading roles. The quality of empathy is as important as its strength. When an actor creates the wrong empathies, we say he is 'miscast.' If the cast is well chosen, the desirable empathies will largely take care of themselves. This is fortunate, as the director often has enough difficulty in avoiding the unpleasant empathies. I once did technical work on a play in which an insane steel-worker caught a 'red-hot' rivet in his bare hand. The rivet was cold iron painted red, and we worried lest it should seem unrealistic. Actually it seemed only too real, and created such violent empathies that many spectators became physically ill. One really bad empathy like that is enough to ruin a production.

Emotional Values—C. Emotion through Memory

Closely allied to empathy, if not identical with it, is the process of arousing emotions by means of memory. For example, an actress may be able to make herself cry by recalling her childhood sorrow over the death of a pet kitten, or the spectators may be placed in a somber mood by the sight of a coffin on stage which brings back the emotions they have felt at funerals.

ESTHETIC VALUES

Esthetic values which have nothing to do with the emotional and intellectual values of the play are sometimes added to a production for their own sake. With a trashy play this may do no harm and may even help, but it is never wise if the play is worth while. Many productions of *Cradle Song* have been ruined because the director became so fascinated by the opportunity to group the nuns in beautiful pictures that he let the physical beauty distract attention from the spiritual beauty in which the real greatness of the play lies.

An esthetic value that is an integral part of the play never stands alone. It grows out of some intellectual or emotional value and at the same time reinforces or increases that value. Thus, if the actress who plays Juliet is beautiful, the spectators will enjoy her beauty for its own sake; at the same time it is an integral part of the charm which makes them fall in love with her and feel that her death is a tragic event.

Clarity, emphasis, relationship, symbolism, repetition, empathy, and emotion through memory are all used in the expression of esthetic values. 'Selection' and 'arrangement,' the two remaining principles of expression, are usually treated as being purely esthetic. Actually, they concern intellectual and emotional values as well and are intimately connected with the principles of clarity, emphasis, etc. Because of their universal application it will be well to discuss them in a separate section.

COMPOSITION

Selection and arrangement according to some principle is a basic requirement in art and in most, if not all, natural beauty—a magnified snowflake forms a hexagonal pattern, a sunset consists of a set of orange and red tones contrasted with the complementary blue of the sky. The process of selection and arrangement in art is called 'composition.' In the theater composition is an important means of clarifying and intensifying the intellectual and emotional values of the production. When the composition gives pleasure in itself, it creates esthetic values.

COMPOSITION—A. PRINCIPLES

Anything is easier to understand if its parts are selected and arranged in accordance with some principle. Five dollars in quarters, stacked in five neat piles of four coins each, can be comprehended at a glance. Five dollars in miscellaneous small change scattered on a desk would require a minute or two to count. In fact, many people could not count it at all except by arranging the coins in some way, such as by separating each coin from the rest as it was counted.

Compositional principles take a wide variety of forms. We have already seen that a play is improved if it deals with a single theme, i.e., if the elements of the play are selected on the principle that they must conform to the theme. Unity of spirit and unity of style are other compositional principles that guide us in selecting and arranging the material for our play.

Principles which deal primarily with arrangement usually take the form of a pattern. All music is based on two kinds of patterns: (1) a time pattern, such as the one-two-three of a waltz, or the one-two-three-four of a march, and (2) a pitch pattern formed by the scale and the key.

Time patterns are common in the theater. In *Twelfth Night,* II, 5, Maria, Fabian, Sir Toby, and Sir Andrew are hiding, but stick out their heads to watch Malvolio. If the heads appear at random, the effect is weak, but if the first three pop out in one-two-three order, and Sir Andrew (the last) waits two counts and appears on 'six,' the audience will laugh. Also the pause itself characterizes slow-witted Sir Andrew. Both the laugh and the characterization are produced by the purely abstract time pattern.

Color schemes are really color patterns, and the various 'color wheels' sold to help beginning artists and interior decorators are devices for selecting colors according to some principle.

Patterns in line are extensively used by the architect, the painter, and the scene designer. Ninety per cent of all buildings are designed on an axial system (Fig. 5, Pl. V, p. 18) in which the walls are set at right angles and the principal elements are alined or 'placed on axis' with each other. A page in a book is also designed on an axial pattern: the block of type is bounded by straight lines which meet at right angles and which are parallel to the edges of the page; the principal lines of the letters are perpendicular to the lines of print. A page of italic type is difficult to read because a third (slanting) axis is introduced and this tends to confuse both the eye and the mind. Paintings are often based on geometrical forms; many of the greatest paintings of the Renaissance have the figures arranged to fill a triangle. Other types of line patterns will be seen

in Pl. X, p. 62. Actors and directors use these types and also a
number of nongeometrical line patterns, such as the floor patterns
in Pl. XV, p. 102.

The fact that many of the principles underlying composition are
definite patterns does not make composition itself mechanical.
The principles to be used in any particular case must be appropriate
both to the subject matter and to each other, so choosing them requires taste and discrimination. Also, the patterns used in composition can be applied in an infinite number of ways. For example,
most of the settings shown in this book are based on axes, yet they
differ widely from one another. Finally, the underlying pattern is
often disguised in some way, so that whatever mechanical features
it may have are not evident. Thus, the walls of a set may meet at
right angles, but the effect is not mechanical because the set is seen
from the front and all the angles are changed by perspective. Another way of disguising a pattern consists in making small de-
partures from it; e.g., a music box keeps strict time, but a fine
musician varies his time slightly and so avoids a mechanical effect.

COMPOSITION—B. PICTORIAL COMPOSITION

At any given moment in a play the scenery, actors, props, costumes, make-up, and lights form a 'stage picture.' The composition
of a stage picture obeys, to a large extent, the laws of pictorial composition worked out by students of painting, although there are
other factors—such as movement—which must be taken into account. Some aspects of pictorial composition (e.g., color) are more
the province of the designer than of the actor or director, but the
actor and director must understand at least the elements of color
theory if they are to make the most of the designer's ideas. To take
an extremely simple example, if a designer gives an actress a bright-
colored petticoat, she should understand that it is to be used for
emphasis by displaying it at certain important moments and by
keeping it hidden under her skirt the rest of the time.

Abstract Elements. Every stage picture can be analyzed into
the following elements, each of which is used in special ways in
composition.

LINES. These may be real, like the line made by the edge of a

1. DOMINANT HORIZONTALS SUGGEST CALM AND CONTEMPLATION

2. CONFLICTING DIAGONALS CONNOTE ACTION AND STRIFE

3. PALE TONES AND LIGHT MASSES SUIT LIGHT. GAY MOODS

4. HEAVY MASSES AND DARK TONES CREATE SOMBER MOODS

table, or a length of wire. They may be composite (i.e., made up of several lines). In Fig. 3, Pl. X, p. 62, the hill L. is a continuation of the top line of the fence R.; the line of the crossbar on the well passes through the scarecrow's bent knee and then along the top of the second fence panel from L. There are at least two other composite lines in the sketch. Lines may also be imaginary, like the relationship lines which run from one character's eyes to another's face.

SHAPES. These are thought of as if the stage picture were painted on canvas so that everything was flat. In Fig. 2, Pl. X, the shape of the ottoman R. is an ellipse, though the actual ottoman is round, as Fig. 1, Pl. XV, p. 102 shows.

MASSES. These are the various objects on stage when thought of as having both weight and three-dimensional bulk. A mass is usually bounded by several shapes. Note that although both a penny and a marble could be indicated by the same shape—a circle—their masses would be entirely different. The 'esthetic weight' of a mass has some connection with the apparent physical weight of the object, but the two are not identical. Dark objects have more esthetic weight than those painted in pale colors, and the form and function of the object also play a part. The only way to deal with mass is to be guided by your own feelings. If something seems heavy to you, it will probably seem heavy to the audience.

TONES. These are colors, including black and white and all shades and tints. A tone has three qualities: 'hue,' i.e., the place of the tone in the spectrum, such as red, blue, orange, etc.; 'value,' i.e., the lightness or darkness of the tone (note that 'value' here has an entirely different meaning from that given it in acting and directing); and 'intensity,' i.e., the tone's vividness or grayness (see tone chart on p. 207).

SPACE. This is the emptiness which separates the other elements and which is of as much importance in composition as the solid objects themselves.

Connotations. These abstract elements of composition create powerful emotional effects. Horizontal lines induce an empathy of complete relaxation, so a scene in which horizontal lines predominate (Fig. 1, Pl. X, opposite) tends to bring the audience to a mood of calmness, quietness, and peace. Diagonal lines (Fig. 2) are dynamic and so are gentle curves (Fig. 3). Full, intertwining curves are associated with ideas of opulence and luxury.

Memory also plays a part here. Everyone associates red with blood and fire. It is the color of danger signals and the banners of revolution—so it may be used to rouse the appropriate emotions in the audience. Memory effects, however, are not reliable unless guided by other symbols. Red means blood and danger when connected with some melodramatic situation or set off by black and somber grays. In other contexts it connotes red-plush luxury. In still others it suggests warmth and brightness. Its connection with holly berries even makes it an appropriate hue for Christmas. More important than the effects produced by the individual hues is the fact that yellow, orange, and red are warm (or hot) and exciting, whereas green, blue, and violet are cool and formal.

Heavy masses (Fig. 4) always connote emotional weight, but a man standing on massive rocks will be supported by them and convey a sense of security, whereas heavy masses overhead—as in a cave or dungeon—will cause a feeling of oppression. Every element of composition has some such emotional effect: tones of high or low intensity or of light or dark value (Figs. 3 and 4); voices of high or low pitch; fast or slow tempos; etc. Each of these must be studied, because if they are not chosen to create the right emotions they will create the wrong ones.

This problem is not as difficult as it may seem. Your reactions will be much the same as those of your audience, so by keeping alert to these effects you can avoid serious errors. Also, you can develop your sensitivity by noticing how you are affected by the elements used in the plays and pictures you see. Whenever you do a production yourself, or even a classroom exercise, try to think of the lines, tones, masses, etc. which you associate with the emotional values it contains.

Harmony and Contrast. When the lines, the shapes, or the tones of a stage picture are similar, they are said to be harmonious. Thus, a set of costumes in various shades of green would be harmonious. Elements which differ sharply from each other, as do red and green, or round curves and straight lines, give an effect of contrast. As far as possible the elements should either harmonize or form a definite contrast. If they do neither one nor the other, the effect will be meaningless. Ideally, the degree of contrast in the stage picture would equal the amount of conflict in the scene.

Balance. If a grouping seems unbalanced, it will create bad empathies just as a crooked picture does. The principle is simple; think of the stage as a seesaw pivoted on the center line. The masses on one side should balance those on the other. A small mass far from the center on one side will balance a large mass near the center on the other side, just as on a real seesaw. The chief masses with which the director deals are his actors. As these can be moved easily, stage pictures are not difficult to balance. Furthermore, groupings that occupy only one or two areas balance themselves. With such small groupings the spectator's eye does not cover the whole stage, but concentrates on the grouping and instinctively selects the right center of balance.

Stability. Groupings of more than five or six characters often seem unstable, as if they were about to float away. This curious psychological effect must be prevented by placing one or more characters in either or both of the downstage corners. The number of characters needed to stabilize a grouping depends on its size. A large crowd may require two or three figures in each downstage corner (Fig. 4, Pl. XIII, p. 90).

Use of Space. Realism tends to crowd the stage and even to clutter it; nothing is left empty or bare (see photograph, p. 139). Classicism and romanticism, however, need space. Shakespeare is less effective on a small stage, even though there is ample room for the action. The depth of the stage picture is an important space consideration. Fantasy and farce call for shallow groupings, with the actors kept close to the tormentor line. Deeper plays, and also plays which need to appear deeper, demand deeper groupings. Actors tend to work downstage and, unless the director is vigilant, will end by lining up along the footlights.

Composition—C. Beauty

The influence of composition on a spectator may be entirely subconscious. The man who assumes that the conflicting diagonals in

GARDEN OF TIME

Too much beauty stifles drama. Few directors could cope with a setting as lovely as this. The strongly diagonal effect gained from a skillful arrangement of lines which are actually horizontal is technically interesting. However, the lack of any conflicting diagonal weakens the dramatic effectiveness of the setting. Note how the cyclorama simplifies both the design and the construction of scenery.

Fig. 2, Pl. X, p. 62 are accidental is affected by them as much as the man who realizes that they follow a definite principle and were introduced to produce a definite emotional effect. The spectator's awareness of composition does, however, have a direct bearing on the matter of whether or not he will consider a thing beautiful.

Philosophers disagree as to the nature of beauty, but for practical purposes in the theater we can lay down the following working rule. Any element (a stage picture, a gesture, a speech, or even the whole play itself) will be considered beautiful to the extent that the audience is aware that it is selected and arranged according to some principles (i.e., composed), provided: (1) that the composition is not made so obvious it becomes cheap or uninteresting; and (2) that no jarring note spoils the effect. In other words, if you wish to increase the beauty of a stage picture, you can do so by decreasing the contrasts and complications. This automatically increases the simplicity and harmony and makes the composition more apparent. Another method is to choose simpler compositional motifs; most people would find a waltz more beautiful than a piece in five-eight time.

Long lines, including composite lines made up of several elements (Fig. 3), make for simplicity and therefore for beauty, because one long line is easier for the eye to follow than several short ones and the total number of lines is reduced. Rich tones in the costumes and scenery, and strong colors in the lighting, are beautifying elements. This is due to the fact that strong, rich tones harmonize only when their color scheme is fairly simple, whereas the more subdued tones permit subtle harmonies which may easily be overlooked.

In most arts there is serious danger of being too obvious, but the composition of a stage picture will be accepted even if it is as obvious as a colored postcard. This makes stage beauty easy to attain.

Beauty is by no means always desirable. It is usually out of place in realism or theatricalized realism, and it is fatal in melodrama or farce. Such plays demand the more subtle types of composition.

Composition—D. Summary

Composition is a study for a lifetime. The bibliography (p. 289) lists books which will serve as an exciting introduction into some of its many possibilities. Do not let the complexities of the subject frighten you. You will find that they afford opportunities, not difficulties. The important thing to remember is that *when anything is arranged according to a principle or pattern, it is easier for the director to conceive, easier for the actor to remember and execute, and easier for the audience to comprehend.*

Chapter VI

Principles and Methods

A number of principles and methods apply to so many facets of
our work that it seems best to bring them together here, rather
than to deal with them in connection with some special topic such
as interpretation or movement.

VARIETY

A play needs unity if it is not to break down into a series of
vaudeville acts, but it must have variety if it is to hold its audience
at all. Unless the groupings, movements, business, inflections, and
pace are changed frequently, the attention of the spectators will
wander. Variety is not opposed to unity; but unity restricts us to
those variations which are appropriate to the concept, spirit, and
style of the production. We are also limited to those variations which
fit the particular situation. For example, we need one sort of grouping for a love scene and another for a quarrel. In practice we rarely
think of variety as such; we notice the monotonous places and
'break them up.' A designer breaks up bare walls by hanging pictures. A director may break up a static scene by adding movements,
business, etc.

Invention and Selection. A full-length play will need at least five
hundred different poses, not to mention the requirements in the
way of movement and business. Directors and actors cannot provide such variety if they wait for inspiration to strike. They must
have a practical method of stimulating and controlling their imagi-
nations.

Pl. XI, p. 71, shows how this can be done. Sit in a chair and take
various poses at random. Suppose you think of only the six shown
in the first row. Each of these can be varied in a number of ways.
You may change the angle that the pose makes to the audience;

Fig. 7 is very different in effect from Fig. 1 but the pose is the same. Another method is to keep the same position but change the angle of the chair. Sometimes the difference is slight, as when Fig. 2 is changed to Fig. 8; sometimes the original pose will be altered almost beyond recognition, as when Fig. 4 is changed to Fig. 9. Tipping the chair will produce a new series of variations—Fig. 10 is really another version of Fig. 4. Any change in the type of support used will open up more possibilities—Fig. 11 is Fig. 2 on a table, and Fig. 26 is still another variant of Fig. 4.

Of course, only a few of these poses will fit any particular situation, but the rest may be used for other characters or other parts of the play. This method is particularly useful when you need a number of related ideas, such as the kisses in a long love scene. You invent several times as many ways of kissing as you need, choose the most suitable ones, and arrange them in the most effective order.

For practice, try to think of twenty ways of taking a drink—of smoking a cigarette. Then think of twenty things to do with a cigarette besides smoking it. Try other common props—a handkerchief, a coin, a watch. Do not neglect eccentric ideas. The fact that they are not generally useful keeps them fresh and makes them particularly interesting when they do happen to fit the situation.

TOUCHES

A 'touch' is a single, isolated effect which is interpolated at some key moment, and which can be instantly appreciated by the audience. Touches may be developed in any production element. Noel Coward's farce *Blithe Spirit* affords a comic costume touch. Charles, the hero, after the death of his second wife, appears with *two* black mourning bands, one on each sleeve. A tiny moustache is an excellent make-up touch, for it announces instantly that the character is unsympathetic. A supernatural character, like Death in *Death Takes a Holiday,* can use an effective lighting touch by seeming normal in every way except that when he strikes a match for his cigarette, it burns with a green flame.

Touches for Emphasis. Touches create great audience interest and so are always emphatic. Their use must be restricted to those characters who are important at that particular moment. If some unimportant character is given a touch, he will automatically 'take stage' and move into the foreground. On the other hand, a touch is so brief that it is an ideal way of bringing a background character into momentary prominence, particularly if the touch is in some way connected with the principal figure. In one production of *Julius Caesar,* the dying Caesar clung to a platform until Casca stamped on his fingers. This gave Casca brief prominence and at the same time threw extra attention to Caesar.

Touches for Conveying Information. One touch may tell more than a thousand words. A character may be shown to be lying if he hesitates slightly at an important moment in an otherwise plausible story.

Touches for Enrichment. When a scene is dull, it may be given interest by adding touches. Often you can find a master touch from which little touches will grow. In *First Lady,* the dignified principal characters may get down on the floor to examine the law books. This produces a laugh, but the effect is over in a moment unless you renew it by adding other touches on the same idea, such as having the pompous butler walk across the floor on his knees.

Pointing. The abstract gestures, pauses, and tricks of inflection that are used to call attention to particular words or situations are closely allied to touches. Using such abstract effects is called 'pointing' (i.e., giving point to) a speech or situation. A movement of the shoulders or a slight turn of the head at exactly the right moment often turns a dull speech into an electric one by bringing out an important idea that might otherwise have been missed.

MOTIVATION

One of the oldest and best rules of the theater is: Do nothing without a purpose. Originally this advice was directed at young actors, who have a tendency to fidget and wander aimlessly, but it should be taken to heart by everyone. In fact the rule should be enlarged to read: *Do nothing that does not serve both a technical purpose and some purpose of the character.* The character's purpose is called his 'motivation.'

Technical Purposes. The chief technical purposes are: (1) To put the actor in a position required by a grouping or from which

Plate XI   71

POSES
VARIETY – EMPHASIS
Except for Figs. 21 and 26 these
are separate poses, not groupings.

he may carry out some part of the mechanics of the action; thus a character may have to be near a door in order to open it, or he may have to sit in a particular pose to complete a grouping. (2) To provide some abstract effect of variety, emphasis, build, or symbolic movement. (3) To prepare for some such movement in the future.

Character Motivations. Motivations arise out of relationships. When a movement is necessary for some technical reason, and the required relationship-motivation is not present, one must be created. Frequently the motivation is already available and needs only to be realized, as when a character goes to the fireplace and holds out his hands to the blaze to show that he moved for warmth. Often a motivation may be supplied by locating a prop, such as a telephone or a matchbox, in the desired position. In difficult cases, it may be necessary to regroup the characters in order to provide some essential motivation.

INTERRUPTED MOTIVATIONS. If the motivation is clear, a movement may serve its purpose without being completed. Thus, a character standing L. who wishes to walk C. for technical reasons may motivate this by filling his pipe and searching in his pocket for a match. Finding none, he starts toward the matchbox on the mantelpiece R. However, when he reaches C., he is interrupted and stops. He may drop the pipe in his pocket and forget it, or he may save the motivation for a later movement to the mantel.

NEGATIVE MOTIVATIONS. Sometimes a character has an overwhelming motivation for doing something which, for technical reasons, he must not do. I once judged a contest play in which a gunman wished to escape through a door guarded only by two unarmed men. The plot required the gunman to remain on stage, but the director failed to find a reason why he should not shoot the two men and leave. By staying without a motivation, the gunman became ridiculous, and the play lost the contest. There are no rules for dealing with problems of negative motivation. The whole situation must be studied until some loophole is found.

Steals. When technical considerations require something for which no motivation is available, the difficulty may be evaded by doing the thing so unobtrusively that the audience does not notice it at all. Such evasions are called 'steals.' Thus, an actor wishing to make a movement for which he can find no motivation may steal into position while the attention of the audience is fixed on the opposite side of the stage. Steals are never desirable, but they cannot always be avoided.

THE INTEREST CURVE

The attention of the audience should be continuous. However, it will not remain at the same level and so must proceed in waves (Pl. XII, p. 74). The crest of each wave is a minor climax and the crest of the highest wave is the main climax. To some extent the interest curve is inherent in the script, but the production elements must be used to reinforce and correct it.

Build. Forcing the interest curve to rise is called 'building.' A build is produced by steadily increasing some element from the beginning to the end of the desired rise in the interest curve. We may increase:

(1) The emotional tension in the characters.

(2) The degree of emphasis on the principal characters.

(3) The concentration of the emphasis on the principal characters.

(4) The number of actors on stage.

(5) The number and length of movements.

(6) The amount of light.

(7) The volume of sound.

(8) The pace.

Normally only a few of these methods of building are used in any one sequence, and even those few are used sparingly. For the ordinary sequence a slight build in emphasis, pace, and tension will suffice.

Scenes of rising interest make the greatest appeal to the audience, and the steeper the rise the better. One of the director's main duties is to provide the play with an interest curve which devotes the maximum time to rising action and the minimum to falling action and which makes each rise as steep as possible. In doing this he will need to recognize a number of limitations.

(1) The desired height of the main climax varies with the play. A thundering climax is appropriate to a Shakespearean tragedy as at

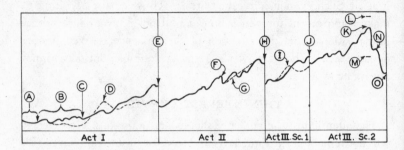

TYPICAL INTEREST CURVE

The height of the line marks changes in the height of the audience interest as the play progresses. The heavy line shows an ideal curve. Dotted lines indicate mistakes.

A. 'Warming-up' period. Do not attempt to create much interest.

B. Introduction. This is usually dull. Interest must be artificially stimulated by touches.

C. Real interest of play starts here. This is usually a definite spot, and the director should note it carefully. It often coincides with the entrance of the principal character.

D. This sequence has been made too dramatic for its position in the play. As a result, the rest of the act seems dull by contrast.

E, H, J, and O. Curtains. Note that the interest is always rising as the curtain falls, and that the next scene begins at a lower point. There is more interest-drop between acts (E and H) than between scenes in the same act (J).

F. Sharp drop in interest after dramatic sequence. Such drops usually occur when an important character leaves the stage.

G. Long, continuous build. Note that the rise in interest is less steep than when the interest increases in waves.

I. Climax of scene reached too soon. This makes the rest of the scene seem uninteresting. In this case, the tension at I should have been held down so that the point of greatest dramatic excitement would not have been reached until the moment before the curtain started to fall.

K. Height of main climax in normal play.

L. Height of main climax in heavy drama.

M. Height of main climax in delicate comedy.

N. Sequence of rising tension after main climax. Without this the audience will lose interest, and the ending will seem flat. When the main climax occurs at the very end of the play, this extra build may be unnecessary. On the other hand, if the main climax comes early, as it does in some Shakespearean plays, you may have to contrive several extra builds to maintain interest until the final curtain.

Even the most thrilling play cannot keep its audience at fever heat from curtain to curtain. A prolonged strain will tire your spectators; you must give them frequent opportunities to relax. Also, the exciting scenes will seem still more exciting when they are contrasted with scenes of comparative calm. Tense scenes in the early part of the play must not be made too thrilling, or the later scenes will seem anticlimactic.

L in the diagram, but would ruin one of Sir James Barrie's delicate comedies (*M*).

(2) During an act, each wave of interest should rise higher than the one before it. Also, the climax of each act should be higher than the climax of the preceding act. If an early scene is permitted to build too high, the later scenes will suffer (*D*).

(3) Long rises overstrain the spectators, sometimes to a point where they laugh at dramatic moments through sheer hysteria. Some sort of relief is necessary, and this is furnished by the falling sections of the interest curve. Relief is almost instantaneous, and, as falling action is dull, it should be gotten over with as quickly as possible. Sharp drops (*F*) are especially desirable if not used too often.

(4) Interest will drop as soon as the build stops. If you reach the end of your build (*I*) before the climax of the scene, the climax will not stand out on the crest of the wave, but will be lost in the falling action on the other side. A common example of this fault is the use of the DC. area. This is the most emphatic part of the stage and normally should be saved for those scenes where the contending forces of the play meet head on. Many actors, however, particularly star actors, make for the DC. area like homing pigeons. Then, having reached the most emphatic position available, they are like the bridge player with a no-trump hand who leads his four aces and then asks, "What do I do next?" A similar mistake occurs when an actor uses his most moving inflections at the beginning of a long speech and then wonders why he cannot hold his audience.

Conservation. The art of starting low, dropping when possible, and avoiding premature exhaustion of your technical resources is called 'conservation.' It is far more difficult than building, and should be given correspondingly more attention.

METHODS OF CONSERVATION. Locate the main climax and the more important minor climaxes. Decide on the height of each. Mark in the script the point where the build to each of these climaxes should begin. Apportion your technical means of building to the length of the scene and do not permit yourself to get ahead of schedule. If the scene runs three pages, and the only available movement is from UC. to DR., as in Fig. 4, Pl. XIV, p. 97, you should not reach DR. before the middle of the third page. It may require ingenuity to do this without feeling nailed to the floor when everything urges you forward, but anything is better than reaching your climactic position too soon and *then* feeling the urge to go farther when you have no place to go.

During the build, look for all possible opportunities to drop back in tension or in one of the production elements. Situations in which such retreats are appropriate are often difficult to find and must be searched for diligently.

Suspense. Suspense is largely a mechanical effect due to skillful management of the interest curve. A climax is approaching. The audience realizes this and wants to race ahead to meet it. However, instead of arriving at the expected time, the climax is delayed. A mere delay of the climax would end in boredom, so the director makes each retarding episode provide a minor climax. Finally the true climax is allowed to arrive. The number of false climaxes varies widely, because the suspense may involve only a short scene or may occupy the greater part of the play.

Shape of the Interest Curve. No two plays call for the same curve, but the following general suggestions apply to all of them:

(1) Do not attempt any build during the first three or four minutes while the spectators are settling down and getting their ears attuned to the theater (*A,* Pl. XII, p. 74), but start the first rise as soon as possible after this 'warming-up' period (*B*).

(2) Vary the time allotted to each wave.

(3) The interest must always be rising when the curtain falls (*E, H, J,* and *O*). If the playwright has not taken care of this with an effective 'tag line,' the director must find a touch strong enough for the needed final 'punch.'

(4) Place the main climax, *K,* as late as possible to avoid the dullness of falling action. In older plays it is usually wise to cut a good deal of the dialog after the main climax.

APPROACHING THEATRICAL PROBLEMS

Every production involves many thousands of problems, ranging from the interpretation of the whole play to the inflection of a single word. With so many things demanding attention, it is easy to waste time on trifles and reach opening night with major difficulties unsolved. The best way to handle this is to make a list of fifteen or twenty problems and then number them in the order of their importance. The importance of a problem does not rest on its difficulty but on the way in which it blocks further progress. When several problems seem equally serious, start with the one that involves the most territory; a problem affecting the whole of Act II would come before one which concerned only the climax of Act III. When half the problems on your list are solved, make out a new list, adding any new problems that have come up and assigning new numbers to all the problems, old and new. If you work in this way, you may not solve all your problems, but you will solve all the important ones. Furthermore, you will avoid *the beginner's most common mistake* of adding extra touches to scenes that are going well, instead of correcting the faults of scenes that are going badly. In writing out your problems, do not be content with brief notes, but state the difficulty in full. A written problem automatically has some clarity, but there is no limit to the vagueness of a problem kept in your head.

Never dodge problems. A problem is a sign that something is wrong. Until you have solved it, you cannot be sure you understand it. You may even be thinking about the wrong problem. If you form the habit of meeting problems squarely, you will be amazed at the frequency with which solving a problem pays an unexpected bonus. Solving a minor difficulty in one act will often clear up a major difficulty in another.

Chapter VII

CASTING

A cast should be chosen for the benefit of the audience, not as a method of rewarding or bribing actors.

PRELIMINARIES

If the best actor available is to be found for each role, the work of casting must begin long before the tryouts are held.

Qualifications. An actor's fitness for a particular role depends more on his suitability than on his technical acting ability. The value of a key depends much less on the quality of its metal than on the way it fits a particular lock. An actor's stage personality may duplicate his everyday personality or it may be radically different. Moreover, his stage personality may change from role to role, even when the roles are superficially similar. What counts is the reactions which the actor, *in that particular role,* is able to rouse in the spectators. If he plays Romeo, he must win their sympathy and persuade them that he is a hotheaded, romantic lover. If he plays Iago, he must avoid their sympathy and make them believe he delights in evil for its own sake. The only safe test is to have each candidate read and act out some scene of the character for which he is being considered. Fortunately, even a little experience with this test will enable a director to apply it with almost certain results.

Casting Committee. The actor affects his audience largely through empathy, and many actors have different empathic effects on different people—especially where sex is involved. This explains why Bette Davis and Robert Taylor stir women more deeply than they do men. A director cannot rely solely on his own responses, but should check them against those of a number of other people

THE YELLOW JACKET

Setting by Norman Zelman

This scene reproduces the stage of a Chinese theater. Almost everything you see is a 'touch.' Note: (1) Comic touch of riding on a wheelbarrow. (2) Property touch of using solid wheel. (3) Scenery touch of using Chinese writing. (4) Character touches in the position of each figure. (5) Production-plan touch in use of property man, L., considered by Chinese convention to be invisible.

who differ in sex, age, and taste. Such a group of empathic guinea pigs is called a 'casting committee.'

Candidates. About a week before tryouts are to be held, the director meets with the committee and outlines the requirements for each character. Everyone is asked for suggestions, and a list of possible candidates for each role is prepared. Candidates on this list are notified of the time and place of tryouts. Announcements through newspaper stories and posters will bring other candidates, and committee members are urged to scout new talent, particularly for those roles which show the weakest prospects.

Scripts. The director should choose his tryout scenes in advance. Scenes of four to eight characters in which the lines are shared equally are useful. So are scenes between the leading female characters, because these roles will draw many candidates. Every important character must appear in at least one of the scenes chosen.

Minor roles which have only a few scattered lines, and which permit enough latitude in interpretation so they can be characterized to fit the actor, may be cast from those candidates who fail to receive a major role. If the exact characterization of a minor role affects the meaning of the play, it must be cast with as much care as the leads.

TRYOUTS

Tryouts are divided into two parts, 'preliminaries' and 'finals.' The preliminaries weed out the unsuitable candidates and reduce the number to workable proportions. They also give the director an over-all picture of the available talent. The only decision to be made about a candidate at the preliminaries is whether he is to be eliminated or called back. This can be settled by a brief reading—five minutes or less, and as several candidates are tested at once, it is possible to hear about fifty candidates in a two-hour tryout.

Preliminary Tryouts. When each candidate arrives, his name, address, and telephone number are recorded by a committee member stationed near the door. A second member lists the candidate's name under the role, or roles, for which he has been suggested or in which he expresses an interest. Candidates who have not been suggested and who have no preference of their own are listed under the roles for which the committee member considers them best suited.

While the listing is going on, the rehearsal furniture is set up (Fig. 3, Pl. XXV, p. 174).

The director opens proceedings with a brief talk in which he:

(1) Outlines the plot, makes a few comments on each important character, and describes the set.

(2) States that the listings already made are tentative and that everyone may try for any part in which he is interested. This policy wastes some time, but it does much to convince candidates that they are receiving a fair trial. Also it frequently brings to light unsuspected talent.

(3) Explains that familiarity with the play is neither necessary nor desirable. Advance preparation tends to obscure those innate qualities on which the choice will be based.

The director then announces the first scene to be used and the characters involved. The first candidate listed under each of these characters is called and provided with a script. The temporary cast thus formed is instructed to go through the scene with all the emotions and actions, just as they would in a rehearsal. Those who are on stage at the beginning of the scene start reading. The rest wait in the wings.

The candidates should invent their own movements and business. The director makes suggestions only when they get into difficulties or when someone seriously misinterprets a character. When the director reaches a decision about a particular candidate he dismisses him and calls for another to replace him. The new candidate goes on with the scene where his predecessor left off. Sometimes a whole batch of candidates may be replaced at one time. When the scene is finished, it may be repeated or a new scene may be chosen. Usually, a candidate is not allowed to read for a second character until everyone has had an opportunity to read once.

Judging Candidates. At preliminary tryouts the candidates tend to huddle in a group and read with a minimum of expression. By contrast, a candidate who is able to give a flashy but unsound reading shows up better than he deserves. For this reason consideration of technical acting ability should be reserved until the final tryouts. During preliminaries a candidate can be judged on three points:

(1) Does he 'come across'? That is, does he rouse empathies? This is apparent at once because a promising candidate seizes the attention whereas a poor one is almost unnoticeable. Candidates who do not show at least fair ability on this point are eliminated without further consideration.

(2) Is the candidate physically *un*suited to the role? A 5′6″ actor cannot play Lincoln, nor will a 200-pound actress succeed as Ophelia. Positive physical qualifications may be noted in the actor's favor, but are less important as they can usually be supplied by the costume and make-up.

(3) Is the candidate believable in the role? If he is trying out for Romeo, would Juliet fall in love with him at first sight? Would it seem reasonable for him to fight a duel? Or take poison? If there is comedy in the role, do the spectators tend to laugh at the funny

lines? Even at a first reading a candidate for a comic character should raise at least a smile.

When the preliminary tryouts are over, the director checks his reactions with those of the committee. He should not ask, "Shall we cast John?" but rather, "Did you think John was funny (or romantic, or whatever the character requires)?"

Call-backs. After the unsuitable candidates have been eliminated, a list of those to be called back for final tryouts is prepared. If there are more than four candidates for a role, the weaker ones should be dropped. If there are only two or three, the weaker ones may be given the benefit of the doubt. However, do not call back a candidate for a role if another candidate has shown himself definitely superior. A candidate may be called back for more than one role. Those called for the finals may be notified by telephone or by a posted list. If there are no promising candidates for a role, the committee members must find new candidates. These need not be given preliminary tryouts, but can be tested like regular call-backs.

Finals. The first step is to check each candidate's suitability for his role in detail. Scenes which are characteristic or difficult should be chosen, and the director should make frequent suggestions and note the candidate's ability to respond. If a role contains more than one mood, candidates for it should read a typical scene for each mood; e.g., for Lady Macbeth both the murder scene and the sleep-walking scene should be read. Sometimes a candidate will be brilliant in one mood and hopeless in another. No one should be cast who is not fairly good in all the required moods. A candidate need not demonstrate his suitability continuously. If he shows some necessary quality for only an instant, he must have it, and the director can develop it during rehearsals.

Acting ability will have been demonstrated during the readings. However, care should be taken to test each candidate for his ability to make himself heard in the back row of the auditorium without loss of vocal quality. For the ordinary realistic role, this is the only technical acting skill required. Emotional roles and roles in stylized plays need more, such as precision and freedom of gesture, vocal variety, ability to let go emotionally, etc. Often special tests have to be devised for these, such as having the actor go through a bit of pantomime or read a scene in a certain way. If ability to sing, dance, or perform some acrobatic feat is required, it may be more convenient to test this at a special tryout. Anyone who may be called upon to appear in a revealing costume should be viewed in shorts or a bathing suit. Dress rehearsal is too late to discover that Romeo is knock-kneed or that Rosalind's thighs can only be deplored.

Each actor must not only suit his own part but fit with the cast as a whole. Actors who look alike, or who have similar voices, should not be used in the same play; the hero should be taller than the heroine; the loser in a fight must not be disproportionately muscular; etc.

At final tryouts, advice from committee members should be given due weight, but the ultimate decision rests with the director.

Supplementary Tryouts. Final tryouts rarely end with a complete cast. Usually one or two roles, which may range from walk-ons to leads, are unfilled. I have rehearsed for two weeks with one lead missing, but troublesome as this is, it is far better than giving a role to an unsuitable actor. Candidates found after final tryouts may be tested individually or in a regular rehearsal. In the rehearsal test they are simply handed a script and treated as if the role were already theirs. If some special test is needed (such as a scene which is not being rehearsed) it can be held at a separate time.

For individual tryouts, the candidate is given a scene and allowed to read it over to himself so that he understands the flow of it. He is then asked to go through his role in the scene, reading his own lines aloud and either skipping the lines of the other characters or reading them silently. The director will usually find it necessary to help the candidate with encouragement and suggestions, but he should not read the other lines himself or he will lose his critical attitude. A carefully conducted individual test is as accurate as a regular tryout, but it takes much longer (at least half an hour) and is more of a strain on both actor and director.

Chapter VIII

GROUPINGS

Usually the director finds it convenient to plan his action as a series of groupings or tableaux, like the pictures in a comic strip (Pl. IX, p. 52). As the rehearsals progress, the groupings are blended into each other with movement, so that they cease to have any separate existence and become part of the flow of the play. Each grouping should express its situation so clearly that the spectators can follow at least the main outline of the play even if they miss the words (that Deaf Old Lady). Notice in Pl. IX that each grouping represents literally the words which would be used to describe the situation figuratively. In Fig. 1, *A* 'finds *B* and *C* together'; in Fig. 2, *C* 'confronts' *A* while *B* 'stands back of' *C*; etc. If you have a scene where the 'other woman' 'comes between' the hero and the heroine, arrange a grouping in which she literally comes between them. If two characters are 'on opposite sides' of a question, try to find something that will symbolize the question and then place the characters on opposite sides of it. You can hardly overdo symbolism of this sort or make it too clear for the Deaf Old Lady in the Back Row, provided that the positions of the characters are adequately motivated.

THE MECHANICS OF THE ACTION

The most vital requirement of a grouping is that it must satisfy the essential mechanics of the action: if two lovers must kiss, they cannot be placed on opposite sides of the stage; if someone is to play the piano, the grouping must permit him to sit on the piano bench; when a character speaks his last line before he exits, he should normally be by the door, in order to avoid a silent and probably uninteresting cross. Mechanical requirements of this sort

Community Theater, Harrisburg, Pennsylvania

POMEROY'S PAST

Setting by Henning Nelms

Even the simplest grouping should avoid obvious symmetry unless the style of the play calls for it. Note how the spacing between the figures varies. The effectiveness of this grouping also depends on the fact that the figure on the sofa points her knees in one direction and turns her head in another. This makes her a link between the single figure, R., and the rest of the characters. Note also how the characters are distinguished by the way they contrast in type and size. See Fig. 1, Pl. XXV, p. 174.

are vital and, unfortunately, they often conflict with other factors that must be considered in arranging groupings.

CHOOSING AREAS

Each area (see Pl. IV, p. 17) possesses definite qualities of its own. These qualities influence scenes played in the area to an extent that seems incredible at first thought, but which you can easily observe for yourself once the qualities are pointed out to you. As far as the essential mechanics will permit, each grouping should be arranged in the area which will best convey its fundamental qualities.

Qualities of Each Area. (1) Areas vary in inherent strength from R. to L. See p. 17. This means that, other things being equal, when two characters are in conflict, the one standing in a R. area will seem stronger than the one standing in a C. or a L. area. (2) The upstage areas are remote from the audience, which makes them cold and distant. (3) Areas near the walls of the set are soft and intimate, whereas the DC. area, which is isolated from the set, is harsh. (4) The L. areas are, for some reason, colder than the R. areas and often suggest something sinister.

Taking all these elements into account, the individual areas have the following characteristics:

UL. is soft, remote, weak. It is used for unimportant scenes. It is effective for horror scenes because it softens them, and for ghost scenes because it gives them an other-world quality.

UR. is similar to UL., but stronger and not so well suited to horror and ghost scenes. Minor scenes are often played here.

DR. is intimate, warm, strong—excellent for love scenes and scenes of humanity and kindliness. Fireplaces are often located here because of its strong 'hearth and home' connotation.

DL. is also intimate, but weaker and colder than DR. It is used for secondary love scenes, but it is particularly suited to secrets, scandals, jealousies, and conspiracies.

UC. is remote and cold but quite strong—a good area in which to begin important scenes that will move downstage later.

DC. is strong, cold, bare, emphatic. It is used for scenes in which the forces of the play meet face to face, and should usually be reserved for that purpose.

The inherent characteristics of an area may be counterbalanced by other effects. For example, platforms UL. or UR. add strength and emphasis to these areas.

When several areas are occupied, you need consider only the qualities of the area which contains the principal characters. When the principal characters are located in two or more areas, the effect of the individual area is weakened to a point where it may usually be ignored.

RELATIONSHIPS

Groupings should show the relationships of the characters to each other and to any symbolic objects on stage. Furthermore, the various indicators should be focused in such a way that the spectator's eyes go automatically to the center of interest. This can usually be handled in small groupings by having the silent characters look at the speaker's face or at whatever other point happens to be important. In large groupings this treatment is monotonous, and therefore one or two characters usually face away from the center of interest. However, these characters should look at other characters who are looking at the center of interest. Normally it is bad for one figure to face entirely away from the group, as does the girl L. in Fig. 1, Pl. X, p. 62. If you cover this figure with your finger, the effect is much more satisfactory. Now, everyone looks at the standing figure except the man on the sofa. He looks at the man DR., who in turn looks at the standing figure. In this way the spectator's eye is led back to the center of interest no matter where it happens to wander.

If the center of interest is off stage, it can be brought into the stage picture by having a character look at it, as does the girl L. in Fig. 1, Pl. X. However, in this case either: (1) everyone else should focus on the figure who is looking offstage, or (2) there should be no center of interest among the group. Two simultaneous centers of interest are always bad. The audience can watch only one spot at a time.

EMPHASIS IN GROUPING

The distribution of emphasis (see p. 51) is particularly important in connection with grouping, and there are a number of forms of emphasis which apply only to this field. The different forms sometimes support each other and sometimes conflict. The director must balance them to obtain the desired result.

Emphasis of Area. A character in the UL. area receives the least emphasis. UR. is more emphatic, and then comes DL. The UC. and DR. areas are almost equal. The DC. area is the most emphatic.

Relationship to Audience. The more closely a character is related to the audience, the more emphatic he is. This relationship may be made: (1) by nearness to the audience, (2) by turning toward the audience. Turning toward the audience has a greater effect than nearness. In Fig. 4, Pl. V, p. 18 both characters make the same angle with the audience, so the woman is more emphatic because she is downstage. However, realism usually compels the downstage character to turn toward the upstage character, as in Fig. 3. Here the man is more emphatic, because the fact that he is almost facing the audience, while the woman is nearly profile, outweighs his upstage position. Fig. 2, Pl. XXI, p. 150 shows the relative order of emphasis given by the various angles an actor makes with the direct axis. F is more emphatic than G because the actor is set squarely on the stage axis. Turning toward the audience is called 'turning out'; turning away is 'turning in.'

A character can decrease his relationship to the audience not only by turning in but also by tipping his head up or down (Fig. 1, Pl. XXI). The strongest position (*C*) is when the actor looks directly at the face of the balcony, if there is one, or about three feet above the heads of the last row of the audience in auditoriums having only one floor.

Elevation. The higher a character's head is, the greater the emphasis. The third line of Pl. XI, p. 71, shows how the emphasis rises and falls with the height of the figure.

Isolation. Setting a figure off from its surroundings provides a powerful form of contrast. The emphasis of the DC. area is partly due to its isolation from the walls of the set. Isolation may be obtained by placing one character alone and massing the others in one or two groups. However, this should be done only when such an arrangement pictures the relationships of the characters. Do not follow Ethel Barrymore's practice of gaining isolation emphasis for a death scene by having the sorrowing relatives avoid the sufferer as if they feared smallpox. Isolation may also be secured by separating a figure from its surroundings by a frame, such as a doorway in the back wall of the set.

Colors. Light and brilliant colors tend to be more emphatic than those which are dark and dingy.

Size. Large figures tend to be more emphatic than small ones. I once substituted a large understudy for a small actor and the entire emphasis of the play was upset.

Support. A figure in a grouping may gain emphasis not only by contrast but also by support. When the figures in a group focus on the principal object of interest, they give it emphasis through support. This form of emphasis is of great practical utility in shifting the attention of the audience quickly from one spot to another.

REPETITION. A figure in a doorway is emphatic not only because it is set off by the frame but also because its line is repeated by the line of the door jambs. A similar effect of repetition is produced when an officer is followed by one or two guards.

BORROWED SIZE. The effective size of a figure may be increased by associating it with something else. When a character leans on or even touches a piece of furniture, he adds the emphasis of its size to that of his own. (Notice the central figure in Fig. 1, Pl. X, p. 62.) This increase in effective size more than makes up for the loss in isolation.

COVERING

When one figure or object is hidden behind another, it is said to be 'covered.' Ordinarily a covered object loses emphasis. Intentional covering is often used to obscure the knife-thrust of a murder, both to disguise the fact that it is faked and to soften the effect of horror.

When an actor speaks, his lips are normally the center of interest and should be visible even though he is eating, drinking, smoking, sobbing, telephoning, or embracing. In such cases the actor may cover his mouth during pauses and uncover it when he speaks, or he may adopt a pose which leaves the mouth uncovered (Fig. 9, Pl. XIII, p. 90).

An actor who turns more than 90° away from the audience automatically covers his own face. If he speaks in this position (*F* or *G*, Fig. 2, Pl. XXI, p. 150) he is said to 'talk upstage.' If he speaks in any other position he is said to 'talk downstage.' Talking upstage involves a number of disadvantages: (1) The voice is muffled so that unusual volume and distinctness are needed to keep words from being lost. (2) When the spectators cannot see the actor's lips move, they find it difficult to tell who is speaking. (3) By turning his back, the speaker loses emphasis just when he needs it most.

These disadvantages are not serious when the action duplicates the words; e.g., a character says, "Have a cigarette," and at the same time extends his pack. Speaking upstage is also practical when the audience does not expect to understand the words or is not interested in them. This happens with mob cries and in cases where the speaker is incoherent with rage or terror, uses a foreign language, or keeps repeating himself.

COVERING—A. MOTIVATIONS FOR TURNING OUT

In most situations, however, the problems involved in talking upstage are so difficult that it is far simpler to arrange for the actor to talk downstage (i.e., at least in profile). The only difficulty here is that of providing a motivation for turning downstage, or rather of

Plate XIII

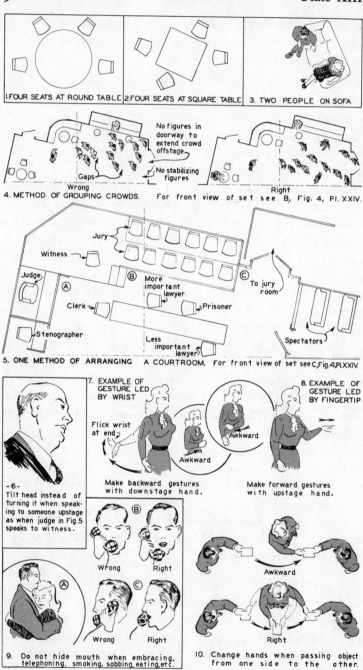

1. FOUR SEATS AT ROUND TABLE

2. FOUR SEATS AT SQUARE TABLE

3. TWO PEOPLE ON SOFA

No figures in doorway to extend crowd offstage.

No stabilizing figures

Gaps

Wrong

Right

4. METHOD OF GROUPING CROWDS.   For front view of set see B, Fig. 4, Pl. XXIV.

Jury

Witness

Judge

(A)

(B) More important lawyer

(C) To jury room

Clerk

Prisoner

Stenographer

Less important lawyer

Spectators

5. ONE METHOD OF ARRANGING A COURTROOM. For front view of set see C, Fig. 4, Pl. XXIV.

7. EXAMPLE OF GESTURE LED BY WRIST

8. EXAMPLE OF GESTURE LED BY FINGERTIP

Flick wrist at end

Awkward

Awkward

Make backward gestures with downstage hand.

Make forward gestures with upstage hand.

-6-
Tilt head instead of turning it when speaking to someone upstage as when judge in Fig.5 speaks to witness.

(B)

Wrong   Right

(A)

(C)

Wrong   Right

Awkward

Right

9. Do not hide mouth when embracing, telephoning, smoking, sobbing, eating, etc.

10. Change hands when passing object from one side to the other.

overcoming any natural tendency the character may have for turning upstage. This can always be done by means of one of the methods given below. Problems of this sort are extremely common, and every actor and director should learn to master them.

Grouping for Motivation. As far as possible, plan all groupings with the motivations in mind. This means that every speaker should be at least as far upstage as the person to whom he speaks. If a character has a decided majority of the lines in the scene, he should be given the upstage position (Fig. 3, Pl. XIII, opposite). If two characters have the same number of lines, they should be placed on the same transverse axis (*B*, Fig. 6, Pl. XXIV, p. 170).

Speaking to Character Farthest Downstage. When a speech is addressed to any one of several people or to a group in general, the speaker should face the person farthest downstage. On the same principle, any imaginary offstage object which a character faces while speaking should be thought of as being far enough downstage to permit the speaker to turn well out (Fig. 7, Pl. XXIV, p. 170).

Turning Away. People who have their feelings hurt, or who are shy or ashamed, naturally turn their backs on those to whom they are speaking. By placing such characters downstage, the whole group will be enabled to turn out (Fig. 5, Pl. IX, p. 52).

Countermotivation. When a character has some motivation for facing upstage, a second motivation may often be supplied which will overcome the first and permit the actor to turn out. One way of doing this is to have him lie or sit in such a position that turning upstage would require more effort than the situation warrants. (See girl at desk in Fig. 1, Pl. XXII, p. 153.) Another method is to give the speaker something to do which will turn him downstage. Often the merest trifle is enough. A woman may place a knitting bag on the floor by the downstage side of her chair. On her lines she fumbles in the bag or examines her knitting.

Comedy lines are most effective when spoken directly toward the audience. This may be made to appear entirely natural if two motivating factors are provided, one on each side of the speaker. In Fig. 4, Pl. IX, p. 52 the girl can turn from *C* to *A* and by a carefully rehearsed 'accident' arrange to be facing front just as she delivers the laugh line.

Steals. When an actor speaks to another who is slightly upstage (e.g., when the judge in Fig. 5, Pl. XIII, p. 90 speaks to the witness) he does not look directly at the listener but faces straight across stage. The difference in angle is so small that the audience does not notice the steal. The effect is much better if the speaker tips the top of his head upstage, as many people in real life actually do tip their heads instead of turning them (Fig. 6).

SPECIAL GROUPING PROBLEMS

There are a few difficult grouping problems which occur so frequently that every director, actor, and scene designer should know the methods used in solving them.

Seating at Tables. Fig. 1, Pl. XIII, p. 90 shows how to seat four people at a round table. When four people must be seated at a square table, it is almost necessary to rake the table as in Fig. 2. An oblong table is more satisfactory than a square one.

When a number of people must sit at a long table, as in the jury room scene of *Ladies of the Jury,* nothing is gained by raking the table, but other devices must be adopted:

(1) If the number of characters is odd, place the extra character on the upstage side.

(2) The most important character sits at the R. end and the next most important at the L. end. The remaining characters are seated partly according to size and partly according to importance. Small and/or unimportant characters sit downstage; large and/or important ones sit upstage and also have cushions placed in their chairs to give them extra height.

(3) Keep the downstage seats vacant as much as possible, particularly the seat in front of an upstage speaker. Motivations can usually be found to delay the seating of a downstage character or to have him leave the table.

(4) Both up- and down-stage characters should rise to speak whenever circumstances permit. Downstage speakers should address their lines to the other downstage characters or to the person at the far end of the table.

Little Theater, Houston, Texas

LADIES OF THE JURY

Setting by Jack C. Hayes

This set is the one shown in Fig. 5, Pl. XIII, p. 90 and also at C, Fig. 4, Pl. XXIV, p. 170. Court-room scenes present many difficult problems in grouping the characters. For this reason, you should plan the groupings first and then design a setting that will make these groupings possible.

(5) When an upstage character must speak while the person below him is in place, the latter should bend over to write a note on the table or to pick up something dropped on the floor.

Two Characters on Sofa. When two characters sit on a sofa that runs more or less up- and down-stage, the upstage position is given to the character with the greater number of lines. This character sits on the edge of the sofa while the other sits far back (Fig. 3, Pl. XIII).

Important Character without Lines. Occasionally a character who is important in a scene will have few lines or none at all. The simplest solution is to place this character in the center of the group. Then, as the attention moves from one speaking character to another, some of it will fall on him. If the character must be separated from the group, the others should focus him frequently both with looks and gestures.

Courtroom Scenes. These are difficult because they present many motivations for turning upstage and few for turning out. The arrangement of the set will depend on whether or not a jury is re-quired, and also on the relative importance of the characters. Fig. 5, Pl. XIII shows an arrangement used for *Ladies of the Jury.* The judge, the witness, and the jurymen are about the same distance from the tormentor line and can talk to each other or to the lawyers without turning upstage. The less important lawyer must rise and walk upstage when he examines a witness. Speeches to the jury can be made from points *A, B,* or *C.*

Crowds. When a principal plays a scene with a crowd, he is usually on one side of the stage with the crowd on the other (Fig. 4). Important crowd characters are placed in front or on the downstage side. If the crowd must surround the principal, he should stand on a chair, table, or platform. If the crowd is mere background, it is put upstage while the main characters are downstage.

The following suggestions will make a stage crowd seem larger (Fig. 4): (1) Avoid gaps by placing a screen of actors downstage and scattering the rest to give depth. (2) Have a few actors (or stage hands) in the entrances to suggest that the crowd extends offstage, and let the speaker address this imaginary offstage crowd as much as possible. (3) Actors should keep as far apart as possible and avoid any tendency to bunch. (4) Overcoats, or other bulky costumes, help.

VARIETY IN GROUPING

Grouping demands great variety. Not only should the poses of the various characters within the grouping differ, but the arrangement of the figures should never be repeated even with different characters except in those cases where the director wishes to call attention to the fact that one scene echoes another (see p. 56). This means that a play will need between one and two hundred groupings, not counting minor variations.

Variety in Areas. One way of obtaining variety is by changing the area. The first grouping can be arranged in a single area, the second may take the full stage, the third may occupy three areas, the fourth may again be in a single area, but in a different one from the first, etc. There are 63 possible combinations of the six areas, and although 16 of these are not of much practical use, 47 remain, so there is no excuse for repeating the same area combination over and over again in any one production.

The director may build by starting in an unemphatic area and moving into more and more emphatic ones. As usual, conservation is more difficult than building, so reserve the DC. area for important scenes. However, the value of this area is not spoiled if it is occupied by minor characters or used for transition scenes.

In plays with a single set, it is wise to reserve one area—usually UR. or DL.—for the last act, so that something fresh can be given the audience.

Three Characters. Characters should almost never be placed in a straight line. This means that three characters can be arranged only in a triangle. A play like *Anna Christie,* which has a number of three-character sequences, is likely to become monotonous unless the director takes advantage of all the ways in which triangular groupings can be varied. These possibilities are listed below. All of them, except the first and fifth, are illustrated in Pl. IX, p. 52. (1) Move the triangle to a different area. (2) Change the size of the triangle. (3) Turn its apex up- or down-stage. (4) Change the shape of the triangle. (5) Reverse it. (6) Have the figures face in different directions relative to the triangle. (7) Use poses which disguise the triangular shape. (8) Change the level of one of the figures so that the triangle made by their heads is tilted.

PLANNING GROUPINGS

Every director should learn to plan his groupings on paper as shown in the little diagrams in Pls. VI and VII, pp. 26 and 27. This enables him to work without his actors and keep an accurate record of his thoughts. Furthermore, many matters are clearer on paper than they are in rehearsal. This is especially true of floor patterns, including those involving axes and areas. In fact, if a grouping looks well on the floor plan, it is almost certain to look well on stage.

In planning groupings, the director should begin with those in which some character is required to be in a particular spot by the mechanics of the action, such as being near the door when the moment comes for him to make an exit. Next, the pivotal scenes and climaxes should be planned so that they may be played in the appropriate areas. The less important scenes can then be filled in. In doing this the director should work for a smooth flow of movement and not plan groupings which require an actor to jump from one side of the stage to the other and back again without reason.

Chapter IX

MOVEMENT

Movement takes place when a character yields to a relationship motivation (see p. 72). Every situation contains motivation for some movement.

TYPES OF MOVEMENT

Each movement should correspond exactly to the motive which causes it; e.g., when we are repelled, we step back. Movements should also show the strength of the motive.

Straight Movements. When motivations are strong and simple, movements are straight. The need for conservation makes it desirable to reserve such movements for important moments. Overuse of straight movements produces an exaggerated effect suited only to burlesques of old-fashioned melodramas.

Curved Movements. A straight line is the shortest distance between two points, but a path across an open field is always curved. People dislike moving in straight lines, so when their motivations are not compellingly strong, they normally move in curves. A person also follows a curve when he is acted upon by more than one relationship. In Fig. 1, Pl. XIV, p. 97, the man is drawn to the fireplace for warmth, but his relationship to the sofa (fear of bumping into it) makes him curve away from it (*A*) although a straight movement would have been possible. If he had suddenly seen his long-lost sweetheart in front of the fireplace, the attraction would have been so much greater that he would have ignored the sofa and moved in a straight line (*B*).

Curved movements have two important advantages: (1) They are more graceful than straight lines. (2) By choosing the appropriate curve, an actor can end his movement facing at any desired

Plate XIV   97

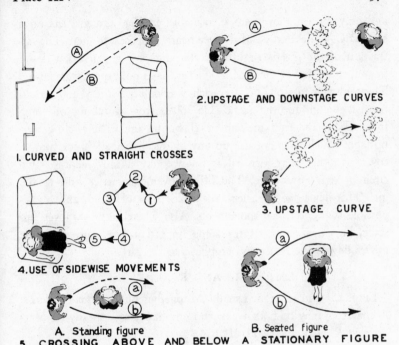

1. CURVED AND STRAIGHT CROSSES

2. UPSTAGE AND DOWNSTAGE CURVES

3. UPSTAGE CURVE

4. USE OF SIDEWISE MOVEMENTS

A. Standing figure

B. Seated figure

5. CROSSING ABOVE AND BELOW A STATIONARY FIGURE

angle (Fig. 2), whereas, with a straight movement, this can only
be done by a turn at the end, which is inconsistent with the direct
motivation implied by the straight line. The 'upstage curve,' i.e.,
the curve which is convex upstage (A, Fig. 2), tends to turn the
actor toward the audience, which is normally advantageous. This
is particularly true when the over-all movement is at an upstage
angle (Fig. 3). Such a curve turns the actor toward the audience
for the last part of his speech, which is desirable if the actor speaks
as he moves, because the last part of a speech is usually the most
important.

Sidewise Movements. Relationships either draw a character
toward something or drive him away from it. When both relationships exist at once, the character tends to circle the object like a
strange dog which is uncertain whether to attack or run away.
Whole circles are rare on stage, but small arcs made with one or
two sidewise steps are common. These show doubt and irresolution.
They are also used technically when a long scene must be played

and only a short movement is available. In Fig. 4, a girl sits on a
sofa DR. while her bashful sweetheart proposes to her. The attraction of the girl is slightly greater than his embarrassed desire
to run, so he moves forward. However, he is only three steps away.
Three movements of one step each would lack variety and would
not be enough for the scene. He solves this by taking one step
forward for the first movement. Then he makes a circling step
upstage, which does not use up any of the distance left for him to
cover. Another step forward is followed by a movement of two
circling steps downstage. The fifth movement carries him to the
girl. This device adds variety, shows his state of mind, and makes
possible two additional movements. Also when the boy moves upstage, he gains emphasis for some important line, and when he
moves downstage he throws emphasis to the girl.

EMPHASIS AND STRENGTH

Emphasis and strength usually go together but are not the same.
A character may be both weak and emphatic; e.g., the dying Mercutio in *Romeo and Juliet,* III, 1.

The comparative strength and emphasis of different movements
is simple to determine, but every movement involves other factors
which may conflict with the effect of the movement itself. Movement from a low level to a high one is intrinsically strong and
emphatic, but if it makes the actor turn his back on the audience
the total effect may mean losses in both strength and emphasis.
The result of such conflicting factors can be learned only by experiment, but the better you understand the intrinsic qualities of the
various movements the less difficulty you will have.

Emphasis. Every movement by a character gives him some emphasis. Long movements are more emphatic than short ones. The
effect is increased by movements which add contrast, carry the
character to a higher level or to a more brightly lighted area, or
increase the intrinsic emphasis of the character's pose (Fig. 12 to
Fig. 17, Pl. XI, p. 71), angle (*F* to *A,* Fig. 2, Pl. XXI, p. 150), or
position on stage (UL. to DC.).

Strength. Aggressive movements show strength. Retreating
movements show weakness. Curved movements are weaker than

straight ones; the deeper the curve the greater the weakness. Movements from L. to R., or from a low level to a high one, are inherently strong, but the effect may be overcome by conflicting factors.

Strength is neither good nor bad in itself, but should be appropriate to the strength of the character in the scene. In scenes where there is no conflict, problems of strength do not arise unless the character's latent strength or weakness must be shown.

Movement Endings. The ending of a movement has much more effect on its emphasis and strength than has the movement itself. When a man sits, the movement is from high to low and therefore weak, but if he slumps a little as he sits and then straightens up smartly, the effect is as strong as if he had risen. Conversely a strong movement with a weak ending is weak.

The ending of a gesture is particularly important. Die-away endings are always weak. A finish of any sort gives strength. Experiment with the following finishes. They are arranged in ascending order of strength and emphasis.

(1) Make a little extra gesture at the end, such as a slight flick of the wrist.

(2) Stop the gesture abruptly by locking your muscles. This is useful only with straight, direct gestures.

(3) Make a noise at the end of the gesture by snapping your fingers or pounding your fist on something.

The strength of each gesture should match the spiritual strength of the character at that moment. Gestures which are slightly too strong or too weak show that the character is insincere (or that the actor is incompetent). A serious discrepancy between the strength of the gesture and the strength of the character produces a burlesque effect.

LENGTH OF MOVEMENT

When a director says, "Take one step," he really means, "Take one step, plus the half step necessary to bring you back into normal standing position." Such 'single' steps are used chiefly for adjustments where there is no real change of grouping. A movement which is long enough to make a real change is called a 'cross.' The term covers movements which are up- or down-stage, as well as those which go across stage. However, crosses which come straight downstage are rare, and those which go straight upstage are almost unknown. In a normal cross, each step taken with the upstage foot opens the actor slightly out, and each step taken with the downstage foot turns him in. As the first step in any cross is normally taken with the upstage foot, and as it is normally desirable to end turned slightly out, it follows that a normal cross contains an odd number of steps. If you will experiment with crosses, you will find that the movement causes the interest curve to rise for the first three steps, but that the curve then drops sharply, so that a cross of five or more steps tends to be dull. This leads to the conclusion that a normal cross should contain three steps (really three and a half). Actors usually follow this rule subconsciously. A three-step cross covers about 5′. If a longer cross is made by a background character, such as a bellboy in a hotel lobby, the interest drop after the third step is really an asset. However, long crosses by important characters must use one of the following techniques to sustain interest:

(1) Break the cross into three-step units, even if the pauses between the units are only momentary.

(2) Have the character do something at the third step, such as begin a speech, glance over his shoulder, etc. The slightest touch is enough to keep the interest alive.

(3) Have some other person start to speak or supply a touch, using the crosser's third step as a cue. Here of course the attention goes to the other actor at least momentarily.

(4) Use either very quick or very slow steps, so that the usual accent on each step is destroyed.

FLOOR PATTERNS

The floor pattern of a cross or of a series of crosses is of great importance.

Crossing Above and Below. We have already seen that the normal cross is made in a slight curve which is convex upstage. This applies both to crosses on a bare part of the stage and to crosses around ordinary furniture. However, when one actor crosses

Little Theater, Houston, Texas

JULIUS CAESAR

Setting by Henning Nelms

Modern-dress productions of Shakespeare introduce many style elements which must be carefully blended. This setting was designed with the groupings in mind, but the chief consideration was the movement pattern. The arrangement of steps and entrances made it natural for the characters to move in sweeping curves which simplified the direction and accentuated the violent spirit of the tragedy.

another, the situation is more complicated. (1) If the stationary character is standing and the crossing character is speaking, the cross should be made downstage (*b* in *A*, Fig. 5, Pl. XIV); otherwise the standing character will cover the crossing one. (2) When a cross above a standing character cannot be avoided, the crosser should stop talking while covered (dotted line in *a*, *A*, Fig. 5) and begin again on the other side. (3) If the stationary character is seated, and the crosser speaks to him directly, it is better to cross upstage, as this provides a natural motivation for opening out (*a* in *B*, Fig. 5). (4) Unimportant or furtive characters normally cross upstage.

Movement Patterns. Movement is not merely a method of getting from place to place; it is a language in itself. Often it is better to plan the direction of a scene or a play as a pattern in movement and then devise groupings to fit, rather than to plan the groupings first. Movements, like groupings, should be literal translations of the figurative expressions you would use to describe the scene.

Plate XV

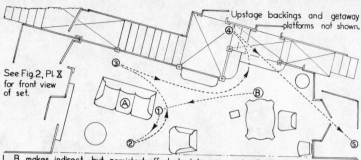

Upstage backings and getaway platforms not shown.

See Fig. 2, Pl. X for front view of set.

1. B. makes indirect but persistent efforts to take command of the home, symbolized by the hearth R. At the end she is defeated and driven out the door L.

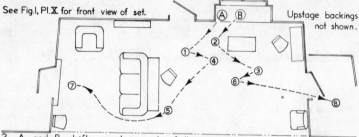

See Fig. I, Pl. X for front view of set.

Upstage backings not shown.

2. A. and B. drift apart in spite of their repeated attempts at reconciliation.

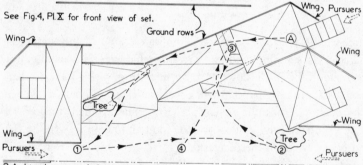

See Fig. 4, Pl. X for front view of set.

Wing   Pursuers

Ground rows

Wing

Tree

Wing

Wing

Pursuers

Tree

Pursuers

3. A. tries to escape but is surrounded. Pursuers are heard but do not enter until A. reaches ③.

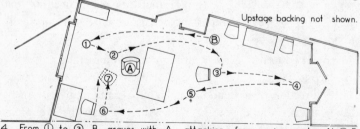

Upstage backing not shown.

4. From ① to ③ B. argues with A. attacking from various angles. At ④ B. withdraws but at ⑤ he returns to the attack. At ⑥ B. pretends to yield in order to 'get around' A. At ⑦ B. approaches A. from his other side.

Fig. 1, Pl. XV, p. 102 is a movement pattern for *Guest in the House,* which shows the general movements of the Guest, *B* (unsympathetic character), in the play as a whole, and is the actual path she takes in the last scene when a character seated at *A* drives her out of the house by a psychological trick.

Fig. 2 shows a pattern appropriate to a scene where two characters drift apart. The numbers show the order of the movements. Notice how at the end they are separated by the sofa, which symbolizes the barrier between them more effectively than mere space. This basic pattern could be used whether the characters go through a series of violent quarrels and reconciliations, or merely discover that they are uncongenial.

The pattern in Fig. 3 symbolizes the idea of being surrounded and trapped. If *A* is a hunter pursued by Indians, he will probably follow the path in the diagram almost exactly. If he is a bashful youth trying to avoid the girls at a Sunday-school picnic, he would use the same general pattern but would break it up into small nervous movements.

Pacing Scenes. The movement pattern is especially important in a scene where a character paces up and down (Fig. 4, Pl. XV). Such scenes are sure to be monotonous unless the pattern is varied as much as possible. It should never repeat itself unless an effect of repetition is deliberately sought. The pattern should permit the moving actor to face downstage when he is speaking. He should pause when the stationary actor speaks, and at that time should be in such a position that the speaker is not compelled to talk upstage.

GESTURE

Although gestures are abstract, they are not without significance. A shrug is significant; so is tearing one's hair. The actor usually does not have to plan the meaning of gesture, because *if he feels a thing strongly and lets himself go, he will automatically gesture expressively.* This is the real answer to the question, "What shall I do with my hands?" If the actor is in character, the question of what to do with his hands would no more occur to him than it would to the character himself.

Freedom. Unfortunately, most Americans and Englishmen are badly inhibited in their gestures. Their elbows seem frozen to their sides, and their hands either do not move at all or jerk in short arcs. After a lifetime of that, *rigor mortis* will not come as a novelty.

To cure this fear of gesture, begin by learning a ten- or twelve-line speech, preferably a bombastic one such as that of Brutus which begins, "Remember March" (*Julius Caesar,* IV, 3), or that of Katherine which begins, "The more my wrong" (*Taming of the Shrew,* IV, 3). Practice in private; your own room will do, but a stage or other large open space is best. Exaggerate the speech as much as possible. Stamp up and down and wave your arms wildly. Pay no attention to whether the gestures are appropriate; in fact try not to notice them except to be sure that they are great free-arm swings, not mere twitches. At first your gestures will be ridiculous and awkward, but that only proves that the exercise is necessary. After a little practice you will notice that your gestures lose some of their stiffness and begin to swing in graceful arcs. Also, without any effort on your part, your gestures will become appropriate to the lines. Do not be afraid that you will carry exaggeration too far. A director constantly says, "Let yourself go"; he rarely says, "Don't overdo it."

Leading Points. Every gesture should involve the whole body, although the participation of the more distant parts may be imperceptible. Paradoxically, the effort to use the whole body in a gesture is the direct cause of many inhibitions. I doubt if anyone can move his whole body at once deliberately, or even his whole arm. Too many muscles are involved, and when the brain tries to give orders to all of them at once, the result is awkwardness. The proper method is to *concentrate on the part of the body that leads the gesture* (Figs. 7 and 8, Pl. XIII, p. 90). It may be the thumb, or the palm of the hand, or the chin. Whatever it is, move that in the required direction and let the rest of your body take care of itself. In an extremely graceful gesture, favored by dancers, the lead is the back of the wrist (Fig. 7). Imagine that your wrist is an iron ball, your hand a loose flap, and your arm a length of soft but fairly heavy rope. Now swing your iron-ball wrist around. Do not worry about your hand and arm; let them drag behind. If you succeed in doing this, the result will automatically be graceful. Then imagine that the iron weight is your fist or the end of your index finger (Fig. 8) and toss these around. See how easy it is?

Centers of Gesture. When you are working in a historical play, you will find it helpful to know that each period has a center from which its characteristic gestures spring. Thus, for Greek tragedy the center is the upper plane of the chest. For Greek comedy it was in the belly, as scores of figurines and vase paintings testify. For romantic plays, the center is the front of the chest — the heart. Mannered plays of the 18th century, like *The Rivals,* also use the heart as the center, but because the characters live on the surface and never get to the heart of things, they gesture as if their own hearts were surrounded by an invisible ball of glass a foot in radius. The arms never swing free, as they do in classical and romantic plays, because the gesture cannot get a real start, and also because these people were afraid to let themselves go. Actors in old-fashioned melodramas either were fencers or imitated other actors who were fencers. This resulted in gestures made from imaginary sword hilts—one on the left hip for the right hand and one on the right hip for the left hand.

If you are working in an unfamiliar period or style, start by reading the lines with free gestures. When you strike a gesture which seems characteristic, notice the center from which it springs. If a number of characteristic gestures start from the same center, you can use this fact as a guide in criticizing poor gestures and in inventing more good ones.

Chapter X

STAGE BUSINESS

Nothing does so much to bring a play to life on the stage as appropriate and well-executed business.

INHERENT BUSINESS

Some business is absolutely required by the plot—Romeo must fight Tybalt, Juliet must stab herself. The method of performing such 'plot business' may demand much thought, but the need for it is always obvious.

Business Incidental to the Action. Romeo must produce a sword in order to fight Tybalt. He may pick up Mercutio's, draw his own, borrow one from a friend, or seize one from an enemy, but he must have one. Most of this incidental business suggests itself automatically.

Business for Realism. This is usually demanded by the lines or the situation. Thus, the banquet scene in *Macbeth* requires a certain amount of eating and drinking. The breakfast scenes in *Life with Father* need a great deal more. Some of this is indicated by lines such as "Give Mrs. Day some bacon and eggs," but still more needs to be worked out. Usually such business is unobtrusive, and although its absence would be felt, its exact nature makes little difference.

Realism often requires business which is dramatically unimportant; e.g.:

BUTLER. Would you like me to mix you a dry martini, sir?
NEIL. I would indeed. I am dry, very dry. It is one of the paradoxes of life that there is no cure for dryness like a dry martini. (*Sipping martini.*) Ah, delicious!

Here the lines do not allow time for the cocktail to be mixed, but we cannot afford to hold up the play for such necessary but un-important business. Such situations are often difficult, but some combination of the following suggestions will always solve them.

(1) Take time for the business but enliven it with touches; e.g., make a ritual of the cocktail mixing by chilling the mixing glass and the cocktail glass, stirring the mixture with elaborate gentle-ness, placing the olive with precision, crushing lemon rind on the rim of the glass, etc. An expert comedian can do wonders with this sort of thing, but with amateurs it is rarely worth the trouble.

(2) Begin the business earlier. In the example, this would mean having the butler start mixing on some earlier cue and changing his line to read "Would you like a dry martini, sir?"

(3) Delay the moment when the business must be finished. This could be done either by cutting Neil's line "Ah, delicious!" or by using it in some later speech.

(4) Eliminate all unnecessary details or even some necessary ones. The old-fashioned trick of writing a stage letter with three scratches of the pen carried this too far, but judicious elimination is quite practical.

(5) Try to group items; e.g., a man packing a suitcase can have his shirts neatly piled and put them all in at once instead of one at a time.

Business mentioned in the lines need not always be carried out. Playwrights often make the mistake of starting a scene with the words, "Won't you sit down?" If the person spoken to sits, variety of grouping becomes impossible until an excuse can be found for him to rise. Usually he simply ignores the line and continues to stand.

Planting. Often an idea must be 'planted' in the minds of the audience before it is used. If Juliet's dagger appears for the first time in the potion scene, the effect will be abrupt and perhaps comic. Therefore Shakespeare makes Juliet say in an earlier scene (IV, 1) that she means to kill herself "with this knife" rather than marry Paris. When the playwright does not provide lines for a plant, it can be done through business; e.g., Juliet could draw her dagger while she is thinking of escaping from her marriage to Paris.

Business Explaining Lines. Often a line is meaningless without business. In the potion scene from *Romeo and Juliet* (IV, 2) Juliet says,

> "What if this mixture do not work at all?
> Shall I be married then tomorrow morning?
> No, no; this shall forbid it. Lie thou there."

If we consider only the words, the last line refers to the mixture, which is nonsense. Juliet is actually referring to her dagger, and she should have business of holding up the dagger and then placing it beside her.

Even when the meaning of the line is perfectly clear, the business should echo and reinforce it. Business should be designed as if you expected an audience of deaf people (that Deaf Old Lady again).

ADDED BUSINESS

Even in modern realistic plays, the business required by the plot and lines, or incidental to them, is only a small portion of that needed to 'keep the play moving,' and a great deal more must be invented by the director and actors.

Business for Exposition. Many of the underlying facts of the play are expressed by the business, often without any help from the lines. At the beginning of every act, business must be introduced to show:

NATURE OF THE SETTING. We may have typewriting in a business office, or cooking in a kitchen. Of course, the scenery and lines presumably indicate the locale, but the business should add its statements as well, so that there is no chance of the point being missed, and so that the impression shall be as strong as possible.

TIME. A character may indicate morning by taking in the milk, or winter by blowing on his fingers, etc.

ATMOSPHERE. The business should show whether the characters are cheerful or sad, energetic or lazy, etc.

RELATIONSHIPS BETWEEN CHARACTERS. Are they friendly, antagonistic, indifferent? Does one dominate another? What are their ages, stations in society, etc.?

Revelation of Thought. In earlier days, actors spoke their thoughts aloud. If they were alone, such 'thoughts' were called

Little Theater, Houston, Texas

PERILS OF A GREAT CITY

Setting by Thekla Lockhart

Old-fashioned melodrama went in for elaborate but unconvincing realism, in which the stage was left practically bare and the details were painted on the backdrop. Acting varied from exaggerated realism to frank theatricality. Every bit of drama was squeezed from every bit of business. The actor in the foreground of this picture took over a minute to die. Modern audiences find this funny, but sixty years ago it was considered the very pinnacle of drama.

'soliloquies' and were usually long. If other characters were on stage, the 'thoughts' were usually brief and were called 'asides.' These crude techniques have been largely abandoned, and actors now express thoughts by means of business. In an old-fashioned play a character might turn to the audience and exclaim, "Aha! I have an idea." Today, in a similar situation, he would snap his fingers.

Often business is used to show a motivation. If a character merely crosses to the fireplace, the movement will seem unmotivated, but if he crosses and then holds out his hands to the blaze for warmth, the reason for the movement will be obvious.

Business for Emphasis. Any movement may be used to emphasize a line. Business touches, properly timed, are particularly emphatic. If a character who is polishing his glasses suddenly holds them up and squints through them, the effect will be both more emphatic and more interesting than if he merely threw back his head and paused. Dramatic business, such as sticking a knife in the table, is so emphatic that it tends to melodrama and must be used with caution.

An actor often uses business to attract attention to himself before he speaks, particularly if he has been silent for some time. Before 'making a point' (speaking some line which is vital to the plot and which the audience must not miss), the actor 'takes stage' (attracts all attention to himself). Business is an effective means of taking stage. Actors sometimes use business to take stage when they are not entitled to it. Directors should watch for this sort of thing and stop it before it gets started.

Business for Enrichment. Often a scene, or even a whole play, seems thin and empty. This is always true of 'talky' plays, even when they are crowded with bright lines like those of George Bernard Shaw. Such scenes, or plays, must be enriched with business touches. Many of the touches will be so insignificant that the audience hardly notices them; e.g., a woman may carry her knitting and use it to point her lines. Trifles like this will often turn a dull spot into a sparkling one.

Business for Characterization. Appropriate business helps to make a character vivid. Some typical business should be introduced early for each character, so that the audience may place him at once. The way a thing is done is as characteristic as the thing itself. A man who flaunts his cigarette in a long holder is far removed from the type who conceals his lighted cigarette in his hand.

Comic Business. Appropriate comic business enriches a play by adding extra laughs. In broad comedy and farce it is hard to have too much comic business, but in comedy drama like *The Voice of the Turtle* it is a serious mistake to introduce comic business at a moment when a dramatic value is needed. Never introduce comic business without asking yourself if it is appropriate.

Filling Time Gaps. Occasionally a play will contain a period of a minute or two when the stage is left empty. Such gaps should be filled by having a character come on and perform some minor bit of business.

UNIFYING BUSINESS

If every bit of business is based on a separate idea, the unity of the play will be weakened. This can be avoided by using each important prop for several pieces of business. In *Arsenic and Old Lace* the poisoned wine, Teddy's bugle, the window seat, and other important props are each used over and over again. The more they are used the more familiar the audience becomes with them and the more effective they are.

Combining Business. At first glance it would seem that any attempt to express several ideas simultaneously by one piece of business would be confusing, but this is not the case. A character who rises from his desk and crosses to turn on an electric fan is performing business which (1) motivates his cross; (2) adds a realistic touch; (3) conveys information about the time of year (summer), the atmosphere (hot), and the character's state of mind (suffering from heat). It may also (4) call attention to the fan; (5) suggest that the character is a type that easily becomes overheated; and (6) be comic or dramatic if the surrounding situation makes it so. The more values you can combine in this way, the richer and more vivid the play becomes.

Chapter XI

SPEECH

The actor uses speech to: (1) transmit the words of the play to the audience; (2) give special meanings to these words through inflections; (3) convey information about the nature and mood of the characters (e.g., age, social position, strength; excitement, despair, rage, etc.); (4) control the mood of the audience much as music does; (5) provide variety. Unless your voice accomplishes all these things simultaneously you are not using it to full effect.

PRONUNCIATION

The beginner's most common speech problem is 'pronunciation,' which may be defined as the choice of sounds. Many common words have two or more pronunciations in daily use by educated speakers, and no pronunciation is actually wrong. However, a pronunciation may show ignorance of normal usage, or reveal the locality in which you were brought up. This is normally undesirable in the theater, so it is well to familiarize yourself with the more or less standardized pronunciations known as stage English and use them except for dialect roles.

The only satisfactory way to deal with pronunciation is through the symbols of the International Phonetic Association (IPA) shown on p. 114. The symbols used by ordinary dictionaries are confusing and unscientific. For example, one well-known dictionary uses three different symbols (ĭ, ę̄, ê) for the sound [I] and six (ă, ȧ, ĕ, ĭ, ŏ, ŭ) for the sound [ə]. There are thirty-seven IPA symbols, but sixteen of these are old friends and most of the rest have been selected to suggest the sound and help the memory. You should be able to learn all of them in an hour or two, and you will find them of immense practical value the rest of your life.

A Pronouncing Dictionary of American English (see Bibliography) uses the IPA symbols. The pronunciations marked E (i.e., Eastern) may be accepted as Stage English.

Stage English is marked by the following characteristics:

(1) Pronunciations peculiar to one locality are avoided.

(2) If there are two pronunciations in common use and a compromise between them is possible, prefer the compromise. Thus [ˈsɛkrəˌtɛri] is a better pronunciation for 'secretary' than [ˌsɛkrəˈtɛri] or [ˈsɛkrɪtrɪ], and 'can't' should be [kant] rather than [kænt] or [kɑnt]. However, do not make the mistake of broadening the *a* in words like 'hand' [hænd] and 'plan' [plæn].

(3) 'Long *u*' (i.e., the sound in 'feud' [fjud] rather than that in 'food' [fud]) is used in words like 'due' [dju], 'numeral' [ˈnjumrəl], etc.

(4) Words beginning in *wh* should be pronounced with [hw] (e.g., 'why' is [hwaɪ], not [waɪ]).

(5) The question of 'dropping *r*'s' has been hotly debated. Actually, *r*-like sounds can be made in several different ways, some pleasing, some harsh. Many Americans use an extremely harsh form of *r,* and this one sound often spoils otherwise pleasant voices. Learning to make a new type of *r* is difficult, but dropping unnecessary *r*'s is easy, and produces satisfactory results. The rule is simple: Drop every *r* which is not followed by a vowel sound, including a vowel in the following word. Thus, "Ask Father to order a more varied rhythm" becomes [ask ˈfɑðə tu ˈɔdər ə mɔ vɛrid ˈrɪðm].

VOICE PRODUCTION

All your life you have been learning to pitch your voice so it could be heard by someone five or ten feet away. Onstage you must speak so that the Deaf Old Lady fifty or a hundred feet away not only can hear you but is practically forced to listen. This means that when your voice is loud enough for the audience it will sound *much* too loud to you. Speech teachers often say that what counts is not how loudly you speak but how clearly. In part this is true. It is also true that for years I have been telling actors to talk as loudly as they could without shouting, and I have never met one who overdid it. However, whether you make yourself heard by of the International Phonetic Association (IPA)

Symbols used in Merriam-Webster dictionaries are shown for comparison.

IPA		KEY	M-W	IPA		KEY	M-W	IPA		KEY	M-W
b	baɪ	buy	b	j	ju	you	y	i	kid	keyed	ē [1]
d	daɪ	die	d	z	zu	zoo	z	ɪ	kɪd	kid	i
f	faɪ	fie	f					ɜ	kɜd	curd	[1]
g	gaɪ	guy	g	ʒ	ruʒ	rouge	zh	æ	kæd	cad	a
h	haɪ	hie	h					ɑ	kɑd	cod	ä
l	laɪ	lie	l	ŋ	kɪŋ	king	ŋ	ɔ	kɔd	cawed	ȯ
m	maɪ	my	m	k	kɪn	kin	k	o	kod	code	ō
n	naɪ	nigh	n	w	wɪn	win	w	ʊ	kʊd	could	u̇
p	paɪ	pie	p	hw	hwɪn	whin	hw	u	kud	cooed	ü
r	raɪ	rye	r	tʃ	tʃɪn	chin	ch	ʌ	kʌd	cud	ˡə
s	saɪ	sigh	s	dʒ	dʒɪn	gin	j	ju	kjud	cued	yü
ʃ	ʃaɪ	shy	sh					aʊ	kaʊd	cowed	[1]
t	taɪ	tie	t					ɛə	kɛəd	cared	[1]
ð	ðaɪ	thy	th					e	tel	tail	ā
θ	θaɪ	thigh	th					ɛ	tɛl	tell	e
v	vaɪ	vie	v					aɪ	taɪl	tile	ī
								ɔɪ	tɔɪl	toil	ȯi

[ə] is unstressed [ʌ]. Most unaccented vowels approach this sound.

[a] (M-W ȧ) is midway between [æ] and [ɑ].

[ɒ] is midway between [ɑ] and [ɔ].

[l̩], [m̩], and [n̩] show separate syllables; e.g., symbol [ˈsɪmbl̩], keep 'em [ˈkipm̩], prison [ˈprɪzn̩].

ˈput before a syllable marks the principal accent; e.g., taxi [ˈtæksɪ].

ˌput before a syllable marks a secondary accent; e.g., taxicab [ˈtæksɪˌkæb].

M-W also uses these accents and sometimes employs them to make one M-W symbol represent two IPA symbols; e.g., M-W ˈər-thē = [ˈθɒɪ], M-W ˈhə-rē = [ˈhɜrɪ], M-W ˈkəs-təm = [ˈkʌstəm].

ː put after a symbol shows that the sound is prolonged; e.g., cot = [kɑt], cart = [kɑːt].

[1] Some M-W symbols represent either a different theory of phonetics or different preferences in pronunciation. Thus, M-W writes ər for [ɜ], ə-r for [ɜr], ē (unaccented) for final [ɪ], au̇ (which corresponds to [æʊ]) for IPA [aʊ], and either ˈer or ˈar = [ær] for [ɛə].

OLDER MERRIAM-WEBSTER SYMBOLS

These are used by some dictionaries still in print.

ă, ȧ, ĕ, ĭ, ŏ, and ŭ all = [ə].   â = [ɛə].   ã = [æ] − [ə].

ā̇ is half-stressed [e] = [e] − [ɪ] − [ə].   ĕ = [ɛ].   ĭ = [ɪ] − [ə].

ė̄ is half-stressed [i] = [i] − [ɪ] − [ə].   ô = [ɔ].   ŏ = [ɑ] − [ɒ].

ō̇ is half-stressed [o] = [o] − [ə].   û = [ɜ].   ŭ = [ə].

u̇ is half-stressed [ju] = [ju] − [jʊ] − [jə] as in "superior."

ē̜ = [ɪə] as in "here" [hɪə].   du̇̈ = [dʒə].   tu̇̈ = [tʃə].

ẽ is unstressed [ɜ] = [ə] + slight "r" sound as in "baker."

ŏ̈ = [ɒ] − [ɔ].   oi = [ɔɪ].   ōo = [u].   o͝o = [ʊ].   ou = [aʊ].

'projection' (i.e., by handling your voice properly) or by sheer volume, there are a few basic speech skills which you should acquire.

Breathing. You cannot speak without breath. If you keep your lungs as full as possible without straining, you will: (1) have plenty of reserve air; (2) gain the confidence that goes with such a reserve; (3) improve the quality of your voice, probably because a full chest serves as a resonator; (4) hold your chest up and improve your appearance.

If you keep your chest up you will be forced to breathe with your diaphragm, which is a single muscle and therefore capable of much more accurate control than the many muscles which move the ribs. When you breathe with your diaphragm, your stomach moves *out* when you breathe *in*—and *in* when you breathe *out*. If you have never tried this, you may have trouble at first. Start by lying flat on your back with one hand on your chest and the other on your stomach to feel any movement. Keep the chest raised and motionless while the stomach moves in and out. This should be practiced until it becomes second nature. Diaphragmatic breathing is also good for the health.

Few speakers breathe often enough. You should breathe about every ten words. Mark your script with breath marks as shown in Pl. VII, p. 27, and practice breathing at these points every time you go over your lines. *Notice that your first breath for a speech comes before the end of the previous speaker's line.*

Let the Sound Out! Making beautiful sounds is useless unless they are permitted to reach the open air. Most Americans talk with their jaws and lips nearly closed and the backs of their tongues humped up. What chance does a sound have under such conditions? Drop your jaw. Drop your tongue. Open your lips and let the sound out. The jaw and tongue should be dropped, not forced down. Tension anywhere except in the vocal chords produces harsh sounds. If you need an exercise for this, and you probably do, begin by yawning. Then drop your jaw as if you were half-witted. Then sing a vowel. Open your mouth more and more until the quality of the vowel changes and it is no longer recognizable. Practice this with each of the vowels on p. 114. You will soon find that each one has a maximum mouth opening *and that* *this maximum is much greater than you ordinarily use when making that vowel.* Practice making each vowel with your mouth opened just a little less than the maximum for that vowel. Do this until it becomes second nature.

Diction. 'Pronunciation' is deciding which sounds to use. 'Diction' is making those sounds clearly. The sounds which are most important for clear speech are the 'plosives' [p, b; t, d; k, g]. Unfortunately these are the very sounds which we tend to slur. The plosives come in pairs, as indicated by the semicolons above. The first member of each pair is 'breathed,' i.e., made without vibration of the vocal chords. The second member is 'voiced,' i.e., made with the chords vibrating. Voiced plosives are difficult to make separately, but it will suffice if you practice only the breathed plosives, i.e., [p, t, k]. For practice, use Steele's exercise. Think of each section as a musical bar with each letter as a note and each dash as a rest.

```
p - - -    p - - -    p - - -    p - - -
p p - -    p p - -    p p - -    p - - -
p p p -    p p p -    p p p -    p - - -
p p p p    p p p p    p p p p    p - - -
```

STEELE'S EXERCISE

Each sound should be short and clearcut——[p] not [pʌh] or [ph]. When you can make [p], [t], and [k] crisply and when you actually do pronounce all your plosives sharply in connected speech, you will notice a great improvement in the clarity of your words.

If you have a tendency to hiss when you speak, practice [s, ʃ, z, ʒ] with Steele's exercise. Make each sound as short as possible and chop it off sharply at the end.

Many other special diction defects exist, such as nasality, stammering, and lisping, but little can be done for these without the aid of an experienced speech teacher.

Lip movement is essential for clear enunciation. Move your lips as much as possible. Exaggerate while practicing, so that you seem to be making faces. There is no danger whatever that you will overdo lip movements in ordinary speech. Active lip movements give you an appearance of vivacity and are worth cultivation on this ground alone.

VARIETY

The importance of vocal variety can hardly be exaggerated. It is the method by which a political orator holds his audience even though his speech contains nothing worth saying. It is also the chief secret of the great actor who makes an audience enjoy a poor play.

Variety in Volume. The beginner usually has trouble in making himself heard and must speak near his top 'volume' (without shouting) at all times. However, as his vocal power increases, he acquires a useful range in which the volume can be varied. Try to discover your softest tones which can be heard easily, and then vary between these and your loudest.

Variety in Pitch. Most people have a 'pitch' range of one or two octaves, and men who can control their falsetto registers can increase this considerably. In your normal speech you tend to use one or two notes in the middle of your range and waste your upper and lower notes. Learn to make use of your full range.

Variety in Tempo. Untrained people tend to speak at a fixed rate. They may talk more rapidly when excited or more slowly when bored, but the speed of any particular sentence is as constant as if it were controlled by a governor. Practice changing within the sentence. A particularly effective trick is to change your rate in the middle of a long word.

QUANTITY. The relative length of the individual sounds should also be varied. Many people speak as if they believed that all sounds should have the same length, just as the letters in a line of typewriting are evenly spaced. Actually, sounds have different natural lengths, and these differences should be exaggerated rather than diminished. The plosives [p, b; t, d; k, g] are made instantaneously and are therefore short and invariable. The fricatives [f, v; s, z; ʃ, ʒ; θ, ð; h] tend to be unpleasant when long and so should also be kept short. However, the nasals [m, n, ŋ], the lateral [l], and the

Yale University Theater

ONE SHALL BE

Setting by Lawrence Goldwasser

The type of speech required by a play is closely related to the style. This play obviously calls for beautiful, clear speech. One actor with a noticeable accent, or one with a tendency to colloquialisms like "can't" and "I've," will spoil the effect. In the setting, note the quiet atmosphere produced by the vertical and horizontal lines. Note also the classic symmetry and simplicity of the grouping.

vowels may all vary over a wide range of duration, and even the glides [w] and [j] may be varied to some extent. The sound [r] is not included because it is made in so many different ways; the safe rule is to keep your [r]'s short unless you roll them for a dialect part. Try writing a few sentences in phonetics and then write a number above each symbol corresponding to the relative length of the sound. Consider the length of the plosives as unity.

$$1\ 1\ 3\ 5\ 1\ 2 \quad 1\ 1 \quad 1\ 1\ 1\ 2\ 1\ 1 \quad 2\ 5\ 1 \quad 1\ 2\ 5\ 9\ 1\ 6$$
$$\text{təmɑro} \quad \text{nd} \quad \text{təmɑro} \quad \text{ænd} \quad \text{təmɑro}$$

Variety in Quality. 'Quality' or 'timbre' is the difference in sound between a bell, a violin, and a trumpet when they all strike the same pitch. Most people have a surprising range of vocal quality and can sound childish, rasping, soft, ghostly, etc. at will. Unfortunately they do not use this ability to vary their speech and to suggest the ideas and emotions back of it. Experiment with your own vocal qualities and then try to make your voice harsh when you speak of harsh subjects, melodious when you speak of poetic subjects, dry when you wish to be comic, etc.

Exercise for Variety. One exercise will do for all four forms of variety. Choose a ten-line passage from some play, preferably one of Shakespeare's, but you can use a prose selection from a modern play if you like—or better still use both. Read aloud, trying to get the maximum variety in volume. At this time do not pay any attention to pitch, tempo, or quality. It makes no difference whether they change or remain the same. Work for abstract variation in volume as if you were trying to interpret a piece of music. The changes in volume should be interesting for their own sake. Make no effort to have the volume appropriate to the words. After you have read the passage twenty or thirty times you will find that you are automatically adjusting the volume to the meaning.

Now try this exercise for pitch, reading the same or a different passage. Use the full range of your voice. Then try to make the pitch patterns interesting. After a while you will find that they accommodate themselves automatically to the meaning of the words. When working with pitch, neglect the other three elements.

The same exercise should be used for tempo and for quality. Tempo works much like pitch and volume. Quality, however, presents special features. Changes from a childish to a poetic, to a harsh, to a ghostly quality, etc. sound particularly silly when they are not related to the meaning, and there seems to be no way of discovering at which point such changes should be made. Furthermore, changes of quality in actual speech should be fairly subtle; so the crude changes necessary for an exercise appear badly out of place. However, if you will persist with the exercise, no matter how foolish it seems at first, you will slowly come to see how changes in quality can be used. Then you can make your changes more subtle until you arrive at the correct level of subtlety for stage speech.

Speech Patterns. Volume, pitch, and tempo variations make definite patterns. The notes of a song form a pitch pattern. Fig. 1, Pl. XVII, p. 120, shows a pitch line similar to the notes of music but less definite, just as speech pitches are less precise than those of music. Figs. 2 and 3 work on the same principle. The volume line in Fig. 2 rises when the volume increases and drops when it decreases. In Fig. 3 a high tempo line indicates rapid speech; a

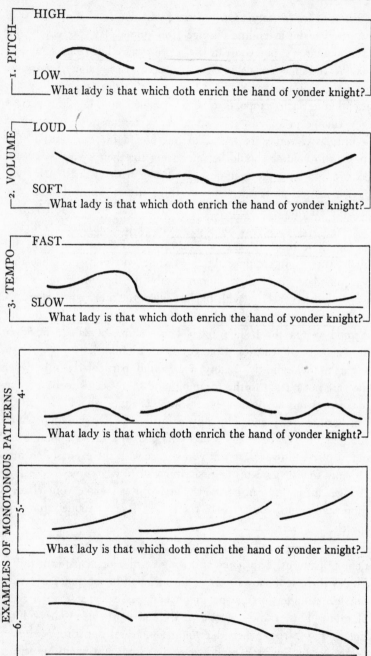

1. PITCH

HIGH

LOW

What lady is that which doth enrich the hand of yonder knight?

2. VOLUME

LOUD

SOFT

What lady is that which doth enrich the hand of yonder knight?

3. TEMPO

FAST

SLOW

What lady is that which doth enrich the hand of yonder knight?

EXAMPLES OF MONOTONOUS PATTERNS

4.

What lady is that which doth enrich the hand of yonder knight?

5.

What lady is that which doth enrich the hand of yonder knight?

6.

What lady is that which doth enrich the hand of yonder knight?

low one indicates slow speech. In Figs. 4, 5, and 6 the curves represent changes of any type.

Variety in speech is not only useless but definitely harmful if it is permitted to follow a monotonous pattern. Fig. 4 shows an uninteresting wave pattern. Fig. 5 shows a monotonously repeated lift, and Fig. 6 shows a repeated drop. Repeating patterns like these will be monotonous whether they are used for pitch, volume, or tempo. Figs. 1, 2, and 3 show how such monotony can be avoided by varying the patterns.

Smoothness. Speech patterns may change smoothly or abruptly. Abrupt changes are much more emphatic and exciting. Use both abrupt and smooth changes to vary your patterns. Staccato effects, when the voice suddenly stops, are effective. Sudden jumps or drops in pitch or volume and sudden changes in quality are even more desirable because they are less hackneyed.

Emphasis. When you emphasize a word, you probably do so by increasing the volume. This works, but it is monotonous. Emphasis is gained by contrast, and a word may be made emphatic by changes in pitch, tempo, and quality, as well as in volume. A word may also be emphasized by lowering the volume, i.e., pronouncing the word softly in a loud sentence. Experiment with all of these and learn to use them. Also learn to emphasize a word by putting a brief pause before and after it.

Indicating Breaks. Breaks in the thought may be shown by pauses or by sudden changes in pitch or volume. The methods of marking breaks in a script are discussed on p. 48, and illustrated in Pl. VII, p. 27. The intelligent use of breaks will do as much as anything else to make your speech lifelike and vivid.

Speech Builds. A speech of any length should normally build to a climax. This means that one of the following elements should be increased from the beginning of the speech to the climax: (1) volume, (2) emotional intensity, (3) variety, (4) pace. Builds in pitch are also possible, but they are risky, as a character loses strength when he becomes shrill. Building in a single element is technically difficult. Usually it is better to build part of the way with one element and then shift to another, or to build in two or three elements at once.

As in all cases of build, conservation is more difficult than building itself (see p. 75).

Topping. When two or more actors must build together, a device called 'topping' is used. Each actor starts to speak at a higher point in volume, pace, etc. than the last word of the previous actor. This is extremely effective, but it requires practice because the build tends to rise so rapidly that after the third speech a further rise becomes impossible. To avoid this: (1) begin the scene at the lowest possible point; (2) leave room for the rises between speeches by keeping the speeches themselves practically level; (3) use any opportunity to drop back within a speech, but never drop back between speeches.

Chapter XII

TIMING

Timing has a magical effect on an audience, so magical that you cannot quite believe it until you have had the personal experience of timing something perfectly and have felt an audience respond. Skill in timing can be acquired only by experience before an audience. However, you will learn both more easily and more rapidly if you have a thorough understanding of the principles upon which good timing is based.

Setting Cues. In its most obvious form, timing consists in setting cues—that is, deciding on the moment at which something is to be done or said. Even this is not so simple as it seems. An inexperienced actor usually assumes that his cue to speak a certain line is the last word of the previous actor's line. So it is, but he must prepare to speak by breathing, and this breath must be taken several words before the previous actor stops talking (see p. 115 and Pl. VII, p. 27). Such cues are said to be 'anticipated.' The majority of cues require anticipation. When you enter, you start walking toward the door before your cue is spoken. When you exit, you move to the door and turn the knob before you speak your exit line. Cues which are not anticipated are called 'dead' cues. *Every cue should be set in rehearsal.* It never pays to leave anything to chance in performance.

One cue difficulty, which seems improbably stupid but which is too common to be ignored, occurs when the actor whose line contains the cue happens to skip it. Suppose your cue to turn on the radio is 'can't I' in the speech: "I can see, can't I? I have eyes," and the actor who speaks the line happens to say, "I can see. I have eyes." Obviously you should turn on the radio anyway, but an amazing number of actors seem to feel that if the cue words are skipped, the business should be omitted. You can avoid this type of blunder if you learn to think of the cue, not as the cue words themselves but as the place where the words should be, whether they are spoken or not.

CO–ORDINATING MOVEMENTS AND LINES

Movement serves as a kind of punctuation. Emphatic movements break a play up into paragraphs of thought, movements of medium emphasis mark sentences, and minor movements show the individual phrases. The analogy between movement and punctuation is not exact; you cannot use a small movement at every comma, and a medium-sized one at every period. In general, however, the principle holds good that the emphasis of the movement should be proportioned to the importance of the break in the thought.

Movements often come between lines, just as ordinary punctuation comes between sentences. However, if this is overdone, it slows the play, so it is usually necessary for an actor to move 'on his line,' i.e., while speaking. A long movement often comes on an unimportant line that follows an important one. Normally, each actor moves only on his own lines. Otherwise the moving actor will distract attention from the speaker

As far as possible only one actor should move at a time. This makes the action simpler for the audience to follow. When two actors must move at the same time, they should not start or stop on the same cue.

Synchronization. The words and actions of a play go on simultaneously. If they are to be effective, they must be synchronized with each other. Fortunately, even inexperienced actors have a natural tendency to co-ordinate words and movements, so this difficulty is not so serious as it looks on paper. You can make it still easier by learning to watch the points set out below. If you understand the timing situation, the timing itself is usually automatic.

PAUSES. The speech element of our synchronization problem is made up of words and pauses; the movement element is made up of movements and pauses. The pauses are as important as the words or the movements. The happenings of a play should be absolutely continuous. During every instant of the play someone should be speaking, or something should be happening, or there should be *a pause that has significance*. Significant pauses:

(1) Provide emphasis. A pause before a word or movement calls attention to it.

(2) Indicate that a character is thinking; e.g., "Let me see, now. (*Pause.*) I have it!"

(3) Serve as a synchronizing period. Synchronizing pauses are used when several actors take the same cue. When one character says, "Are you with me?" and the rest reply, "We are," "Certainly," etc., they pause for a count of one after 'me,' so they will be sure to start together. Audience reactions, such as laughter and applause, are also synchronized in this way (see Pl. XXIII, p. 164).

When an actor is slow on his cue, or when a legitimate pause is held longer than necessary—in fact, when the continuous flow of the play is broken for any reason whatsoever—we have the phenomenon known as a 'stage wait.' Audiences are extremely sensitive to such waits. A wait of less than a second may make them subconsciously uncomfortable, and one of two or three seconds tells them plainly that something is wrong.

INSTANTANEOUS ACTIONS. Some actions, such as snapping the fingers or pounding on the table, have no appreciable length. Such actions are emphatic and usually come during a pause just before the word or phrase to be emphasized. Sometimes, however, they come either on the accented syllable of the emphatic word, or during the pause following the word or phrase. The timing for any particular case must be determined by experiment. Normally one method gives a much better effect than either of the others.

LONGER ACTIONS. When an action is long enough so that its beginning and its end are felt as two separate things, it should be synchronized with the lines in one of three ways:

(1) If the action comes on a pause, it should exactly fill the pause. Suppose you have a situation like this: "I hear someone outside. (*Cross to window.*) Yes, it's John." As soon as you said "outside" you would start to cross. When you arrived at the window and stopped, you would say, "Yes, etc." Even when the action consists of elaborate pantomime lasting several minutes, it should start immediately after the preceding speech, and the first syllable of the

following speech should be spoken the instant after the action stops.

(2) An action made during a line should generally end on the last accentable syllable of the line. Usually the last accentable syllable is the syllable that would normally be accented in the last word. However, lines exist in which the stress has to be moved earlier. In "He's going to kill you—and *me* also" the last accentable syllable is not 'al-' but 'me.' If you cross on this line, your last step will come on 'me.'

(3) Occasionally the beginning of a movement coincides with the beginning of a line. On a line like "Why, you dirty dog . . ." the speaker would probably start to move on 'Why.' The end of the movement might or might not coincide with the end of the line.

The lines referred to in the last two paragraphs need not be whole speeches, but may be sentences or even phrases. On the other hand, an action may be so long that it occupies several short speeches. You should have no difficulty with such cases if you follow the principles outlined above.

RHYTHM

No one knows much about rhythm, even in music and poetry where the rhythms are obvious. Stage rhythm is more subtle, and the little we do know about it can be summed up briefly. However, that little is important, and fortunately you will find it is easy to use.

Beats. If you sit at a play and tap your foot without making any effort to beat a particular time, you will soon find your foot moving in rhythm with the play. This is a steady beat like that of a metronome and has nothing to correspond with the unstressed beats of poetry or music. Plays do have unstressed beats, but they seem to be highly irregular and you will save trouble by ignoring them unless you wish to undertake a scientific study of rhythm. If you use a waltz tune in a play, do not try to co-ordinate its one-two-three rhythm with anything in the play. In a verse play like *Peer Gynt,* when the meter shifts from trochaic tetrameter to iambic pentameter, do not try to create a corresponding shift in the dramatic rhythm. Any synchronization between the subtler play rhythms and the musical or verse rhythms should be left to work itself out

Yale University Theater

LE BOURGEOIS GENTILHOMME

Setting by Donald Oenslager

When a production is as highly stylized as this, it becomes a kind of spoken ballet. Precise timing and a strongly felt rhythm are essential. Notice the use of a draped sateen cyclorama.

subconsciously. If you try to force it, you will probably do more harm than good.

The beats of a stage rhythm are figured by counting. You do not have to worry about the speed of counting. If you have any rhythmic sense at all, the mere fact that you are associated with the play will make you count at the correct speed.

SPEECH BEATS. Beats fall either on accented syllables or on pauses; unaccented syllables never receive a beat. Not all accented syllables take beats. In "He *jests* at *scars* that *never felt* a *wound,*" all the italicized syllables would be accented, but probably only 'jests,' 'nev-,' and 'wound' would take beats. The beat pattern of a speech can be changed by changing the stress, e.g., the above line might be read with only two beats—'scars' and 'wound.' It is important to find the pattern which best fits the particular situation, and this can be done only by experiment.

ACTION BEATS. Some actions, such as the steps of a cross, fall into obvious beats. Others flow so smoothly that no beat is perceptible.

Even these, however, usually have a definite accent at the end, with which a beat can be associated. Any short, sudden gesture counts as a single beat.

Synchronizing Speech and Actions through Rhythm. The methods of synchronization already mentioned can be both elaborated and made easier through the use of rhythm. Old-fashioned melodrama provides the best opportunity to study rhythm, because the beats are strongly marked and there is no need for subtlety. Here is an example showing how the beats of the action are synchronized with those of the words.

(The farmer has hidden the mortgage money in his coffee pot. The villain has stolen the money and used it to buy the mortgage. When the farmer learns that the villain owns the mortgage, the farmer rushes to get the money to pay it and returns with the coffee pot in his hand.)

                  (*Step*)   (*Step*)   (*Step*)   (*Holds up pot*)
FARMER.   Tear up the mort-gage, Mist-er. Here's the money.

                  (*Leans forward*)
VILLAIN.   Where?

                                                          (*Step*)
                        (*Step*)   (*Step*)   (*Opens lid*)
FARMER.   (*Crossing*) Right   here.

                                                          (*Gasps*)
                                                          (*Removes hand*)
                  (*Puts hand in pot*)   (*Touches bottom*)   (*Looks in pot*)
                  Here   it   is.
                  (*Step back*) (*Step back*) (*Step back*)
                  Why   it's   gone!
                        (*Step*)   (*Step*)   (*Step*)
VILLAIN.   (*Advancing*) Be-ware how you tri-fle with me, sir!

Strength of Rhythm. Realism and theatricalized realism call for lightly marked rhythms. Expressionism calls for strong rhythms. Stress placed on the beats strengthens the rhythm; it is stronger when an actor stamps his feet than when he glides smoothly. Rhythm is also strengthened when several elements coincide. In the scene above, the farmer simultaneously gasps, removes his hand, and looks in the coffee pot. If he took a step at the same time, the effect would be still more marked. Except in highly stylized plays it is usually unwise to have more than two things happen at once.

Suggestions. (1) When a three-step cross is made on a speech, the three steps of the cross should coincide with the last three beats of the speech. The half-step at the end of the cross does not count in the rhythm.

(2) In early rehearsals, pauses should be 'counted' by saying, "One, two, three, etc.," mentally. Short pauses normally last exactly one count. Long pauses may last from five to eight counts. Ten counts may be taken as a maximum, though I once saw a twelve-count pause. When there is a pause at the beginning of an act, *start* counting when the curtain *stops* moving.

(3) Normally, speeches should follow one another without pause. Beginners tend to insert one- or two-beat pauses at each cue. Nothing does more to make a play boring, and the director must check this tendency from the start.

Exercise. The following exercise works wonders in aiding an actor to feel the rhythm of the play, to emphasize and time his speeches, and to co-ordinate his movements with his words. Moreover, it produces almost magical results in curing stiffness and encouraging free, easy gestures.

Say your lines one after another without waiting for cues. As you speak, assume the pose of a boxer and move around the stage, punching out every time you think a word should be emphasized. Soon you will learn what words to emphasize and also that it is easy to punch on an emphatic word and difficult to punch on an unemphatic one. You will also find that some words call merely for short feints whereas others demand great 'roundhouse' swings. A knowledge of boxing does not help this exercise. In fact it rather hurts, because real boxing draws a sharp distinction between the two hands, but for the exercise they should be used indiscriminately. If you prefer, you can substitute a two-handed tennis pantomime for the boxing. When you are not in a play, you can still use the exercise by memorizing a ten-line speech from Shakespeare and saying it over and over. This is the most valuable exercise I know, and anyone who seriously wishes to improve his acting will do well to practice it religiously.

Rhythm an Esthetic Value. Rhythm is not merely a synchronizing device. It adds a definite esthetic value to a production just as beauty does. Furthermore, in some curious way, rhythm makes monotonous passages less boring and also ties together passages that have no real unity. In other words, rhythm makes variety seem more unified and unity more interesting.

PACE

The pace at which an audience can absorb ideas differs with the ideas and with the audience, but it must always be taken into account. If the play moves too slowly, the ideas come too far apart and the audience is bored during the gaps. If the play moves too rapidly, a new idea is presented before the old one is absorbed, so that the audience becomes confused, loses both ideas, and becomes bored for that reason. Boredom, therefore, results whenever the pace is either too fast or too slow.

Amateur actors have a strong tendency to be too slow. However, instead of trying to effect an over-all increase of pace, the director should work for variety of pace by selecting the more exciting scenes in each act and speeding them up until they are definitely faster than the rest. Normally, the pace should not increase suddenly but should build steadily from the beginning to the end of the scene.

If left to themselves, amateur actors are probably never too fast. However, if the director pushes them too much, they may overdo the speed in certain types of plays: (1) heavy dramas with unusually terse dialogue, such as E. P. Conkle's one-act play *Minnie Field;* (2) high comedy, like *The Importance of Being Earnest,* with subtle wit that requires a moment or two for even a clever audience to see the point; (3) old-fashioned melodramas.

Chapter XIII

CREATING THE CHARACTER

After a character has been interpreted, it must be brought to life by being given characteristic movements, business, speech habits, etc. These should not only be appropriate, but should reveal the character's nature and psychological reactions to the situations of the play. Thus, one character may strut when things go well and droop when they go badly, whereas another may maintain a calm demeanor throughout. Many of these effects are extremely subtle, and most of them could not be described in words. Many people believe that the creation of a character requires great ability. Actually, it is not difficult once you understand how it is done.

THE APPROACH

An actor's success in bringing his character to life depends largely on the way he approaches the problem of characterization.

The Objective Method. Some actors seek these characterizing movements and speech qualities 'objectively.' An actor who is to play an old man may study a real old man and find that he stoops and talks with a cracked voice. Or perhaps the actor has noticed that old men in general tend to stoop and to talk with cracked voices. In either case the actor seeks to simulate old age by rounding his shoulders and pitching his voice high. As far as my own experience goes, this method is never successful if used by itself. In a role of any length an actor has hundreds and even thousands of things to do, if every movement and every inflection is counted. An old man does not merely stoop; he moves every joint and muscle in a characteristic way. One false gesture or one out-of-character speech trait is enough to weaken or destroy the illusion, and a dozen such mistakes will ruin the effect of a whole role. No actor is observant enough, or studies his character long enough, to copy every movement and inflection in an entire play. Some bits always come from his own habits, to remind the audience that they are watching an actor instead of a character. Furthermore, movements and inflections must be appropriate not only to the character but also to the physical equipment of the actor. A heavy man imitating the movements of a light one will not be convincing even if he produces an exact copy, for movements suited to a light body are inappropriate to a heavy one.

The objective method is not limited to copying, but includes anything which comes from outside the actor. If you obey the director blindly, or work out the action of a scene on technical principles, you are using the objective method.

The Subjective Method. Because of the obvious failure of the objective method, the opposite or 'subjective' method has been widely advocated, notably by Stanislavsky. In this method the actor does not make any attempt to work out the movements and inflexions of the character directly. Instead he tries to become in complete sympathy with the character, feeling his emotions and thinking his thoughts. As far as characterization is concerned, this method works perfectly, at least in the hands of an expert, but it has two serious drawbacks.

(1) It consumes an enormous amount of time and effort. Stanislavsky's actors at the Moscow Art Theater rehearsed a play for months and sometimes for years before they were ready to perform it. Even making allowance for the high standard that the Art Theater set itself, its methods are impractical for the ordinary company.

(2) It is not enough to produce effects; they must be conveyed to the audience. The actor who identifies himself with his character to the point where he neglects his technique is likely to find that much of his art fails to cross the footlights. The Moscow Art Theater has been severely criticized on this ground. It is worth noting that its successes were scored in realistic plays of character, and that it added little to its reputation by attempts to produce stylized works which made greater demands on technique.

Combined Method. Fortunately, when the objective and subjective methods are both used, each supplies the virtues the other lacks. This is due to the psychological fact that *an actor who learns to perform certain actions in a certain way, and who then comes to feel the emotions of his character, will automatically express those emotions through the actions he has learned, provided that the actions are appropriate to the emotions.*

You can prove this to yourself by using the exit technique in Fig. 1, Pl. XXII, p. 153. Learn the movements mechanically. Then make up your own words for a scene in which you grow more and more annoyed until you finally struggle into your coat and rush out. The movements will come so naturally that you can hardly believe you learned them mechanically. However, if you work up the emotions first, using any movements that the emotions suggest, you will commit technical faults. When you try to correct these faults, you will find that the corrections will not harmonize with the emotions. In other words, it is easy to fit an emotion to a technical pattern, but difficult to make technical changes in the movements which have grown out of an emotion.

An emotion of annoyance happens to be appropriate to the movements in Fig. 1, but if you try the same movements with an inappropriate emotion, say one of tender farewell, you will not be able to make the movements and emotions work together.

To apply these principles, the early work on the production should be done objectively, by reason rather than feeling. This period lasts from the first reading of the script until the tenth or twelfth rehearsal, and covers all the larger aspects of interpretation and action, including: (1) the determination of the theme and treatment of the play, and the nature and functions of the characters; (2) the design of groupings and crosses and the invention of business; (3) all matters in which technique is of basic importance.

There is no sharp break between the objective period and the subjective period which follows it. While the actors are learning their lines, they are beginning to feel their way into their characters. Once the lines are learned, the subjective method becomes dominant. The actors learn more and more to share the feelings of their characters. These feelings are expressed within the framework of the actions already worked out—unless these prove inappropriate, in which case they must be changed. Details, however, will be needed, such as speech inflections and gestures, and these are encouraged to arise naturally from the emotions.

The actors should be entirely subjective in performance, except in cases where:

(1) Something must be faked. If a stage fight becomes too subjective, someone will get hurt.

(2) Some reaction of the audience interferes with the smooth running of the play. This would include prolonged laughter or applause, but not such subtle matters as the responsiveness or coolness of the audience, which the actors should sense and allow for subconsciously.

(3) Something goes wrong and must be corrected. In real life nothing ever 'goes wrong' in this sense, so such problems must be solved objectively.

HOW TO 'FEEL THE ROLE'

If you think the character's thoughts you will automatically feel the character's emotions. I could cite hundreds of examples like the following: In a production of *Anna Christie* which I directed, the actor playing Mat had difficulty with the scene where Anna delivers a three-page criticism of Mat while he stands with his back to the audience. In the early rehearsals 'Mat' gave a good imitation of an actor waiting for a cue, but that was all. I asked the actor what Mat was thinking and he replied. "He's too mad to think coherently, so he's cursing her under his breath." I advised him to write out a string of swear words as long as Anna's speech and actually to repeat them to himself during this scene. After that we no longer had an actor waiting for a cue, but a wild Irishman who had all he could do to keep from springing at Anna's throat.

The 'Silent Script.' To use this method properly, the actor should go over his script—preferably while he is learning his lines—and work out his character's thoughts in detail whenever he is on stage and is not saying anything himself. Sometimes the character is paying strict attention to whatever is being said, and his thoughts are identical with the speaker's words. More often he is making some mental comment on the speaker's words, or perhaps thinking about something entirely different. Once this 'silent script' has been worked out, *the actor should actually 'say' it mentally during rehearsals and performances*. This takes work, but the work is interesting, and I have never known the method to fail where it was given an honest trial. Furthermore, the results are immediate; the actor who spends an hour or two working on his 'silent script' will show a marked improvement at the next rehearsal.

It is neither necessary nor desirable to learn this 'silent script' by heart. Simply familiarize yourself with the ideas and then fit in the appropriate words in rehearsals and performances. This saves trouble and also avoids any tendency to go stale.

The 'silent script' need have no literary virtues, nor need it conform to the language of the play; in fact, half-formed phrases are best because that is the way people usually think. Here is an example taken from *Romeo and Juliet,* I, 1.

The Text	Benvolio's 'Silent Script'
	(*He is off stage when he hears the fight start.*) *A fight! Good Lord, they're at it again! The prince swore he'd—*(*Enters.*)
BENVOLIO. Part, fools! Put up your swords; you know not what you do. (*Beats down their swords.*) *Enter* TYBALT.	Part, fools! Put up your swords; you know not what you do. *Ooop! Damn you* (*knocking down* GREGORY's *sword*), *drop it! If the watch catches you we'll all be in trouble. Unh, unh! Here's*
TYBALT. What, art thou drawn among these heartless hinds? Turn thee, Benvolio, look upon thy death.	*Tybalt. What rotten . . . "Benvolio, look upon thy death."* I do but keep the
BENVOLIO. I do but keep the peace. Put up thy sword.	peace, *you hotheaded idiot.* Put up thy sword.

The 'silent script' should start at least two sentences before the character enters and continue for at least two sentences after he exits or the curtain falls.

The thoughts must be phrased like real thoughts, not as statements made by an outsider. If the actor playing Benvolio says to himself, "Here he (Benvolio) thinks, 'A fight, etc.'" or even, "Here I think, 'A fight, etc.,'" the method will fail, because either phrase reminds the actor that he is standing outside Benvolio, whereas the idea is to get inside Benvolio.

The actor will find it particularly helpful to add a brief silent comment to each of his own speeches, as in the following scene:

ANNE.   Remember that day at the county fair. *What crazy kids we were!*
GREG.   I remember I fell off the merry-go-round, *and tore my pants.*
ANNE.   And you bought me one of those big paper cones filled with cotton candy. *I wish anything tasted that sweet to me now.*
GREG.   And then found out that I'd spent all my money and couldn't pay for it. *Boy! Was the man sore.*

This device helps the actor avoid the common fault of relaxing his tension at the end of each speech. It also focuses his attention on the inner meaning of the lines. Notice how the whole significance of the scene—and the actor's inflections—is altered by changing the silent lines:

ANNE.   Remember that day at the county fair. *The day I met you.*
GREG.   I remember I fell off the merry-go-round, *because I tried to show off so you'd notice me.*
ANNE.   And you bought me one of those big paper cones filled with cotton candy. *I loved you for that.*
GREG.   And then found out that I'd spent all my money and couldn't pay for it, *but I was glad you had the candy.*

Substitute Emotions. Occasionally a role demands an emotion that the actor cannot possibly feel. For example, a scene might show a strictly reared Mohammedan girl suddenly unveiled in front of a strange man. An American actress who has spent a lifetime unveiled cannot hope to duplicate the Mohammedan girl's feeling of shame. The only way to handle cases of this type is to find the most nearly equivalent emotion in your own conceivable experience. In the unveiling example, the actress might imagine herself stripped naked. The emotion would not be quite the same, but it would probably satisfy the audience.

Repressed Acting. Young actors, who have heard repressed acting praised, often try to imitate it by going through their parts without acting at all. Real acting is always hard work, and these unfortunates deceive no one but themselves. Nevertheless, a few roles do demand repression. If you are cast for one of these, your first task is to build up the emotion. This is best done by ranting through the early rehearsals as if you expected to take part in a howling melodrama. Then, when your emotions are set, you can repress them by refusing to permit them to manifest themselves in action or inflection. The strong emotions will be there, but they will be bottled up—which is what repressed acting means. No one can impose emotion on restraint, but it is comparatively easy for an actor to impose restraint on emotion.

Function of the Actor. The actor must do the acting, and it is he who must feel the emotions of the character. Therefore he must be the final judge of whether or not a motivation is adequate. No matter how strongly the director may feel that a certain emotion would result in a certain movement, he should not insist on the movement if the actor does not agree. The director may force the actor to do something, but he cannot force the actor to feel something. When the actor does not feel it, the audience does not feel it either. On the other hand, if the actor does feel that the motivation is adequate, that is usually sufficient even if the director does not agree.

When an actor and director differ, the matter can almost always be settled by discussion. If the discussion consumes more time than the point is worth, the director should let the actor have his way. Usually, however, an agreement is easily reached. I have held hundreds of such discussions with actors and have always either come to the actor's opinion or persuaded him to agree with mine, except in those cases where the actor was guided by personal vanity rather than by a sincere effort to feel the part. Vain actors are often too stupid to realize that the audience is not interested in them personally but only in the character. If such an actor plays a character who is made to seem ridiculous or who otherwise fails to live up to the actor's lofty opinion of himself, he invents all sorts of absurd reasons for interpreting the character in a more glamorous light. Such arguments rarely fool anyone, but the director's only recourse is to get another actor, which is not always practical. Compelling an actor to do something against his will never works.

Chapter XIV

ACTING TECHNIQUE

The term 'acting technique' applies specifically to the technique of movement. This technique is designed to: (1) help the actor to look his best; (2) make the mechanics of movement efficient and unobtrusive; (3) avoid covering the actor or turning him upstage while he is speaking or is otherwise the center of attention.

Even when these ends are not desired, a sound technique is helpful because it permits the actor to choose and control his effects; a competent performer can express awkwardness more vividly than an actor who is naturally clumsy.

CONTROL OF WEIGHT

Both the way you stand and the way you move depend almost entirely on the way you handle your weight. You will be called on for many unfamiliar movements on stage. If you learn to analyze them in terms of weight control, you can solve them easily for yourself; otherwise you must depend on the director.

Center of Gravity.   Every rigid object, such as a piece of furniture, a statue, or an actor with his muscles tense, behaves as if its entire weight were concentrated at one point known as the 'center of gravity.' Thus a hollow statue with a lead ball at its center of gravity would balance in exactly the same way as a solid statue of equal weight. A rigid actor's center of gravity is in his pelvis (see the black dot, Fig. 1, Pl. XVIII, p. 141) when he stands erect. The center of gravity may be outside the object; the center of gravity of a doughnut is in the hole. When an actor bends, his center of gravity may be ahead of him (Figs. 3–6).

Base.   The space enclosed by the supports of an object is its 'base.' The base of a standing actor is his feet and the space between

Community Theater, Harrisburg, Pennsylvania

THE LOWER DEPTHS

Setting by Edwin McKay

Here the designer has managed to produce an extremely interesting and picturesque effect without sacrificing the dirt and ugliness demanded by extreme realism. Realism does not mean copying from the first real-life example you see. It means finding a way to be convincingly real and dramatically effective at the same time. Note the abundance of detail and the unconventional grouping.

them (Figs. 1 and 6). When an actor leans on some support (Fig. 5), the entire area enclosed by his feet and the support becomes the base. When an actor sits, his base is the area between those parts of his body which rest on the chair.

Line of Support. The line joining the center of gravity and the base is called the 'line of support.' When the actor is motionless, the line of support is always vertical, but when he moves (Fig. 7), the line slants in the direction of the movement, and the slant is proportional to the speed.

Balance. As long as the line of support falls within the base, the actor's weight is under control and he is balanced (Fig. 1). When he leans so that the line of support falls near the edge of his base (Fig. 2), he is still in balance but is less stable. The larger the base and the farther the line of support is from the edge of it, the greater will be the actor's stability. If the actor leans so that his line of support falls outside his base, he will topple over (Fig. 3). He may maintain his balance while bending by throwing his hips backward (Fig. 4) and so keeping his center of gravity over his base. However, once he starts to fall, he cannot check himself except by enlarging his base. This may be done by leaning on something in the direction to which he is falling (Fig. 5) or by stepping in that direction (Fig. 6). He may also save himself by seizing something behind him or to one side. In this case the object seized becomes part of his base, but he hangs from it instead of resting on it. A base need not be horizontal.

Although the actor's center of gravity is in his pelvis when he is rigid, there is usually a certain amount of flexibility in the waist. As a matter of weight control, this divides the body into two parts— the part below the waist which acts as a support, and the part above the waist which acts as a balancing element. The center of gravity of the upper part of the body is in the chest near the heart, and normally it is of this that the actor should think when he moves. That is, if you think of your weight as if it were concentrated at your heart, you can ignore the weight of your legs in solving problems of weight control except when you are lying down, in which case the weight of the legs becomes extremely important.

CONTROL OF WEIGHT—A. POSTURE

Good posture will do more for your appearance than almost anything else. It also serves as a basis for graceful and efficient movement. People who waddle rather than walk do so because their posture is faulty. Posture is primarily a matter of weight control. The body has three main weights: the pelvis, the chest, and the head. When you hold a weight off balance (Fig. 8, Pl. XVIII), whether it is your head or an Indian club, you have to strain, whereas you can carry the same weight easily when it is balanced (Fig. 9). When your body weights are out of balance (Fig. 10), you not only suffer this constant strain but your weight falls on your muscles instead of on your bones. At first it may seem more tiring to hold yourself erect, but that is because the small muscles (which maintain your balance) have grown lazy, and the large muscles (which have been needlessly carrying your weight) have grown numb through long abuse.

When your posture is bad, your head hangs out in front of you like that of a tired horse, and the tilt of your pelvis tips your intestines against the wall of your abdomen, pushing it out. At the

Plate XVIII

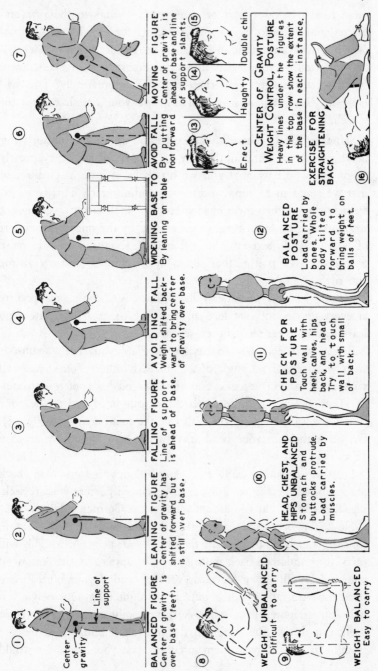

① BALANCED FIGURE Center of gravity is over base (feet).
Center of gravity
Line of support

② LEANING FIGURE Center of gravity shifted forward but is still over base.

③ FALLING FIGURE Line of support is ahead of base.

④ AVOIDING FALL Weight shifted backward to bring center of gravity over base.

⑤ WIDENING BASE TO AVOID FALL By leaning on table

⑥ AVOID FALL By putting foot forward

⑦ MOVING FIGURE Center of gravity is ahead of base and line of support slants.

⑧ WEIGHT UNBALANCED Difficult to carry

⑨ WEIGHT BALANCED Easy to carry

⑩ HEAD, CHEST, AND HIPS UNBALANCED Stomach and buttocks protrude. Load carried by muscles.

⑪ CHECK FOR POSTURE Touch wall with heels, calves, hips, back, and head. Try to touch wall with small of back.

⑫ BALANCED POSTURE Load carried by bones. Whole body tilted forward to bring weight on balls of feet.

CENTER OF GRAVITY
WEIGHT CONTROL, POSTURE
Heavy lines under the figures in the top row show the extent of the base in each instance.

⑬ Erect
⑭ Haughty
⑮ Double chin

⑯ EXERCISE FOR STRAIGHTENING BACK

same time the lower part of your pelvis swings to the rear and carries your buttocks with it. By correcting these faults you will not only improve your appearance, but the weight of your intestines will be supported by your pelvis instead of dragging your chest down. Freed of this weight, your chest will rise automatically. This will increase your lung capacity and improve your breath control for speech.

Standing Erect.   Usually when we stand up after sitting or lying down, we do not stand all the way up. Our heads are heavy (nearly ⅕ of our whole weight) and we lift them as little as possible, so that we stand in a slump instead of standing erect. This is an extremely shortsighted form of laziness; the small effort saved by not straightening up is spent many times over by the unnecessary effort of holding your body weights off balance. Nothing will do more to improve your posture than the habit of standing erect every time you rise.

Posture Check.   Another valuable habit is to check your posture at every opportunity—at least four or five times a day. After you learn how, you can do it in ten seconds.

Find a wall that has no baseboard. Place your heels against it with your feet at an angle of 45° to each other. Touch the wall with your calves, buttocks, and shoulder blades (not your shoulders), as in Fig. 11. Raise the back of your head and at the same time force it back against the wall (see the small arrows in Fig. 13). Do not either tip your head up (Fig. 14) or pull in your chin (Fig. 15).

Let your shoulders hang free. Any attempt to force them back makes for stiffness instead of the easy, relaxed posture you are seeking. Remember that you are an actor, not a German soldier.

Now, slip one hand between your waist and the wall. Try to squeeze your hand by pressing the top of your pelvis back. This will carry your abdomen back with it. At the same time, the bottom of your pelvis will swing forward, 'tucking under' your buttocks instead of letting them 'bustle out.' By straightening your pelvis you will also straighten your spine. A curved spine carries little weight itself, but throws the strain on the muscles. Children's spines are straight. If they allowed them to curve, their young muscles would not be strong enough to carry their proportionately heavy heads. If you cannot straighten your spine, you have a condition known medically as 'lordosis.' This will take a little time and exercise to correct. Start by learning which muscles tip the pelvis back. Open a door 10" and slip through the crack sidewise. In 'making yourself small' you will automatically tilt your pelvis erect by using the muscles in the buttocks and on the inside of the thigh. Learn to control these muscles and try to keep a slight tension on them when you stand or walk, so that they will hold the pelvis erect. It is particularly easy to 'tuck under' when going upstairs, so that is a good time to practice.

If you cannot straighten your back enough to squeeze your fingers against the wall in the posture check, you will need the exercise shown in Fig. 16. Lie on your back with your knees up and your feet flat on the floor. Slide one hand under your waist to feel the arch in your back. Take your hand away and jerk your knees toward your chest one at a time. Six counts with each knee is enough for one exercise period. Now test your arch again. It will probably be flatter. Use this exercise until you cannot get your fingers under your waist when you lie down.

Standing Poses. The posture shown in Fig. 11 is an excellent check, but it is too stiff for ordinary use. After making your check, slide one foot forward until its heel rests against the instep of the other foot, but keep the feet at 45°. Sway forward until your weight comes over the balls of your feet (Fig. 12). Relax—but do not slump. Check for any feeling of strain or stiffness, particularly in your shoulders, to make sure that no unnecessary muscles are in use. You may let your head move forward ½", but keep your pelvis erect. Let your hands hang loosely at your sides.

This is the normal standing position for use on stage. Men usually advance the upstage foot (Fig. 3, Pl. XXI, p. 150), as this opens them out slightly and makes turning easier. Women prefer to keep the upstage foot back, as this makes their feet look smaller (Figs. 4 and 5). This pose permits almost no variety, because nearly every change is a change for the worse, both in the actor's appearance and in his mechanical readiness for movement. If the weight is allowed to drop back on the heels, you will lose the appearance

Plate XIX

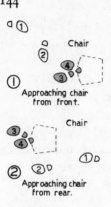

Approaching chair from front.

Approaching chair from rear.

③ Touch chair with calf of rear leg.

④ Have weight on rear leg as you go down.

⑤ Take weight on forward foot when 6" from seat.

⑥ To rise: lean back, then swing forward to bring center of gravity over feet.

⑦ Awkward way to rise or sit. Use only for character roles.

Position for feet

⑧ When you cannot get your feet under chair, move to edge of seat. Bring center of gravity over feet by leaning forward and to the side. Then rise.

⑨ Lifting heavy object.

⑩ Lifting light object.

⑪ Awkward, use only for character roles.

SITTING, RISING, STOOPING, AND KNEELING
—o—
Heavy line under each figure shows the extent of the base.

⑫ Kneel on downstage knee. You will move forward or backward as you sink or rise, depending on which foot takes the weight.

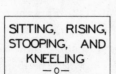

of alertness. If the feet make an angle much greater than 45°, you will seem slue-footed. If the angle is much less than 45°, your base will be so narrow that you will lack stability. Men may stand with their feet apart, but *girls wearing skirts should keep their feet and knees together*. A separation of even an inch makes an actress less attractive. Fig. 23, Pl. XI, p. 71 is the only exception I have ever found to this rule, and it is not a pose of any general utility. Actresses wearing slacks may occasionally stand with their feet apart for variety. Also an actress may separate her feet when she deliberately desires to appear ungainly.

Hands should normally hang at the sides or rest lightly on the back of a chair or some other furniture. Almost any other pose, such as clasping the hands behind the back, putting them in the pockets, or resting them on the hips, will have a definitely characterizing quality and must be judged by its appropriateness to the character portrayed. Folding the hands on the stomach is fatal to anyone's appearance. It should be done only in broad character roles.

CONTROL OF WEIGHT—B. MOVEMENTS

Your movement problems will be simplified if you learn to think of them in terms of center of gravity, line of support, and base.

Sitting. Approach the chair as shown in Fig. 1 or Fig. 2, Pl. XIX, p. 144. Put one leg back so that you touch the seat with your calf (Fig. 3). This will check your position and assure you that it is safe to sit. *Never glance behind you to see if the seat is there.* Moving the leg back also brings the ball of your foot, which is to be your base of support, as near the seat as possible; this is of vital importance in both sitting and rising. Throw your weight on the ball of this rear foot and lower yourself by bending the leg (Fig. 4). When 6″ from the seat, lock the muscles of the forward leg and relax the rear leg (Fig. 5). This throws your weight on your forward foot, and as your center of gravity will be outside your base, you will fall into the chair. When you land, your back should just touch the back of the chair. Practice this every time you sit in daily life until it becomes automatic.

Sitting poses for men give little trouble, but girls usually require poses in which their legs will appear graceful. Figs. 1, 2, 3, 5, 6, and 13 in Pl. XI, p. 71 show the most useful poses. Unless a girl's skirt reaches the floor, she must keep her knees together when sitting, and must also keep her feet together, except when she crosses her legs or sits on one foot. Men may separate both knees and feet slightly but should not sprawl except in character roles.

When your legs are crossed, the upstage leg should be on top unless you have no lines in the scene.

Rising. Your center of gravity must be over your base before you can rise, so draw your feet under you as far as conditions will permit (Figs. 6 and 8, Pl. XIX, p. 144). To rise from a straight chair, lean back and then sway forward sharply. As the momentum brings your weight on your feet, straighten your legs. Keep your weight on your downstage foot and take a short step forward at once with your upstage foot; otherwise, as your legs straighten, they will knock over the chair. Another method is to move to the side of the chair and bring one foot back as shown at *A* in Fig. 1, Pl. XXII, p. 153. By bending to the side you can bring your weight over the foot and rise. You can end this movement standing in front of your chair, at the side, or in back of it, depending on where you place your foot. Fig. 8, Pl. XIX, p. 144 shows how to rise when the seat is low or when you cannot get your feet under it. In this case you must anticipate your cue to rise by sliding to the edge of the chair. Bend slightly to bring your weight over your feet—then rise. If a chair has arms, they may be used to pull yourself forward, but do not lift yourself by pressing on the arms. Never stand or sit by bending forward (Fig. 7) except in character roles.

Kneeling. Normally you should kneel on the downstage knee, as this opens you out. If you keep your weight on the downstage foot, you will move forward as you kneel and backward as you rise (Fig. 12). By keeping your weight on your upstage foot you will reverse these directions.

Stooping. When stooping, keep your weight erect as you go down (Fig. 10, Pl. XIX, p. 144). Avoid bending (Fig. 11) except in character roles.

Lifting. When lifting a heavy object, your own body and the object will act as one weight with a common center of gravity. This

Community Theater, Harrisburg, Pennsylvania

CANDLELIGHT

Setting by M. Dale Smith

This is comedy of situation with a decided flavor of sex. The scenery would express this perfectly, even if no actors were shown. See small sketch Pl. IV, p. 17 and *A,* Fig. 4, Pl. XXIV, p. 170.

must be over your base as you lift. The strain of lifting should be borne by your leg muscles, not by the muscles of your back and arms. Place your feet as close to the object as possible (Fig. 9) and squat. Do not bend over as in Fig. 11. As you lift, lean your own weight backward to counterbalance the weight of the object.

The secret of carrying a person lies more in the one being carried than in the carrier. The person carried (usually a girl) should bring her weight as close to the carrier as possible (Fig. 3, Pl. XX, p. 148), so that he does not have to use any strength in balancing her. To do this, she lets herself go limp and rests her head on his shoulder. If she is not supposed to be unconscious, she locks her arms around his neck and supports some of her own weight.

The stage directions in Shakespeare's plays often require a body to be carried off stage. This should be avoided if possible, as a limp body is never an impressive object and may strike the audience as funny. If you must carry a body, keep the feet upstage. One man can support the shoulders while two take the feet, but it is better to have two men on the shoulders. If six men are available, two of them can carry the hips, which will otherwise sag ungracefully. The whole action should be masked by having other actors stand downstage of the procession. If the attention of the audience can be attracted to another part of the stage, so much the better.

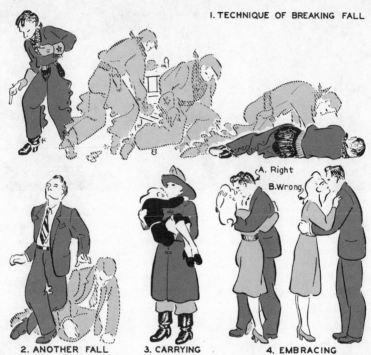

1. TECHNIQUE OF BREAKING FALL

A. Right
B. Wrong

2. ANOTHER FALL   3. CARRYING   4. EMBRACING

Falling. Despite the deep-rooted belief of young actors with a desire to show off, spectacular falls should be avoided except in broad farce and melodrama. The audience never believes the *character* has fallen but wonders how the *actor* did it without being hurt. The climax should occur when the actor is stricken, and the fall itself should be unobtrusive. If possible it should be masked by actors or furniture, and the attention of the audience should be momentarily diverted to some other character. Fig. 1, Pl. XX, above, shows a well-managed fall. The actor's weight is under complete control during three-fourths of the time, and the fall itself is divided into four minor falls so that shock is almost eliminated. These minor falls should be blended so that they seem to be one continuous movement. A fall on a bare stage is shown in Fig. 2. The actor places one foot behind the other and sinks by bending his forward leg. He then rolls to one side and breaks his fall by letting his hand, hip, and the whole length of his thigh strike the floor together. He may remain like this or may roll into the final position of Fig. 1.

Dead or unconscious characters should lie with their backs to the audience and their heads slightly downstage. This makes the body inconspicuous, which is almost always desirable, and helps to hide any movement the actor may make while breathing. The soles of the shoes should never be downstage, as audiences for some reason find them funny.

In order to avoid hurting yourself on a fall: (1) Divide the fall into several stages, as shown in Fig. 1. (2) Keep control of your weight as far as possible and reduce any actual drops to a minimum. (3) If you must fall from a height, land first on your feet and then collapse. (4) Revolve as you fall and roll when you land; this will make your movement seem continuous and it will also soften the shocks.

Walking. Fashion models are taught to walk with their feet parallel and close together (*A,* Fig. 10, Pl. XXI, p. 150). This method may be used on stage, or you may open yourself out by turning your downstage foot slightly toward the audience (*B*).

FOOTWORK

Footwork is as important to the actor as it is to the athlete. Most footwork difficulties are caused by using the wrong foot for the first step. Two simple rules apply here: (1) When you start to walk straight ahead, take the first step with the upstage foot (*A,* Fig. 7). When you start with a turn, however slight, take the first step with the foot on the side to which you are turning. (Fig. 6 shows a slight turn to the actor's left; Fig. 8 shows a wider turn to his right. Note that your first step should never make you cross your legs as in *B,* Fig. 6.)

Young actors often turn their heads 90° or more without moving their feet. This is an awkward habit. Learn to "Let your toes follow your nose" by practicing the turn in Fig. 8 until you are no longer afraid to move your feet.

If one step of a cross is especially important (such as the first step through a door in making an entrance or exit), you should arrange matters so this step can be taken with the upstage foot. The first and last steps in climbing or descending stairs should normally be taken with the upstage foot. However, in some cases the down-

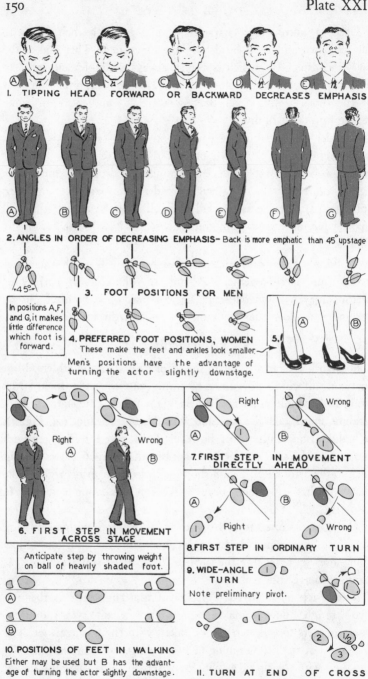

1. TIPPING HEAD FORWARD OR BACKWARD DECREASES EMPHASIS

2. ANGLES IN ORDER OF DECREASING EMPHASIS— Back is more emphatic than 45° upstage

3. FOOT POSITIONS FOR MEN

In positions A, F, and G, it makes little difference which foot is forward.

4. PREFERRED FOOT POSITIONS, WOMEN
These make the feet and ankles look smaller.
Men's positions have the advantage of turning the actor slightly downstage.

5.

6. FIRST STEP IN MOVEMENT ACROSS STAGE

Right (A)   Wrong (B)

7. FIRST STEP IN MOVEMENT DIRECTLY AHEAD

Right   Wrong

8. FIRST STEP IN ORDINARY TURN

Right   Wrong

9. WIDE-ANGLE TURN
Note preliminary pivot.

Anticipate step by throwing weight on ball of heavily shaded foot.

10. POSITIONS OF FEET IN WALKING
Either may be used but B has the advantage of turning the actor slightly downstage.

11. TURN AT END OF CROSS

stage foot is more convenient or more natural, and if experiment shows this to be the case, the downstage foot should be used.

A turn at a wide angle (Fig. 9) is made by pivoting on the foot farthest from the direction of movement. In a quick turn the pivot is made during the turn. For a slow turn the pivot must be made an instant before the turn. This means that there is one moment when the actor stands pigeon-toed, but this effect is not noticeable if the movement is made smoothly and the turn follows the pivot immediately.

Footwork for a turn at the end of a cross is shown in Fig. 11.

Avoiding Upstage Turns. This problem arises only when the actor is facing upstage at an angle of about 45° in one direction and must cross at an angle of about 45° in the other direction (Figs. 4 and 5, Pl. XXII, p. 153). In other situations there is no difficulty in making a downstage turn seem natural. The upstage turn can be eliminated if you can get out of the 45° upstage position by a preliminary turn (*A* in Fig. 5) made shortly before the cross is necessary. If this is not possible, the preliminary turn and the cross can be made as part of the same movement (Fig. 4). In either case a motivation for the preliminary turn must be found, but this is not difficult as the movement is an indecisive one, such as might be made by almost anyone at almost any time.

Crossing Upstage. It is easy to work downstage, but the actor who must move upstage while speaking, without turning his back to the audience, often finds his task difficult. This is especially true if he must start from a downstage position and make an important exit through a door in the back wall. Fig. 1, Pl. XXII, p. 153 shows a number of devices by which this can be done with apparent naturalness. Of course, these devices may be used in any order to suit the conditions. Problems of both footwork and motivation are combined. In the diagram, the door compels the actor to go upstage for his exit, while three other motivations, the girl, the picture (supposedly hanging on the R. wall but not shown in the diagram), and the coat on the hat tree draw him across the stage or turn him downstage.

The basic pattern is a zigzag. If the movement were directly upstage, the actor would find it almost impossible to face the audience as he moved. The first cross-stage movement is motivated by the picture. Presumably it is mentioned in the lines, but if not, the mere fact that the character takes an interest in it may serve as a motivation. The second cross-stage movement is motivated by the coat and the third by the door itself. Crosses C and E curve only slightly upstage, and during them the actor turns downstage to talk to the girl. On the exit F he is turned downstage by the business of putting on his coat. Notice how he takes advantage of every opportunity to move even a little upstage. He gains 2′ by the way he rises from his chair. The two turns B and D are not mere pivots; each of them moves him 1′6″ upstage. He gains another 1′6″ by the way his foot is placed for the third step in E. The serious student will find many hours of study and practice in this diagram.

Fig. 2 shows how two people may face downstage while making an upstage exit together. The man is ahead (and therefore uncovered) as they start, and he naturally turns downstage to speak to the girl. Then he stands back politely to let her go through the door first. She continues to move, facing straight ahead for the first few words of her line (which are presumably unimportant) but turning back to speak the end of her line over her downstage shoulder. The man may either follow her out silently or say a few words as he exits.

The patterns given in Pls. XXI and XXII will meet 99 per cent of your footwork problems. The rest you can solve by asking yourself: (1) "Which foot shall I use?" and (2) "Where shall I place it?"

HANDLING DOORS AND CURTAINS

Open doors are a source of distraction on stage, so you should always close a door behind you unless there is some specific reason for not doing so. For either an exit or an entrance, grasp the knob with the hand nearest the hinges and open the door. Change hands behind you as you pass through and close the door with the hand that was originally farthest from the hinges.

When you enter through draw curtains to make a curtain speech, remember which side of the curtain hangs upstage where they overlap in the center. Near the end of your speech, move about 5′

Plate XXII   153

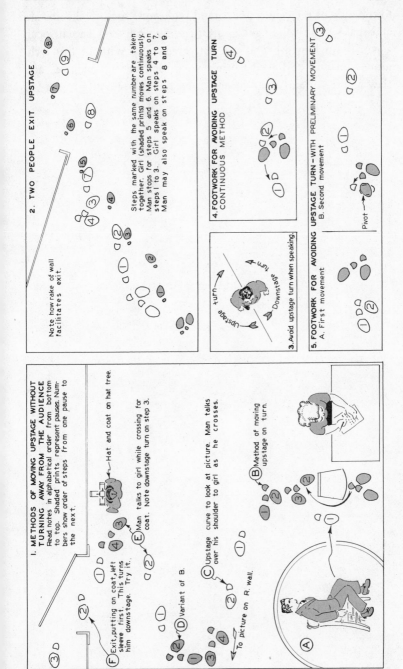

to this side of the center line. Stand with your back to the curtain and strike it with the hand nearest the center line. This will open a gap through which you can exit gracefully. Without this technique you will be forced to turn your back on the audience and claw at the curtains for a means of escape.

Chapter XV

SPECIAL PROBLEMS

Certain types of scenes which present special difficulties are dealt with in this chapter.

SCENES OF VIOLENCE

There is grave danger that a scene of violence will be too violent on the one hand or too tame on the other. If it is too violent, the audience is overstrained and may burst into hysterical laughter at the climax. This is so true that, except in melodrama and farce, long fights and spectacular episodes should be avoided. Furthermore, nothing should ever be done suddenly, as this may cause unwanted laughter. On the other hand, a fight which is too tame to be convincing leaves the audience disappointed. The exact balance is always a difficult problem, and even the best directors sometimes err on one side or the other.

Faking. Stage blows must always be faked. Blows with a dagger are struck directly up- or down-stage and masked by the body of the striker or his victim. Sword thrusts go across stage and pass between the body of the victim and his upstage arm. By clamping the blade between his arm and body, he makes it difficult to withdraw.

Fake blood should not be used unless the plot demands it. Even then it should be as unobtrusive as possible.

In fist fights, blows are always aimed at the point of the jaw. Actually the blow passes just in front of the chin. The 'victim' may clap his hands together to simulate the sound of the blow or he may hold his open palm before his face and let the striker's fist smack against it. If properly done, these movements are too quick to be noticed. At the moment of the blow the 'victim' should jerk his head back as if struck and also stagger a step or two. Precise timing is essential.

Precautions. All violence involves certain physical dangers, and these must be reduced to a minimum, not only for the personal safety of the actors, but because even an injury which is not serious in itself may be enough to keep the hurt actor from going on with the performance. To minimize these dangers the director should demand strict adherence to the following rules:

(1) No reasonable precaution should be neglected.

(2) The actors involved should practice the violence privately and not introduce it into rehearsal until it can be performed without a hitch.

(3) Individual responsibility for *each* move should be fixed; e.g., in a fist fight John should know exactly how and where to hit, and Bill should know exactly when and how to dodge. Never leave anything to chance—or to inspiration.

(4) Due precautions must be taken for the safety of the actors who are not actually involved in the violence, and sometimes for the safety of the technical crews and the audience as well.

Shooting Scenes. At a range of a foot or less, the wad from a .22 blank will knock a hole in a heavy galvanized-iron bucket even if it strikes a glancing blow. It would presumably have a corresponding effect on an actor. Unburned grains of powder are less deadly but have a greater range. Also, they spread like buckshot. Worst of all, guns have a mysterious way of loading themselves. I have had personal experience with three examples of this, and I have read of a case where a gun which was 'known' to be loaded with blanks actually contained six lead bullets. All the following safeguards are worth while:

(1) Have your blanks prepared by a gunsmith. Specify a light load (most blanks are too loud), a thin wad, and fast-burning powder which will be consumed in the barrel of the gun and not scatter sparks around the stage.

(2) Keep the gun unloaded until just before the actor carries it on stage. Then it should be loaded in the presence of the stage manager, the actor, the person in charge of hand props, and the director if he is backstage. When the actor comes off stage after

the shooting, the gun should be taken away from him and unloaded at once.

(3) Never shoot toward another actor or toward the audience. Usually a target about three feet upstage of the actor 'shot' is best. Crew members should not be permitted to stand on that side of the stage.

(4) Make the range as great as circumstances will permit. If possible the actor 'shot' should turn his back or at least turn his head away. The other actors on stage should stand well out of the line of fire.

A fifth precaution, which concerns the play rather than the actors, is that the stage manager should always have a second gun loaded with blanks, so that he can supply the necessary report in case the actor's revolver misses fire.

LOVE SCENES

Love scenes arouse strong empathies, audiences watch them attentively, and every detail is important. For this reason they require much private rehearsal with only the director and the 'lovers' present. However, such private rehearsals are for detail. The general business and particularly the kisses should be used in the regular rehearsals from the beginning. As the actors have their scripts in their hands, kisses in the early rehearsals are mere pecks, but the ice is broken and the actors learn to take such things in their stride. If a director tries to work up to the kisses gradually, he merely makes his actors self-conscious.

Appropriateness is especially important in a love scene. If Romeo and Juliet indulge in tame caresses, the audience is disappointed. On the other hand, if an unsophisticated couple winds up in a Hollywood clinch, the audience is embarrassed.

Sitting poses are much easier to handle than standing ones. The pose for a standing kiss admits of almost no variety and is likely to seem ungraceful even with experienced actors. The pose shown at *B*, Fig. 4, Pl. XX, p. 148 comes automatically to most actors but must be avoided at all costs. *A*, Fig. 4 is much better. The man places his downstage toe between the girl's feet. His upstage foot is thrust forward to provide support; otherwise the girl will tend to fall backward. His downstage arm goes around her body, while his upstage hand supports the back of her head. Hugging must be genuine; the pressure cannot be faked.

SUPERNATURAL SCENES

Scenes using ghosts, fairies, dreams, or other unreal characters must be handled delicately. The basic principle is to introduce the unreal character unobtrusively. Contrast and emphasis should be avoided until the supernatural idea is well established and the audience has accepted it completely. The unreal character normally makes its first appearance UL. If possible, that area should be an alcove or otherwise set off from the main stage. The effect is still better if this portion is reserved for the ghost and is not used for the live characters at all.

The ghost and the live characters stay as far from each other as possible during the early scenes, and never come into physical contact unless it is essential to the plot.

Everything which may remind the audience that the ghost is really a living actor should be avoided. When a ghost sits on a piece of overstuffed furniture and sinks into the cushions, he shows his weight and spoils the illusion. If the furniture is rigid, the idea does not arise. Similarly, when a ghost exits through a door, the spectators are reminded that real ghosts can pass through walls and have no need of doors. This difficulty can be evaded by having the attention of the audience attracted to the far side of the stage whenever the ghost enters or exits. If this is properly done, the ghost seems to appear and disappear, and at worst, attention is not called to the entrances and exits.

Dim lights usually help, but trick effects are risky. Even if they work, the audience stops watching the play and wonders how the effect was produced.

SPECIALTIES

A 'specialty' is a song, a dance, or anything of a similar nature introduced as an episode of a play. It must be kept part of the play and not allowed to stand out like a number in a musical comedy. The actor doing the specialty should never perform for the real spectators, either by facing them or by acknowledging their presence in any way. Instead he should perform for the stage audience. This generally means that the stage audience is on one side of the stage with the performer on the other side facing them. If there is no stage audience, the performer ignores the real audience and behaves as if he were alone.

Special equipment, such as tap or ballet shoes, should not be used unless they are appropriate to both the character and the situation. The performance must also be appropriate to the character. If an ordinary character sings and the actor happens to have a fine, trained voice, then the training and the quality of the voice must be disguised. The specialty is of no value for its own sake but only as part of the play. I have spent hours teaching a trained singer to breathe badly, and I once staged a duet in which two talented musicians obliged by singing off key. If these people had done their best, they would have provided some excellent music—and spoiled the play.

Any tendency to applaud on the part of the audience will ruin the effect. An audience applauds only at the end, so the secret of killing the applause is to avoid a definite ending. This can be done in several ways: (1) Break off the specialty before the end is reached. (2) Have the other characters start to speak before the end. (3) If the action calls for the specialty itself to be carried through to the end, have the accompaniment continue and allow it to fade out under the following dialog.

COMEDY

Philosophers disagree over the meaning of comedy, but for our purpose we may define it as anything the actors do or say which is intended to make the audience laugh and which succeeds. Laugh-getting depends 75 per cent on the actor's technique and only 25 per cent on the point of the joke.

COMEDY—A. FARCE TECHNIQUES

One reason why technique is so important in comedy is that a large part of all laughter is due to things which have no point and cannot be said to be funny in themselves. The best known ex-

Community Theater, Harrisburg, Pennsylvania

AREN'T WE ALL   **Setting by M. Edwin Green**

This is an excellent example of a setting for high comedy. Notice the general symmetry of the arrangement, and the fact that the back wall is parallel to the footlights. The realism, elegance, and good taste are also characteristic of the type of play. P. 147 shows a less typical high comedy.

amples of this are tickling and laughing gas. These are so crude that the mechanical nature of the laughter is obvious. The farce techniques used on stage are similar in effect to tickling, but they are sufficiently subtle to keep the spectator from realizing that he is being tickled and make him think he is laughing at something funny.

Farce Effects. The simplest farce device is the S-curve, in which the actor moves about the stage in wide sweeps at high speed taking long strides. This was the chief trick of the late George M. Cohan and earned him thousands of laughs.

A more generally useful device is the duplicate movement, in which two actors do the same thing either simultaneously or in succession. Normally, the movements are not exactly alike. One may be an unsuccessful copy of the other, as where a boy tries to duplicate the movements of a man; or they may mirror each other, as where one actor gestures with his right hand while another makes the same gesture with his left. Duplicate movements offer almost infinite possibilities for getting laughs.

Another farce device is overprecision in timing, which makes the actor seem like a clockwork doll; e.g., it is not ordinarily comic if three actors put on their hats, but if they put them on in strict rhythm, one-two-three, the audience will laugh. Overprecision occurs automatically in animated cartoons and is one of the chief reasons for their popularity.

The sounds of certain words also come under the head of farce. The laughter at 'Oshkosh' and 'Gorgonzola' is not due to the strangeness of the words, for 'Susquehanna' and 'Roquefort' will not cause a smile.

Farce may be purely abstract, with no more real humor than a demonstration in calculus. One of the funniest things I ever saw was a class exercise in which two students demonstrated variety of pose, like the examples in Pl. XI, p. 71. By sheer accident their movements happened to repeat each other and so fell into the repetition pattern of farce.

Comedy—B. Emotional Laughter

Laughter may also occur without a definite joke when an audience is subjected to too great an emotional strain. Long, tense, dramatic situations are dangerous on this account, because any sudden event, however slight, may startle the spectators and they will relieve their tension by nervous laughter.

Embarrassment is another emotion which is often relieved by laughter. An embarrassed person laughs to relieve his nervousness. Then he tells himself that the laugh is due to sophistication. This relieves his embarrassment and the relief results in fresh and more hearty laughter. Jokes on sex depend on this for a large part of their effect. ' Fifty years ago, when public profanity was less common and therefore more embarrassing, a comedian could count on getting a laugh every time he said 'damn.'

When an unsympathetic character is ridiculed, the resulting laughter is also emotional. At matinees of *The Women,* the audience yelped like a hunting pack every time one of the stage cats got clawed.

Comedy—C. The Point

Farce, overstrained emotions, and embarrassment can cause laughter in situations which are not inherently funny and which may even be tragic. Most laughter, however, is based on a definite joke—something with a specific point that would be recognizably funny even if presented in a different way or under different circumstances.

The secret of 'point comedy' lies in Horace Walpole's statement that "life is a comedy to the man who thinks and a tragedy to the man who feels." Point comedy always begins by making the audience feel. The feeling may be shallow—often it is no more than a mild irritation at some incongruity in the joke itself. The comedy always ends with the audience thinking instead of feeling. The transition is brought about by a sudden understanding which is called 'seeing the point.' Take the line, " 'Tis better to have loved and lost—much better." The first phrase makes the audience feel. The end brings them up short with an emotion of mild annoyance at the apparent incongruity. Then they understand, and they laugh —if the line is properly delivered.

Incongruity. Some form of incongruity, real or apparent, underlies every laugh of this type. Often it is possible to find several types of incongruity—really several different points—behind a single joke. However, one type usually predominates, and the actor should analyze his laugh lines, business, and situations to find this main incongruity and emphasize it. The chief types are listed below:

Simple incongruity. An obvious example of this is a tall thin man standing beside a short fat one.

Collapse of dignity. A pompous politician slips on a banana peel.

Incongruity between treatment and subject. This may be either a light treatment of a serious subject, such as a joke about death, or a serious treatment of a light subject ("I have a left shoulder blade that is a miracle of loveliness"—*The Mikado*). This type includes comic understatement ("I've almost come to the conclusion that this Mr. Hitler isn't a Christian"—*Arsenic and Old Lace*), and also comic exaggeration ("Tall? I'll say he's tall. He has to duck to let the moon go by.").

Incongruity between a character's action and what the audience knows. A character who has been employed by mail may patronize his boss, believing him to be the janitor. Comic misunderstandings belong to this type; e.g., a man describes a hippopotamus, and a fat woman thinks he is talking about her.

Incongruity between expectation and fact. The crowd looks off

L. and shouts, "Hail to the king!"—then the king enters R. Comic anticlimax falls under this head. We expect the climax to come last but it actually comes first; e.g., "When husbands [climax] or when lap dogs breathe their last."

Puns. These are incongruous because they join two thoughts which have no logical connection but which are symbolized by words that happen to sound alike; e.g., "They went and told the sexton and the sexton tolled the bell." Comic mistakes are often based on puns: e.g., a girl says, "Give me a [candy] kiss," and a boy thinks she is asking him to kiss her.

Ridicule. The incongruity here is between a supposedly ideal standard and the victim's actual status; i.e., "Consuelo, my darling, what a lovely evening gown! Did you make it yourself?"

COMEDY—D. COMEDY TECHNIQUE

Even the best joke will not cause a laugh unless it is well presented. The method of presenting jokes is called 'comedy technique.' Farce and comedy techniques may be used together to produce a single laugh, but they are essentially different. Farce technique will cause laughter by itself, just as tickling will; comedy technique is devoted to making the most of a point so that the point may cause laughter.

Analysis. The first step is to find the lines, situations, and pieces of business which may be 'played for laughs.' In doing this you will have to be guided by your own sense of humor. These items are called 'laughs,' although of course they are really potential laughs. Analyze each laugh separately. Does it depend on farce, embarrassment, a point, or some combination? If it has a point, what is the incongruity involved?

Stress. After you have analyzed the laugh, find ways of emphasizing the elements that make it funny. If it depends on a duplicate movement, exaggerate the duplication. In this you must be guided by the style of the play. In broad farce the duplication may be exaggerated to a point where its mechanical nature is obvious. If a laugh of this type appears in a comedy drama, it would require subtle treatment and a definite motivation for the duplication. If the laugh has a point, as in the 'hippopotamus' situation, stress the

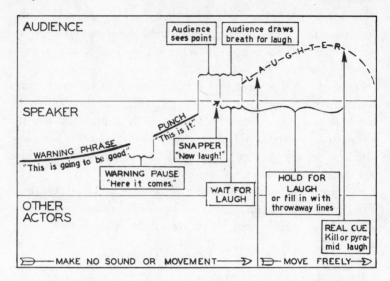

incongruity. The more the fat lady looks like a hippopotamus, the more furious she is, and the more innocent the speaker is—the funnier the laugh will be.

The Comic Line. A laugh line must be short enough to be spoken in one breath, i.e., ten words or less. If the laugh line is a clause at the end of a longer sentence, the actor should pause and breathe before delivering the comic line.

Delivering a Comic Line. There are several ways of speaking a comic line effectively, but one is all you will need. The method given here is used, with minor variations, by the vast majority of comedians. As Pl. XXIII, above, shows, seven separate stages are required.

WARNING PHRASE; e.g., ' 'Tis better to have loved and lost.' This serves to: (1) Take stage; i.e., concentrate attention on the actor and say, in effect, "This is going to be good. Don't miss it." (2) Produce an emotional effect of some sort. (3) Present either the whole incongruity or one half of it.

WARNING PAUSE. This is a one-beat pause after the warning phrase. It says to the spectators, "Look sharp, now, here it comes!"

PUNCH. The 'punch' may be the last word or two of the laugh line; e.g., 'much better' is the punch of the ' 'Tis better to have loved and lost' joke; or it may be a bit of comic business. The punch is always short—one or two rhythmic beats—and if it is spoken it must be the end of the sentence. A single word after the punch will kill the laugh. The punch either presents the other half of the incongruity, or explains an incongruity already present. In any case it makes the audience stop feeling and start to think. An audience is never in emotional sympathy with any character at the moment of laughter, even though such sympathy may be strong immediately before and after the laugh. Empathy also dies during the intellectual phase of laughter; so because we cease to reflect the other person's feelings, laughter is often cruel.

Whenever a motivation can be found, the actor should face dead front at the moment of the punch.

PUNCH PAUSE. The punch should be followed by a one-beat pause, during which no sound or movement is made. It is during this period that the spectators see the point, and their attention must not be distracted.

SNAPPER. When the audience laughs as a unit, crowd psychology increases the effectiveness and volume of the laughter. If the spectators are to laugh together, they must have a definite laugh cue. This is called a 'snapper.' Anything short and emphatic, such as a quick gesture or a snap of the fingers, makes a good snapper.

WAIT FOR LAUGH. The snapper is followed by another pause, during which the actors remain silent and motionless. The spectators are overcoming their mental inertia and drawing breath to laugh. Any distraction at this time is fatal. The last word of the punch is, technically, the cue for some other actor's line. This gives rise to one of the greatest difficulties that the inexperienced actor has to face. If he 'picks up his cue' and speaks promptly, he will kill the laugh. If he waits for the laugh and it fails to arrive, he breaks the flow of the scene and calls attention to the fact that a joke has fallen flat. The experienced actor knows instantly whether the audience will laugh or not, but this ability can only be acquired in actual performance. Rehearsals and exercises are of no value here. My own practice in directing a comedy is to train the actors to pick up their cues, but also to point out where laughs are likely to come and discuss in general the necessity of waiting for them. On opening night the actors usually kill a good many laughs by speaking too soon. Before the next performance, I explain what the trouble was and give specific examples. The second performance shows a marked improvement, and by the third only a few laughs are lost in this way. With inexperienced actors a perfect record is too much to hope for.

HOLDING FOR LAUGHS. No important line can be spoken during the laughter, for it would not be heard. The gap is filled with pantomime. As the length of the laughter cannot be judged until opening night, the actors must 'ad lib' their pantomime, i.e., make it up for themselves to suit the situation. Holding for the laugh is entirely different from waiting for the laugh and is fortunately much easier. Even the most inexperienced actors seem to do it instinctively.

The actors should never join in the laughter, even if the play is realistic and failure to laugh would be definitely rude in real life. Ninety-nine times out of a hundred if the actors laugh, the audience will sit silent.

KILLING THE LAUGH. If laughter is permitted to die away naturally, the spectators will feel satisfied and it will be difficult to make them laugh again. For this reason the laughter should be killed as soon as it begins to weaken. This is the real cue for the speech following the laugh line. If the first words of this speech are spoken in a loud, firm tone, the audience will realize that something important is coming and will quiet instantly to listen to the rest of the line.

If, instead of killing the laugh, a piece of comic business is inserted at this point, a new laugh will result. Unfortunately, such extra laughs can only be worked out after the play has opened and the exact audience reaction is known. Amateur productions rarely run long enough to make this possible.

COMEDY—E. UNWANTED LAUGHTER

When an audience laughs in the wrong place it is called a 'bad laugh.' Bad laughs often occur when the emotional current of the play is broken by some distraction, such as an audible prompt during a dramatic scene, or the rumble of a streetcar just after a character has said, "If only some sound would break the deathly silence of this desert." Some of these bad laughs can be avoided by taking greater pains. The others are simply bad luck.

Another type of bad laugh comes when the audience has been overstrained emotionally by a dramatic situation. Danger spots of this type can usually be located in advance. It is rarely possible to eliminate the risk entirely, but it can be reduced by (1) avoiding any sudden sound or movement as the climax approaches; (2) finding a legitimate chance for the audience to laugh in the middle of the scene; (3) deliberately decreasing the dramatic strength of the scene.

The third type of bad laugh occurs where farce movements are introduced accidentally. This happens during the early rehearsals of almost every play and the director must watch for it and correct it. The most common example is that in which two actors cross simultaneously, either in the same or in opposite directions. The laugh can be avoided by: (1) giving the actors different cues, so that they do not move at the same time; (2) having them move at distinctly different speeds; (3) changing the floor patterns so that they are definitely different; (4) breaking up one of the crosses into two short crosses; (5) having one actor execute a showy piece of business, such as waving his hat, so that he takes all the attention and the other is not noticed.

Silly Laughter. One type of mechanical laughter occurs when two actors, standing close together, look in each other's eyes and giggle. Actors afflicted in this way should stare at each other's chins. The impulse to laugh will stop, and the difference in the direction of the eyes is not noticeable from the audience.

Chapter XVI

SET DESIGN

The design of scenery is of basic importance to the success of the production. When my scenery has been well designed, I have found that directing was easy. Badly designed scenery, on the other hand, presented innumerable difficulties to both director and actors.

FUNCTIONS OF SCENERY

Scenery serves a large number of different purposes, and all of these must be kept in mind by the designer if his set is to be satisfactory.

Background. A play needs a background to shut out distractions. The Broadway production of *Our Town* was done on a bare stage where the brick walls and radiator pipes caught the eye every few minutes and drew it away from the play. An amateur production that I saw later used a plain gray cyclorama as a background, and the effect was much better.

Style. Scenery has the first word in the theater. Unless that word is right, the audience is misled from the start instead of being guided in the correct direction. For this reason scenery should not merely conform to the style of the play; it should definitely strike the style note to put the audience in the proper vein from the moment the curtain rises.

Conveying Information. When the curtains open, the audience should be presented instantly with a great deal of important information. The principal items that can be conveyed by the scenery are mentioned below. Not all of them can be expressed by certain sets, and occasions exist when some of them should purposely be left vague. On the other hand, a designer should always be on the lookout for opportunities to convey some extra bit of information; e.g., the lettering on an office door may reveal the name and position of the tenant, etc.

TYPE OF PLACE. Is it a living room, an office, a street, or a garden?

TIME. Time of day, time of year, sometimes even day of week (newspapers for Sunday, wash for Monday, etc.) can be expressed by the setting.

ECONOMIC, SOCIAL, AND CULTURAL STATUS OF OWNERS. Are they rich or poor, liked or shunned? Is their taste good or bad? An enormous amount of information about the characters can be conveyed by a conscientious designer. They may be shown as neat or careless, friendly or unbending, religious or libertine, etc. Often a single property will express a whole chapter of information; e.g., a large, shining, and expensive toy in a cold, formal living room says there is a child in the house who is pampered in material ways but forced to lead a frigid existence spiritually. This, in turn, says that the parents are rich and unfeeling, and the child is either a brat or an object of pity.

Atmosphere. The atmosphere of a setting colors all the facts, and it must be correct if the audience is to understand the play. A set with the wrong atmosphere may confuse the spectators so badly that they will need most of the first act to straighten themselves out. I once sat through twenty minutes of a heavy drama under the impression that it was a mild burlesque because the atmosphere of the set was too cheery for the play. By the time I discovered the truth, I had entirely lost the key to the action, and the rest of the play was meaningless.

Esthetic Values. A set should certainly please the eye, and if the play calls for beauty the set should be beautiful. However, the attractiveness or beauty of a setting is fatally easy to overdo. It should never be interesting enough to call attention from the play. Donald Oenslager says that if a set is applauded it must be a bad set. Claude Bragdon used to boast that a friend attended a performance especially to see Bragdon's scenery and then became so engrossed in the play that he failed to notice the settings. *Good scenery is unobtrusive.* It should have charms, but if it calls attention to them it defeats its purpose.

Plate XXIV

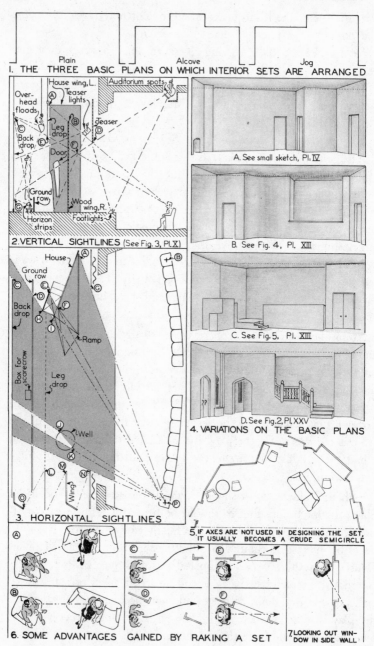

1. THE THREE BASIC PLANS ON WHICH INTERIOR SETS ARE ARRANGED

Plain   Alcove   Jog

2. VERTICAL SIGHTLINES (See Fig. 3, Pl. X)

House wing, L. — Teaser lights — Auditorium spots
Over-head floods — Back drop — Leg drop — Teaser — Door — Wood wing, R. — Footlights — Ground row — Horizon strips

A. See small sketch, Pl. IV

B. See Fig. 4, Pl. XIII

C. See Fig. 5, Pl. XIII

D. See Fig. 2, Pl. XXV

4. VARIATIONS ON THE BASIC PLANS

3. HORIZONTAL SIGHTLINES

House — Ground row — Back drop — Box for scarecrow — Leg drop — Ramp — Well — Wing

5. IF AXES ARE NOT USED IN DESIGNING THE SET, IT USUALLY BECOMES A CRUDE SEMICIRCLE

6. SOME ADVANTAGES GAINED BY RAKING A SET

7. LOOKING OUT WINDOW IN SIDE WALL

A set should be so composed that it seems in balance (p. 65) when no one is on stage. Otherwise the groups of actors will have to balance not only themselves but the set. Unless the set is used only for a short scene, it should not contain a definite center of interest. Where such a center does exist, it must be considered in grouping the actors, and this is impractical throughout a long scene.

MACHINE FOR PRODUCING PLAY

Another purpose of scenery, one which is so important that it deserves a special section by itself, is to provide a physical environment which will make the action of the play flow smoothly. Many designers neglect this. They look on set design as a kind of interior decoration, whereas it is primarily a problem in directorial technique. For this reason the director will usually find it wise to design the floor plans of his sets and leave only proportions, colors, and decoration to the designer. Arranging a set is by no means easy. Even an experienced director sometimes draws dozens of plans before he finds one that satisfies him.

Raking. Should the set be raked? Raked sets have three characteristics as compared to sets which are placed parallel.

(1) They convey a greater sense of realism.

(2) They are more dynamic. (Compare Figs. 1 and 2, Pl. XV, p. 102.)

(3) They simplify the design of groupings and movements and often make them more effective (Fig. 6, Pl. XXIV, opposite; Figs. 2, 3, and 5, Pl. XIII, p. 90; and Fig. 2, Pl. XXII, p. 153).

These qualities are desirable for most plays, so you should normally rake your sets and place one parallel only for a definite reason. There are three main reasons for placing a set parallel:

(1) Variety—in a play of many scenes some sets should be placed parallel to avoid monotony. Also, in a season of plays it would be well to have at least one important set placed parallel.

(2) Style—any play done in a period style, such as an old-fashioned melodrama or a comedy by Molière, would be spoiled by raking the set.

(3) Spirit—the dynamic quality of a raked set is out of key

Yale University Theater

COMPANIONS OF THE LEFT HAND

Setting by Jean Eckart

Note how the designer has considered all the elements of this setting. The play is obviously a romantic melodrama. We are told that it is romantic by the use of curves and by the general picturesque effect. The conflicting angles would announce melodrama even without the German soldiers. The various steps, platforms, and entrances provide magnificent opportunities for groupings and movement. The many planes offer opportunities for interesting variety in the lighting. Finally, the dominant importance of the house, R., is made clear by giving it more details than the rest of the setting.

with some plays. This would include plays of strong emotions but little physical action, e.g., most Greek tragedies and many plays by Eugene O'Neill. It would also include plays in which the intellect is dominant; high comedies like *The Importance of Being Earnest* and *Blithe Spirit* are more at home in sets that are placed parallel.

Usually it does not seem to matter whether the set rakes to R. or to L. In Fig. 1, Pl. XV, p. 102, the set rakes to L. as it forms a symbolic funnel leading to the DL. door. However, this is the only case I have found where the direction of rake was important except in the way it affected the location of openings and the placement of furniture.

A rake of less than 10° may make a set look as if it had been intended to be placed parallel and had been set up crooked by mistake. A rake of over 25° rarely results in a useful set. Between 10° and 25° the amount of rake does not seem to influence either the effect of the set or its utility.

THE SHORT WALL. Raked sets always have one short side wall.

(1) This may be omitted entirely (Fig. 5, Pl. XIII, p. 90), in which case it gives the effect that the set is part of a larger room.

(2) The wall may be placed on set axis (Fig. 5, Pl. V, p. 18). This is realistic and also provides a corner where some necessary but awkward piece of furniture can be stored. When the wall is in this position it should never contain a door, as the door would be invisible to part of the audience.

(3) The wall may be placed on the direct stage axis. This may be considered the normal practice and is exemplified by most of the sets in this book. Such a wall is visible to all the audience for every practical purpose. If there is a door in the wall, some spectators may not be able to see it, but they see characters pass through it and so learn that it is there. A wall placed in this way acts as an intermediate element between the set axes and the stage axes.

Some designers prefer to place this short wall off axis and make it rake onstage with the idea of bringing it into view of the whole audience. To my mind this upsets the axial effect of the set without serving any true purpose. I have used short walls on the direct axis in at least two dozen sets and I have never heard a criticism from actor or spectator. When the short wall is in this position, the furniture near it should also be on the stage axes (Fig. 2, Pl. XXV, p. 174).

When a set is placed parallel, the side walls are normally raked slightly (Fig. 2, Pl. XV, p. 102). This improves the view from the sides of the auditorium and does not disturb the axial effect, because the slanting walls create an illusion of perspective so that the walls seem on axis and the set appears deeper than it really is.

Areas. The set should be so arranged that each important scene can be played in the area best suited to it. *Guest in the House* (Fig. 1, Pl. XV) is the story of a struggle for a home. The hearth as a symbol for the home is of basic importance. 'Home' scenes are most effective when played DR. Therefore, both the hearth and the principal group of furniture are placed in this area. In a set

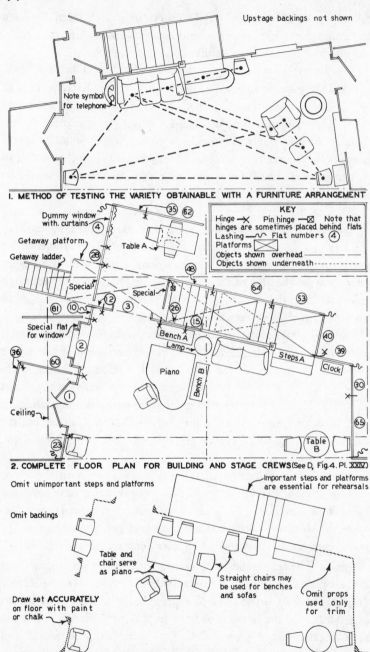

Upstage backings not shown

1. METHOD OF TESTING THE VARIETY OBTAINABLE WITH A FURNITURE ARRANGEMENT

Note symbol for telephone

Dummy window with curtains

Getaway platform

Getaway ladder

Table A

Special

Special flat for window

Ceiling

Bench A

Lamp

Piano

Bench B

Steps A

Clock

Table B

KEY

Hinge ⟶✕   Pin hinge ⟶⊠   Note that hinges are sometimes placed behind flats
Lashing ⟶⌇   Flat numbers ④
Platforms ⊠
Objects shown overhead ——————
Objects shown underneath -----------

2. COMPLETE FLOOR PLAN FOR BUILDING AND STAGE CREWS (See D, Fig. 4. Pl. XXIV)

Omit unimportant steps and platforms

Important steps and platforms are essential for rehearsals

Omit backings

Table and chair serve as piano

Straight chairs may be used for benches and sofas

Omit props used only for trim

Draw set **ACCURATELY** on floor with paint or chalk

3. FURNITURE, PLATFORMS, AND STEPS ARRANGED FOR A REHEARSAL

where the ideas of 'home,' 'warmth,' etc. are not involved, it would usually be better to place the fireplace and the principal furniture group DL. In Fig. 1, note also the stiff, office-like furniture group DL. and the fact that DC. is kept fairly open so that the actors will have room to move during scenes of conflict.

FURNITURE. Areas are normally outlined by the way the furniture is placed. An area which contains a group of furniture is called a 'furniture area.' Most sets require at least two of these—one upstage on one side of the set, and one downstage on the other. Fig. 2, Pl. XXV, opposite, has four furniture areas—UR., UC., DR., and DL. Furniture areas that can be combined by rearranging the characters add greatly to the possible variety of groupings. In Fig. 2, if one character is placed on bench B, another on the love seat, and a third in the chair DL., the whole C. and L. of the stage becomes one large furniture area.

Another device for making a furniture arrangement more flexible is to have a chair that may be considered as belonging first to one furniture area and then to another, depending on the way its occupant faces. Thus, the chair C. in Fig. 4, Pl. XV, p. 102 is shown as part of the DR. area, but if it were turned to face L., it would become part of the UL. area. If it is carried DL., a DL. furniture area will be created.

The dotted lines in Fig. 1, Pl. XXV, opposite, show how the grouping possibilities of a furniture arrangement can be tested. In this set there are only twelve pairs of seated positions, and the seats in many pairs are too far apart to be of much use. The possible groupings for three seated characters are even more limited and unsatisfactory. Now, make the same test on the set in Fig. 2. Both sets have the same general shape and both are about equally expensive and difficult to build. However, in Fig. 2 the connecting lines are much shorter and the groupings they permit are far more unusual and interesting. Also the possibilities for interplay between the furniture areas are decidedly greater than those in Fig. 1.

Try this test on the sets in Fig. 5, Pl. V, p. 18 (both desk chairs swivel), the small sketch in Pl. IV, p. 17, and Figs. 1, 2, and 4, Pl. XV, p. 102.

The groupings for important scenes must be taken into account when furniture is arranged. In this connection it will be well to re-read the chapter on Groupings, especially the section on Special Grouping Problems (pp. 92 ff.), and to study the drawings referred to there.

Young directors often find it desirable to make a rough model of the furniture and act out the play with dolls made by sawing off the bottoms of the prongs of clothespins.

As far as possible, furniture should not be placed downstage of an important door in the back wall, as it will hide entrances and exits. However, low chairs downstage of doors in the side wall are satisfactory and often desirable. Avoid having chairs face upstage. Of course, there is no objection to having a chair face upstage at the rise of the curtain, if it is moved before anyone sits in it. Moving furniture during the action is an excellent means of obtaining variety. On the other hand, never move furniture between the acts (if the set is not changed) unless the reason for the move is explained in the dialog.

Except in crowd scenes (Fig. 4, Pl. XIII, p. 90), there should always be enough seats so that everybody can sit at once. The director may not need such a grouping, but if he does, it is usually too late to add extra chairs after the play is in rehearsal.

In selecting each individual piece of furniture, thought must be given to the poses it makes possible. In Pl. XI, p. 71, note that the poses in Figs. 8 and 9 are impossible with an armchair, and that the poses in Figs. 12, 13, and 14 cannot be used with a straight chair. Chairs with half arms are particularly useful. The pose in Fig. 19 could not be taken in a straight chair, and that in Fig. 20 would be impossible in a chair with full arms, but both can be used with the half-arm type. Stools and hassocks permit a wide variety of poses, as they can be sat on from any angle (Fig. 25) and can also be used as footrests (Fig. 18). Sturdy coffee tables (Fig. 2, Pl. XV, p. 102) are convenient because they can serve either as tables or as stools. Rocking chairs allow almost no variety of positions, but they let the actor point his lines by rocking or sitting still at appropriate moments. Furthermore, he can swing forward to attack and backward to retreat. A sofa offers much more variety than a love seat. Round and oval tables permit a greater range of chair arrangements than rectangular ones, but they weaken the axial effect of the scene. The more these possibilities are considered in the design of the set, the easier it will be for the director and actors to work out groupings in rehearsal.

Openings. The openings in a set exert so much influence on the groupings and movements that they are as important as the furniture.

Doors. A plan or picture of the Broadway production will enable you to form a tentative idea of the number of doors in the set, but you should check this by listing the places to which the characters go and from which they come. Draw a floor plan of the house and work out a logical arrangement of the rooms. Even in the most fantastic play the geography of the situation should be clear.

I have used as many as seven doors in a set, but two to four is the normal quota. A large number of doors not only complicates the design but is likely to confuse the audience. Also, the doors occupy wall space, which is usually at a premium. You can often reduce the number of doors by having a corridor that leads to several places. If you wish to be more specific, the corridor can lead to one place L. (e.g., front door), to another R. (e.g., kitchen). There can be a flight of stairs (to the upstairs bedrooms) and a door in the back wall of the corridor (leading to a porch).

Next, list the important entrances and exits from each doorway. Dramatic entrances are best made from upstage, so doors for this purpose should be in the back wall if possible. On the other hand, dramatic exits are difficult to make upstage. Doors for this purpose should be in the side wall, preferably near the tormentor. When both important entrances and important exits must be made through the same door, it should be in the side wall, as it is easier to make a dramatic entrance from the side than to make a dramatic exit through the back.

Doors through which the audience is to see something must be placed in the back wall. This applies to a multipurpose corridor like the one described above. However, such a corridor can be located behind a raked side wall if the meaning of the action does not depend on a specific indication of the various places.

In locating doors you must also remember 'that they will serve as motivations for many movements. This means that if there are only two doors in a set, it will usually be a mistake to place them close together, or to place both of them upstage or both downstage. In Fig. 1, Pl. XV, p. 102, the door DL., the archway URC., and the door UC. are all fixed by their relation to the floor pattern. (The arch URC. can be seen more clearly in Fig. 2, Pl. X, p. 62.)

Stage doors normally swing offstage. Doors of this type are easier to build and less likely to stick at a crucial moment. Also, they make the action flow more smoothly if only because actors are more accustomed to them. This practice is normally followed even where it is actually unrealistic. Real entrance doors, both to residences and apartments, almost always swing in, but on stage the doors are usually hung to swing out. I have never heard a spectator criticize this arrangement or even indicate that he noticed it. As far as I know there are only three reasons for having a door swing onstage:

(1) When great realism is desired.

(2) When some special effect is involved, such as having a character hide behind a door, or having two lackeys 'swing wide the portals' so that the king can enter. If the lackeys pushed the doors instead of pulling them, their movement would be contrary to that of the king and so would resist his entrance psychologically rather than welcome him.

(3) When mystery plays build suspense by using doors in the side walls that swing onstage and hinge downstage. The audience sees the door swing and imagines that something horrible is going to enter.

Doors that swing offstage in side walls always have their hinges on the upstage side. This arrangement automatically masks the backing, and it also makes the movements of the door itself less distracting. A low gate like that in Fig. 5, Pl. XIII, p. 90 may be hinged downstage if it happens to be mechanically more convenient. When the back wall rakes, doors in it usually hinge on the upstage side, but the need to provide for an easy flow of movement may require a downstage hinging. Notice the door URC. in Fig. 4, Pl. XIII, and observe that a quick entrance or exit would be easier if the door were hinged on the other side, especially if the movement involved several people at once. Flow of movement governs the swinging of doors in a back wall which is placed parallel.

Windows. When the audience must see some action through a window, the window must be in the back wall. However, if the action can be conveyed by shadows, as in *Arsenic and Old Lace,* the window may be put in a side wall.

If an actor must see something through a window and describe it, the window should be in the side wall. Otherwise the actor will be forced to use an elaborate technique to avoid speaking important lines with his back to the audience (*E* and *F,* Fig. 6 and Fig. 7, Pl. XXIV, p. 170).

When a person exits through a window he naturally backs out. This makes exits through upstage windows entirely satisfactory, so a window used for entrances and exits may be placed either in a back or a side wall, whichever is more convenient.

Fireplace. A mantel or fireplace is a valuable source of motivations both for crosses and for interesting groupings if it is placed in a side wall and downstage. A fireplace in the back wall is little more than an ornament, because to approach it an actor must turn his back to the audience.

Steps and Platforms. The location of stairs in an interior set depends on their length, their breadth, whether or not they have a railing, and the rake (if any) of the set. The nature of the production is also important and complicates the matter so much that only general observations can be given here.

(1) A single step is of little value. Three or four steps can be used almost anywhere, as the actors can sit or stand on them to form effective groupings.

(2) Long flights of narrow stairs are most satisfactory when they run along the back wall. If they run along a side wall with the foot of the stairs downstage, the actors must turn their backs to the audience when climbing the steps. If the foot is upstage, the stairs themselves hide the actors.

(3) Broad stairs usually rise toward the back wall. If the set rakes, and the actor climbs the steps at an angle, he can avoid turning away from the audience.

Community Theater, Harrisburg, Pennsylvania

THE WARRIOR'S HUSBAND   ·   Setting by Henning Nelms

High schools often use draperies for scenery. This setting shows how appliqued patterns and a slight departure from the usual arrangement can lend interest even to conventional draperies. Of course, both the scene depicted and the style of play must be in keeping with this treatment.

(4) Irregularities such as turns, landings, etc. (Fig. 1, Pl. XV, p. 102) add interest both to the steps themselves and to the groupings and movements of the actors.

(5) Railings are often required by realism, but they are usually undesirable from the director's point of view as they limit the groupings that can be arranged on the steps.

GETAWAY PLATFORMS AND STEPS. When steps lead up to an opening, a 'getaway' platform must be provided on the offstage side of the opening so the actor will not walk off into space. Fig. 1, Pl. XXV, p. 174 shows a case where the stairs themselves extend far enough to make a getaway platform unnecessary, but this is rarely possible. Sometimes the actor merely stays on the getaway platform and waits for his cue to enter, but usually access to the platform is made possible by a getaway ladder (Fig. 2) or getaway stairs.

PLATFORM SETS. Sets which consist chiefly of platforms (Fig. 3, Pl. XV, p. 102) are extremely effective. Designing such a set has been described as "deciding where the actors are to stand and then building platforms under them." In other words, decide which areas are to be given emphasis by raising them on platforms. Movement patterns should also be considered, as the steps must facilitate movement along desirable paths. Movement along undesirable paths is often made difficult or impossible in order to provide the characters with an obvious motive for not taking these paths.

In sets of this type the platforms and steps usually act as furniture on which seated groupings can be arranged. It is well to plan many of these groupings in advance and keep them in mind while the set is being designed.

Some of the platform lines should follow the stage axes and some should follow the set axes. If only one pair of axes is used, the effect will be formal and probably monotonous. If more than two pairs of axes are used, the set is likely to become confused and meaningless.

The lines marking the edges of a platform usually coincide with those marking the surrounding flats. For that reason, platforms are shown by drawing their diagonals (Fig. 3, Pl. XV, p. 102). Of course, this is merely a convention; the diagonals do not appear in the set itself.

VARIETY IN SCENE DESIGN

Nonaxial sets are almost always roughly circular (Fig. 5, Pl. XXIV, p. 170) and tend to force their furniture into a semicircle. Axial sets fall into one of three general plans (Fig. 1, Pl. XXIV).

Providing Variety. Although the number of basic plans is limited, unlimited variety of effect may be obtained by using some combination of the methods listed below:

RAKE. A set that rakes R. (*A*, Fig. 4, Pl. XXIV) is different from one that rakes L. (*B*, Fig. 4) and also from one placed parallel. The direction of the jog provides another type of variation (*B* and *C*, Fig. 4). A change in the amount of rake is of little importance.

PROPORTION. If a wall is long in one set and short in another, the entire effect will be changed. (Compare the alcove in the small sketch Pl. IV, p. 17, which includes nearly the whole back wall, with that in Fig. 5, Pl. V, p. 18).

COMBINING BASIC PLANS. *B*, Fig. 4, Pl. XXIV, p. 170 combines a jog and an alcove. In *D*, Fig. 4, an alcove in the back wall exists but is suppressed in effect by the stairs. This makes the alcove seem separate from the main set, which is plain in plan. Note, however, that this set has a shallow alcove in the R. side wall.

CURVED AND SLANTING CORNERS. These decrease the strict axial impression of the set (*B* and *C*, Fig. 4, Pl. XXIV, p. 170).

LOCATION, SIZE, AND SHAPE OF OPENINGS. These make a great difference. Windows and open archways give a feeling of space which closed doors and blank walls deny. Sometimes an entire wall is omitted as in Fig. 5, Pl. XIII, p. 90. Large doors are more formal than small ones and have more esthetic weight. Notice also the Tudor arches in *D*, Fig. 4, Pl. XXIV, p. 170, and think how the appearance of the set would be changed by round or Gothic arches, or by rectangles like the doors in the other sets.

STEPS AND PLATFORMS. These introduce a third dimension and also make the set more complicated. Note how uninteresting *C*, Fig. 4, Pl. XXIV would be if the platforms and railings were omitted.

DECORATIONS. Even if two sets are structurally alike, they can still be changed in appearance by altering the color and decoration of the walls. In fact, some producing groups have only one set which they repaint for every production. Differences in trim, such as window draperies, pictures, flowers, etc. will also have a profound influence upon the looks of a set.

FURNITURE. The amount, type, and arrangement of furniture are potent elements of variety. Figs. 1 and 2, Pl. XXV, p. 174 are almost identical in structure, but Fig. 2 was used for a heavy drama and Fig. 1 for a light comedy. The color and decoration of the walls made some difference, but the furniture was the chief means by which the great contrast in spirit between the two plays was reflected in the settings.

CEILINGS. Beamed or sloping ceilings create a marked change in the appearance of a set, but if your auditorium has a balcony, half your audience will be unable to see the ceiling.

TECHNICAL CONSIDERATIONS

Beginners frequently think of scene designing in terms of a picture on paper. For one of my productions a professional artist turned in a 'scene design' which consisted in a sketch of four men seated around a table. No background was indicated. Such a picture is not a scene design. A scene design is a set of directions to the technical workers, showing them how to construct, paint, and light the scene. It must be thought out in terms of real materials—wood, and canvas, and scene paint, which can be cut, and glued, and brushed into place by real workers, shifted on your stage, and lit by your stage lights. The designer must also know which parts of his set are to be 'practical,' that is, capable of being used as their appearance suggests. A practical window can be opened; a practical rock can be stood on. 'Nonpractical' scenery is easier to make and places fewer limitations on the designer's fancy, but even nonpractical scenery must be built and shifted and lit. The designer who forgets this is creating trouble for others and disappointment for himself.

This means that while the design is being made, the designer must be constantly aware of the way in which the actual scenery will be built, used, and lit. He must take into account the cost and difficulty of each piece, and weigh them against the effect he hopes to produce. In amateur practice, the designer rarely has the technical knowledge required for this, so he must work in close collaboration with the director or the technical director.

Drawings and Specifications. In order that the designs can be understood by the workers who are to execute them, the designer should provide a floor plan (Fig. 2, Pl. XXV, p. 174), a sketch like those in Pl. X, p. 62, and whatever working drawings and diagrams are necessary to explain the construction involved. If the construction is simple, the working drawings can be merely freehand sketches.

Scenery specifications for an amateur group are usually standardized by custom, so that it is not necessary to mention the kind of lumber, the grade of paint, etc. When special specifications are necessary, they can be written on the drawings near the item to which they refer.

Principles of Scene Construction. A real house is built as one piece; the only separate parts are things that must be free to move, such as doors and windows. A stage set, on the contrary, is composed of separate units, and these in turn are made up of smaller units joined together more or less temporarily. The walls of the set in Fig. 2, Pl. XXV, p. 174, consist of five groups of hinged flats called 'books.' These books include a total of seventeen individual flats (fifteen numbered flats and two special flats). There are also eight offstage flats, arranged in three books and a single flat. These are called 'backings.' The single flat, 61, is a 'window backing,' or it may be referred to as an 'exterior backing' or a 'sky backing.' Flats 36 and 60 make one 'door backing,' or 'interior backing.' The remaining five flats, taken together, also make a door backing. The set also includes: (1) a door frame and two doors (we might call this a door 'thickness,' as it has no facing); (2) two thickness pieces for the window alcove, the special window flat, the window frame (with one practical sash), and the window seat; (3) the arch thickness URC.; (4) three platforms, three sets of steps, a get-away ladder, and a 'cover flat' (this is the irregular scene unit which masks the sides of the steps and platforms; the one in this set includes a railing); (5) a ceiling.

An exterior set, like that in Fig. 4, Pl. X, p. 62, is made up of steps and platforms; a 'back drop,' which is a large sheet of painted canvas hung upstage of the rest of the set; 'borders,' which are flat valances of painted canvas hung overhead to represent leaves, etc; tree trunks; and cutouts. A cutout is a kind of flat with irregular edges. Horizontal 'cutouts', which represent things like distant mountains, are called 'ground rows.' Vertical cutouts used to mask the sides of the stage are called 'wings.' Wings which represent trees are called 'wood wings.' Note the distinction between 'a wing,' which is a piece of scenery, and 'the wings,' which is the area at the side of the stage. Scenery wings mask the wings and keep the audience from seeing the sides of the stage. There is no special term for a cutout which stands alone in the center of the stage. It is called simply a 'cutout.' Fig. 3, Pl. X shows two other types of scene units. One is the 'ramp,' which is a sloping platform. The other is the 'leg drop,' which is a drop with the center cut out so that it acts as a border and wings combined. Most drops of this type have two legs, but in Fig. 3 the L. leg is not needed as it would be hidden by the house. A type of unit not illustrated is the 'grass mat,' which is a mat made of raffia used to simulate grass. These are ex-

pensive but can sometimes be borrowed from florists, window dressers, or undertakers.

The flat (Fig. 1, Pl. XXVI, p. 194) is the fundamental scene
unit. Its construction is typical of most scenery and consists of a
piece of canvas stretched over a wooden frame. This method of
construction can be applied only to planes or to objects made up
of planes. In general, the designer may consider it an axiom that
anything made up of planes will be easy to build, whereas anything
requiring curved surfaces will be difficult.

Standards. Most amateur scenery is built of stock units which
are reassembled and repainted for each production, with one or
two special pieces added to provide individuality. If the stock pieces
are to work well together, they must be standardized. Such stand-
ardization may seem a handicap to the designer, but in actual practice he will find it a convenience.

FLATS. Usually all flats should be the same height, though some
theaters have two sizes of flats, a short one for ordinary scenes and
a tall one for impressive scenes. The ideal flat height is 12', but if
your auditorium has a balcony you may need to make yours 14'
high, or, if you are unfortunate enough to work on a stage with
a low ceiling, you may be limited to flats of 11' or even less.

Flat widths should not be standardized. Some groups standardize on widths in even feet (1', 2', etc.), but this limits the designer
and gives him no way to make a wall of odd length such as 8'7''.
A much better system is illustrated by the list of flats on p. 186.
These can be arranged to fit any play. You need not use these exact widths, but you should follow the general principle of having
one flat for each two or three inches in the range between 1' and
5'9''. For anything less than 1' you can use a board instead of a
flat. The upper limit is 5'9'', because this is the greatest width that
can be covered with a single piece of 72'' canvas (allowing for
shrinkage), and also the greatest width which a stagehand can
handle easily. Special flats for windows and fireplaces are not
needed, as the flats with door openings can be used for these purposes by partially plugging the holes (Fig. 5, Pl. XXVI, p. 194).

Note that each flat has a number for identification and that this
number suggests the width of the flat. When a set is not made up

of standard flats but is to be used in only one production, it is more convenient to omit the individual flat numbers and number the books instead (Fig. 5, Pl. V, p. 18). These numbers should start DL. and run upstage and R. so that they will appear in normal order to anyone looking at them from behind. Backings should be assigned letters rather than numbers, so that they will be distinguished from the set proper.

Door Flats

No.

1	5'9" wide, 4'4" × 9'6" opening centered.					
2	"	"	"	"	"	"	"
3	"	"	"	"	"	"	"
4	"	"	3' × 7'	"	"
5	"	"	"	"	"	"	1' from R. of flat.
6	"	"	"	"	"	"	1' " L. " "
7	4'0"	"	"	"	"	centered.

Plain Flats

No.	Width	No.	Width	No.	Width
10	1'0"	23	2'3"	36	3'6"
11	1'1"	25	2'5"	39	3'9"
12	1'2"	26	2'6"	40	4'0"
13	1'3"	28	2'8"	43	4'3"
15	1'5"	29	2'11"	48	4'8"
18	1'8"	30	3'0"	50	5'0"
19	1'9"	32	3'2"	51	5'1"
20	2'0"	34	3'4"	53	5'3"
21	2'0"	35	3'5"	57	5'7"

Also six to ten 5'9" flats numbered 60, 61, etc.

Doors. The opening in the frame of a single door should be 2'8" wide and 6'8" high. If the door itself hangs on the back of the frame, it must be 2'9½" wide and 6'8" high. If the door hangs in the frame to swing onstage, it must be 2'7¾" wide by 6'7¼" high. Frames for double doors should have openings 4' wide by 6'8" high. Each door should be 2'¾" wide by 6'8" high.

Steps. Standardize on 7" risers and 10" treads. This makes a fairly steep stair, but on stage you usually need to get a maximum of height in a minimum of space.

Platforms. Make two 10' × 4' platforms; two 7' × 5'; one 7' × 2'; and two 7' long which can be put together to form a 7' × 5' rectangle. One of these should taper from 4' on the R. end to 1' on the L.; the other should taper from 1' on the R. end to 4' on the L. You can make these any height you like simply by providing each platform with a set of legs 1" shorter than the desired height of the platform. These seven platforms can be arranged in a wide variety of ways, and, when supplemented by one or two special pieces, their range is almost unlimited (Fig. 3, Pl. XV, p. 102—note that some of these platforms overlap).

SIGHTLINES

The designer must know what parts of his set will be visible to the whole audience and also what parts will be hidden from the whole audience. This is done by means of drawing 'sightlines.'

Horizontal Sightlines. We will begin with the horizontal sightlines (Fig. 3, Pl. XXIV, p. 170). Tracing paper is placed over the floor plan of the set, and the seats at the ends of the first row are located (B and P). Lines are drawn from P, as in the diagram, touching every part of the set which might mask something from a spectator seated at P.

Lines to the near side of the set indicate the parts of the stage that we might like to have visible but which will be hidden from some of the spectators. Obviously, important action must not take place here. In Fig. 3 the posts of the well interfere with the view of the UR. area, which therefore becomes almost useless. On the other hand, line J tells us that the scarecrow can be seen by everyone.

Lines to the far side of the set ($C, H, I, E,$ and A) indicate parts that we might like to have hidden but which can be seen by some spectators. In Fig. 3, a spectator at P can see the back wall of the stage house between the backdrop at C and the point H. This means that the drop must extend farther offstage L. At the same time line H shows us that the ground row is unnecessarily long (D). The line to the corner of the house at I shows that some of the backing H can be seen. If many people could see this, it might be well to bring the house farther onstage. However, in the present case the designer might decide to paint the backing to represent the outside of the house. The line past the downstage edge of the door F shows us how far the backing must be carried offstage at E. The

line past the tormentor G tells us that the house extends far enough
offstage to mask.

I have shaded the diagram to show the part of the stage that is
visible from P. Such shading would not be necessary in working
out the sightlines for an actual set.

Similar sightlines should be drawn from the other sightline station B. In this set, only those to the leg drop L, the wing M, and
the tormentor N are important. These tell us that the wings O and
M will mask, but that the leg drop must be carried farther offstage.

Vertical Sightlines. The method of determining vertical sightlines is shown in Fig. 2. Usually only the sightline station in the
front row is important. However, in balcony scenes and other cases
where the top of the set must be visible, sightlines are drawn from
the back row of the orchestra and the back row of the balcony if
there is one.

For vertical sightlines we need a kind of X-ray view showing the
important parts of both sides of the set. In Fig. 2 this is relatively
simple, but in a set like D, Fig. 4, the drawing would be rather
complicated. Fig. 2 shows that the leg drop E masks the top of the
back drop C, and that the teaser D masks the top of the leg drop.
Also, all the lighting instruments are masked. Unfortunately, we
also learn that the wood wing B must be at least 14' high, and that
the house must be at least 16'5". Probably a designer would decide
to make the house shorter than that and give it a cutout top. He
would then hang a short foliage border behind the house to provide
the necessary masking.

PUBLISHER'S NOTE. Drawing is essential for every form of stage design and technical planning. It is almost equally valuable to directors and actors (see Pls. VI and
VII, pp. 26 and 27). If you have trouble with drawing, *Thinking with a Pencil,*
written by Henning Nelms and published by Barnes & Noble, explains simplified
methods which bring all types of theatrical drawing within easy reach of anyone
who has enough skill with a pencil to write his own name.

Chapter XVII

SCENERY

The making of scenery is an ideal task for the amateur craftsman because so much can be accomplished so easily.

EQUIPMENT

An adequate supply of good tools does much to speed up the work and make it more pleasant. The equipment required is not expensive, and if the handles of all tools belonging to the theater are painted red no one will carry them off by mistake.

Carpenter's Tools. Any carpenter's tool kit is sufficient for scene building if one or two special items are added. However, the following check list and specifications may prove helpful. Tools are listed roughly in the order of their importance. More than half of those listed could be omitted, though each will prove useful in special cases.

Clinching plates—iron plates ⅛" thick, cut in the shape of right triangles 12" on a side. See p. 196. Must be made specially by some local iron worker.
Brushes—(1) for gluing canvas, a No. 1 varnish brush; (2) for varnishing corner blocks (p. 191), any 2¼" flat brush.
Rules—(1) 6' or 12' flexible steel rule; (2) 50' steel tape. Do not use cloth tapes; they are not sufficiently accurate.
Saws—(1) crosscut, eight or nine teeth to the inch, 26" or 28" long; (2) hack, pistol grip, with 10" blades; (3) combination, with keyhole and compass blades; (4) rip, five or six teeth to the inch, 26" or 28" long; (5) power saw with 8" circular blade and ½ horsepower motor (smaller motors are unsatisfactory).
Hammers—(1) ripping, 16-oz.; (2) tack, 4-oz., magnetic; (3) 'stapling machine' or 'tacker' (the best quality is needed to stand rough usage). A stapling machine is really an automatic hammer that drives staples, which are a cheap and convenient substitute for tacks in scenery built for only one production.
Squares—(1) steel; type with white markings is best; (2) try, 6" combination try-and-miter type; (3) sliding T-bevel, 6".
Brace and bits—10" ratchet brace; 7/16" bit is size most used.
Screwdrivers—(1) Perfect Handle type, 7" blade; (2) spiral-ratchet, spring-return type, 20" long when extended.
Canvas knife—small paring knife or large jackknife.
Drills—(1) egg-beater hand drill with ¼" chuck; (2) automatic or 'push' type; (3) ¼" power hand drill (many accessories are now available for these

drills, including jig-saw for making cutouts and 5″ circular saw for general use).
Twist drills in the 7/32″ size will be most used. A ½″ countersink for metal
will also be needed. Push drills take special fluted drills usually sold in sets of 8.
'Butterfly' drills in ⅛″ sizes from ⅜″ to 1″ are available for ¼″ power drills;
they are ideal for boring wood.

Plyers—machinist's (1) 6½″; (2) 10″.
Pipe wrenches—17″; two needed.
Vice—combination swivel vice, pipe vice, and anvil, 3″ jaws.
Miter box—may be homemade.
Center punch—⅜″ × 6″.
Files—iron handle with detachable blades: (1) 6″ flat file; (2) 4″ triangular
file; (3) 17″ wood rasp, or Stanley 'Surform.'
Tin snips—10″ straight or duckbill.
Chisels—¼″ and ½″ with plastic handles.
Wrecking bar—2′ long, ¾″ thick.
Plumb bob—small, iron.
Draw knife—10″.
Plane—8″ long, 1⅝″ blade.
Carpenter's level—18″.
Upholsterer's needle—6″, curved.

Painter's Equipment.   These must stand rough treatment, so a
durable grade is economical.

Brushes.   The three types shown in Pl. XXVIII, p. 207 will meet all ordinary
needs. A house painter's 4″ 'wall brush' with 4″ bristles (Fig. 1) will be used for
most work. A No. 8 'chiseled sash tool' (Fig. 2) is used for details such as leaves,
brick, etc. Lining and other fine work calls for 'angular liners' (Fig. 6), ½″ and
¾″ sizes.

Pails.   Galvanized 12-quart pails are used for mixing glue and for holding the
larger quantities of paint. Small quantities call for smaller containers such as lard
pails or saucepans.

Stove.   A two- or three-burner gas, electric, or kerosene stove is needed for heat-
ing glue and paint.

Sink.   A sink with running water is essential.

Paint bins.   A separate bin should be provided for each pigment. Boxes, drawers,
or metal drums may be used. Each bin should be furnished with a scoop for dip-
ping out the pigment.

Ladders, etc.   Painting can be done from ladders, but a rolling platform 6′ high,
10′ long, and 2′4″ wide with a ladder built in each end is a great convenience.
Such a platform can also be used for rigging overhead scenery and lights.

Miscellaneous.   A number of cheap yardsticks, wooden stirring paddles, and a
ball of cord complete the equipment.

MATERIALS

A knowledge of the materials used in scenery, and of the sources
from which they can be obtained, is an essential part of stagecraft.

Lumber.   Steps and platforms may be built of any wood that is
strong and straight. White pine is best because it is lightest, but
spruce, yellow pine, and fir are all satisfactory. For all other types
of scenery the wood must be not only strong and straight, but light

and not easily split. Unfortunately, the only wood that meets these requirements is (white pine,) or its Brazilian equivalent, Porono pine. Both of these are scarce and expensive. No substitute is satisfactory. However, if you are forced to use one, the possibilities rank in this order: (1) cypress, (2) New England native pine, (3) spruce, (4) ponderosa pine.

Lumber sells by the 'board foot,' which is 12″ × 12″ × 1″. This is figured on the nominal size, which represents rough lumber. The actual, or 'dressed,' size is always smaller. Actual sizes vary. This will throw your measurements out, unless you agree on standards with your dealer. The following sizes are satisfactory:

FOR STEPS AND PLATFORMS		FOR ALL OTHER SCENERY	
Nominal	Actual	Nominal	Actual
1″ × 6″	¾″ × 5⅝″	1″ × 2″	¾″ × 1⅝″
1″ × 10″	¾″ × 9⅝″	1″ × 3″	¾″ × 2⅝″
1″ × 12″	¾″ × 11⅝″	1″ × 4″	¾″ × 3⅝″
2″ × 4″	1⅝″ × 3⅝″	1″ × 6″	¾″ × 5⅝″
		1¼″ × 3″	1″ × 2⅝″
		lattice strip	5⁄16″ × 1⅜″

All sizes are sold in lengths of 12′, 14′, or 16′.

Lumber grades vary with the locality. A fair grade will serve for everything except 1″ × 2″ and 1″ × 3″ pieces. These are most economically bought in 'shop grade' and 'random lengths.' Some pieces in this grade will be knotted or bent, and only the 'clear' portions of these can be used. Even so, you will save 25 per cent compared to the cost of lumber that is clear throughout.

Profile board. The irregular edges of cutouts (Fig. 10, Pl. XXVII, p. 200) should be sawed from 'profile board,' which is a plywood ·7⁄32″ or ¼″ thick made of white pine or basswood. Ordinary plywood is too heavy for use in scenery. For most purposes light 'wallboard' may be substituted at a considerable saving. An even cheaper substitute is the 'corrugated board' used for cartons. This has the advantage that it can be cut with a knife, but it is too fragile for use on scenery which must be shifted.

Profile blocks. These are cut from profile board and are used to join the structural members of flats (Pl. XXVI, p. 194). There are two types: (1) 'corner blocks,' which are right triangles 10″ on a side, and (2) 'keystones,' which are 8″ long and taper from 4″ at one end to 3″ at the other. If smaller blocks are needed they are cut from these standard types. Profile blocks are beveled on one side. They should be given two coats of waterproof varnish before you use them. This will double their life and that of the scenery on which they are used.

Molding. Small variations are not perceptible from the audience, so one type of molding will meet *all* requirements. The shape shown in Fig. 5, Pl. XXVII, p. 200 is ideal. It is not stocked by most lumberyards and must be specially made, but even so it is economical because the pieces can be used over and over again.

Canvas, etc. Your choice here will depend on the use to which your scenery will be put. I have seen admirable drops made of Manila paper, but they were good for only a few performances, whereas canvas drops can be repainted for a dozen plays.

Canvas. The most satisfactory material for covering flats is 8-oz. 'canvas' or 'duck' 72" wide. *Feltdux* made by John Boyle & Co., Inc., 112 Duane St., New York, N. Y., is excellent. Muslin costs less per yard but is difficult to handle and so much less durable that it is more expensive in the long run.

Padding. The cheapest padding for platform tops is 'cotton batting' held in place with 8-oz. tacks driven through small squares of cardboard. The jute and 'waffle' types of rug padding are more durable but much more expensive.

Gauze. Transparent drops for special effects are made of 'gauze,' also called 'bobbinet' and 'scrim.' This is 30' wide, has a hexagonal weave, and is entirely different from the fabric called 'theatrical gauze.'

Wire. Trees, rocks, etc. are shaped with 'poultry netting' with a 2" mesh. Window glass is usually omitted entirely but may be simulated with No. 14 mesh 'wire screen.'

Builder's Hardware. The following items should be kept on hand:

NAME	SIZES	REMARKS
Clout nails	1½" or 1¼"	Used for attaching profile blocks. *No other nail is satisfactory.* Clout nails must be about ¼" longer than the combined thickness of the block and the lumber. Ordinary ¾" lumber and ¼" blocks require an 1¼" nail.
Common nails *Finishing nails*	4d, 6d, and 8d	Read "fourpenny," etc. Sizes indicate length: 4d = 1½", 6d = 2", 8d = 2½"
Tacks	8-oz.	Use only cut tacks, not wire tacks.
Screws	⅞" × 9 1½" × 9	Flat-head bright. Size 9 screws are 3/16" in diameter and fit most stage hardware.
Bolts	3/16" × 2"	Flat-head stove bolts with washers.
	⅜" × 4" ⅜" × 6"	Carriage bolts with washers and wing nuts.
Hinges	2" × 4⅜"	Tight-pin backflaps.
	6", heavy	Strap hinges.
Mending plates *Corner plates* *Corner irons*	¾" × 3" ¾" × 3½" ¾" × 3"	Used for making joints.
Screw eyes	No. 10–⅜" No. 5–⅜" No. 108–⅜" No. 105–½"	Nos. 105 and 108 are stronger than Nos. 5 and 10. Dimensions refer to diameter of eyes.
Turnbuttons	2"	For holding plugs in place (*A*, Fig. 1, Pl. XXIX).

Harness snaps	Medium	Attached to ropes for quick release.
Door locks	3⅛″ × 4″	Horizontal-rim type.
Casters	3⅛″ wheel	Rubber tired. Used under heavy scenery.
Strap iron	3/16″ × ¾″	Used for sill irons (Fig. 4, Pl. XXVI).

Special Stage Hardware. Many hardware items needed on stage are made only by J. R. Clancy, Inc., of Syracuse, N. Y. Their catalog numbers are given and also the page of this book on which each article is described.

NAME	PAGE NO.	CAT. NO.	PURPOSE
Stage braces	212	135 } 235	Bracing scenery. No. 135 extends from 5′ to 8′4″; No. 235 extends from 6′ to 10′4″.
Foot irons			
Solid	213	42 }	
Hinged		142 }	Attaching scenery to stage floor.
Flat	200	542 }	
Stage screws	212	230	Attaching braces and foot irons to floor.
Brace cleats	212	438	Attaching stage braces to flats.
Lash cleats	211	439	Joining flats.
Lash hooks	211	939	Tying off lash lines.
Ceiling plates	198	98	Joining and rigging roll ceilings.
Picture-frame hangers	212	577 677 977 1077 }	These are hook-and-eye devices used for attaching pictures and light objects to flats.
S-hooks	212	64	Bracing flats.

Rope. Braided sash cord (¼″) is used for lash lines and for many other stage uses. It cannot be depended upon to bear weight where a break would cause damage. In these cases use Manila rope and bind the ends with friction tape to prevent unraveling.

Paint, Glue, etc. Do not use ready-mixed kalsomine for painting scenery. It is both expensive and unsatisfactory.

Pigments. These are the 'dry colors' sold in paint and hardware stores. The following list will meet ordinary requirements:

Whiting	Chrome green	Burnt umber
Drop black	Chrome yellow	Venetian red
Ultramarine	Yellow ocher	Permanent red

'Hercules black' may be substituted for drop black. Cheap yellow ocher is muddy, so get the better grade known as 'French ocher.'

Glue, etc. Cake or flake glue is used for the 'size' which is mixed with scene paint. Granulated glue is usable but less satisfactory. To make size: fill a pail two-thirds full of glue. Cover the glue with water and leave overnight. Put a few inches of water in another pail. Put the glue pail in this, making a double boiler. Heat the glue until it melts. It will harden when cold but may be reheated. Size will keep indefinitely but spoils rapidly when mixed with paint.

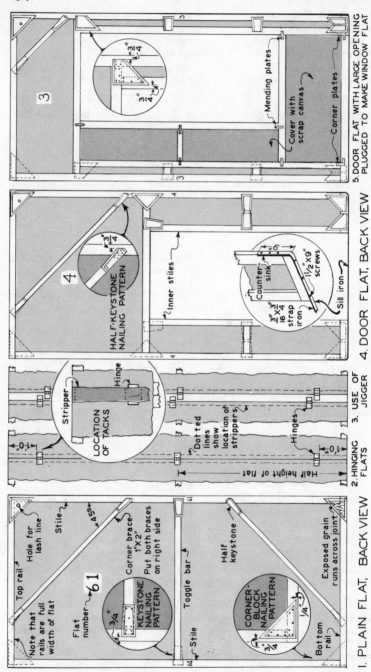

1. PLAIN FLAT, BACK VIEW

2. HINGING FLATS

3. USE OF JIGGER

4. DOOR FLAT, BACK VIEW

5. DOOR FLAT WITH LARGE OPENING PLUGGED TO MAKE WINDOW FLAT

Canvas for permanent scenery should be attached with 'plastic resin glue.' For temporary work, 'cold-water paste' is more satisfactory. Stir the powder into water a pinch or two at a time. Paste is thick enough when the stirring paddle leaves ripples. Melted glue can be used for canvasing if 1 part of glue is mixed with 1 part of paste and 1 part of whiting. Never use melted glue alone; it strikes through the canvas and ruins the surface for painting.

Chalk, etc. Colored chalk and artist's charcoal are excellent for adding details to a paint job. Preliminary guide lines should be drawn with a 'copying' or 'indelible' pencil, which will show through several layers of paint.

SCENE BUILDING

The processes described here are short cuts. Any further simplification is likely to produce flimsy results.

SCENE BUILDING—A. FLAT CONSTRUCTION

This is the basis of all scene building and should be thoroughly mastered. Pl. XXVI, opposite, shows the important points.

Measuring. The 'rails' are the full width of the flat. Therefore, the 'stiles' are shorter than the flat by twice the width of the lumber. Also the 'toggle bar' is shorter than the rails by the same amount. Flats over 12′ high require two toggle bars. Flats over 14′ high must be built of 1¼″ stock. 'Corner braces' are about as long as the rails, but the measurement need not be exact and can be made by eye.

Squaring. If the corners of a flat are not perfectly square, it cannot be properly joined to other flats and will cause endless trouble. Assemble the flat face down on the floor. As each member is placed, nail it to the floor with 4d common nails driven part way home. Square each corner carefully with a steel square. Sight along the stiles to make sure they are straight. Check by measuring the diagonals, which should be the same.

Joining. Profile blocks are placed as shown in the plate. Note that they are 'held back' ¾″ from the outside edges of the stiles. Otherwise, when two flats are placed at right angles like Nos. 26 and 10 in Fig. 5, Pl. XXIX, p. 210, the profile blocks will hold them apart.

The pattern in which the nails are driven is of the utmost importance. A nail in the right place strengthens the joint; one in the wrong place weakens the wood. One nail should be driven in each corner of the block and two on each side of the crack of the joint.

Other nails are placed wherever the blocks show a tendency to pull away from the lumber. Correct patterns for the various blocks are shown in Pl. XXVI, p. 194.

The nails are clinched by placing a clinching plate under the joint and driving the points of the nails against it (Fig. 3, Pl. XXIX, p. 210). Once the nails are clinched they cannot be withdrawn without damaging the wood. Scenery intended for only one production should be joined with ⅞″ screws instead of nails, so that it can be taken apart and the lumber used again.

Canvasing. The canvas of a flat covers only the front of the frame and is not carried around the edges. The piece of canvas used should be about 3″ longer and 2″ wider than the flat. Turn the frame over and lay the canvas on its face. Hold the canvas in place temporarily with a tack at each corner. It should be slack but not wrinkled, and the threads must lie parallel to the stiles and rails. Attach the canvas to the stiles with a row of tacks 6″ apart and ¼″ from the inside edge. Drive a tack in the center of each rail ¼″ from the inside edge; then drive tacks in the centers of the spaces on either side; then in the centers of the spaces left. This method divides the slack evenly.

The loose flap of canvas outside the row of tacks is now glued or pasted to the wood. When the glue is dry, drive a second row of tacks 1′ apart and ½″ from the outside edge of the flat. Trim the waste canvas with a knife. The knife does not really cut but acts as a ripping aid. The secret lies in pulling the waste canvas away with the left hand at just the right tension and at just the right angle.

Door and Window Flats. These require an inner frame around the opening (Fig. 4, Pl. XXVI, p. 194). Unless the flats are to be used for only one production, special flats for windows, fireplaces, etc. are unnecessary. Door flats can be made to serve these purposes by plugging any part of the opening which is not needed (Fig. 5). When the same walls are used for two or more sets in the same play, unwanted openings can be filled by temporary plugs like that shown in Fig. 1, Pl. XXIX, p. 210. These are small flats with a lip of wallboard 3⅝″ wide, nailed on the face to cover the crack between the plug and the flat. The canvas is glued over the lip.

Plugs must be painted at the same time as the flat; otherwise they will not match.

The 'sill iron' makes it necessary to cut the four stiles, and the bottom rails, $\frac{3}{16}''$ shorter than they would otherwise be. The iron can be bent cold by putting it in a vise and hitting it with a hammer. The outer dimension of the iron after bending must be the exact width of the flat. Screw holes are bored after the iron is bent. They are reamed out so that the screws will be countersunk and fit flush with the face of the iron. Note that twelve screws are used in groups of three. Screws will not hold in the end grain of the rail.

The small toggle bars between the inner and outer stiles are essential for rigidity.

Use three pieces of canvas. Those for the legs are placed first so that the top piece will overlap them. If the leg pieces overlap, the scene painters tend to pull up the flap with their brushes.

Hinging Flats.   Walls are usually made up of two or three flats. These must be joined so that the cracks will not show. The flats are laid face up on the floor and hinged together with tight-pin backflaps. One hinge is placed 1' from the top, a second in the center, and the third 1' from the bottom (Fig. 2, Pl. XXVI, p. 194). Next the crack is covered by a narrow piece of canvas called a 'stripper.' This should be 4'' wide and a little longer than the height of the flats. Wet it and wring it out until it is barely damp. Lay it on a piece of 1'' $\times$ 6'' and smear it with paste (not glue, unless you intend the job to be permanent). Brush paste along the crack so that it covers 2'' of each flat. Two workers grasp the ends of the stripper and turn it over. One holds his end high while the other places his end over the crack, flush with the bottom of the flats, and fastens it in place with four tacks or staples. The stripper is then smoothed in place, using a fairly dry paste brush. Note that the ends of the hinges are not covered. This does no harm, as scene paint will stick to the hinges, and if the stripper were too broad it would tend to work loose. The stripper must not be stretched or it will pull free when it dries. Four more tacks or staples are driven below and above each hinge and at the top of the flat. If part of the stripper hangs over at the top, it is turned under and pasted down before being tacked.

Jiggers. If three or more flats the same size are hinged together, they will not fold. To correct this, a $1'' \times 3''$ the height of the set must be inserted between two of the flats. It is treated like a small flat and is hinged to the flats on both sides. The 'jigger' and both cracks are covered with a stripper $7''$ wide (Fig. 3, Pl. XXVI, p. 194).

Cutouts. These are made by attaching a strip cut from profile, wall, or corrugated board to the edge of a flat or of an irregular piece of scenery built to some special shape (Fig. 10, Pl. XXVII, p. 200). In order to make such a shape rigid, the members must form triangles. The bottom must be a continuous piece so there will be no rough places to catch on the floor when the cutout is moved.

Scene Building—B. Hung Scenery

Certain types of scenery must be supported from above, usually by being attached to the pipe battens with snatch lines.

Ceiling. The same ceiling is normally used for all the sets in a play. It is made like a large flat, without corner braces, and with the members joined by ceiling plates instead of profile blocks (Fig. 4, Pl. XXIX, p. 210). The seams in the canvas should run lengthwise. The lumber should be $1\frac{1}{4}'' \times 3''$ rather than $1'' \times 3''$. As the long members (corresponding to the stiles of a flat) will be about $30'$ in length, they must be made of two pieces. This joint can be made by using a $2'$ piece of the same lumber as a 'fishplate' and another as a 'stiffener.' The canvas is glued and tacked to the end 'stretchers' (rails) but is merely tacked to the long members. When the ceiling is dismantled for storage or transportation, the canvas is rolled on the end stretchers.

Drops. As R, Fig. 5, Pl. XXIX, p. 210 shows, drops are made of several widths of canvas with the seams running horizontally (J). The 'battens' at top and bottom are made by placing pieces of $1'' \times 3''$ or $1'' \times 4''$ on both sides of the edge of the canvas and screwing them together (G). Several lengths of wood are needed for each side. The joints on the two sides must come in different places. Each joint is reinforced with a mending plate held in place with bolts. The nuts must be countersunk and the ends of the bolts cut off. The sides of the drop should be trimmed so that it tapers

1″ in every 1′ from top to bottom (*O*). This taper helps to avoid the wrinkles which appear in the corners of rectangular drops.

Borders.   These are like drops except that they are shallower and have no bottom batten. If they represent foliage, the bottom is cut in an irregular leaf shape (Fig. 4, Pl. X, p. 62). Cut the leaves so that they hang almost straight down. Any overhang will curl back. As some curling is inevitable, the cut edge should be painted on both sides so that no bare canvas will show.

Scene Building—C. Doors and Windows

The simplest type of door is made like a small flat with a toggle bar of 11″ × 6″ held in place by corner irons (Fig. 12, Pl. XXVII, p. 200). By attaching panels of molding to the face of such a door, a satisfactorily realistic effect can be obtained. A more elaborate door is shown in Fig. 13. This is made of 1″ × 6″ and the canvas is applied before the profile blocks. A strip of molding is nailed inside each panel.

Door Frames.   These are of 1″ × 6″ joined as shown in Fig. 11, Pl. XXVII. A notch is cut for the sill iron of the flat. The door sill itself is 1″ × 3″, beveled on both sides to keep actors from tripping. It is held in place with one corner plate and one corner iron on each side. A bent brace cleat is screwed to the side of the frame as a catch for the lock.

The door is hinged to the frame with loose-pin backflaps (*B*, Fig. 11). One leaf of each hinge is screwed to the door with the bent part sticking past the edge. The other leaf is turned over so that the countersunk side is toward the back of the door. The frame is laid face down on the floor. The door is placed over it flush with the hinge side and ¾″ from the bottom, so it will clear the floor when it swings. Then the free leaves are screwed to the frame.

Windows.   Window frames are like door frames except that they are the same construction at the bottom as they are at the top and have a strip of molding added to provide a lip for the sill. The upper 'sash' is 1½″ wider than the opening and is nailed to the back of the frame. The lower sash is the same inside width as the upper, but as its stiles are of 1″ × 2″ instead of 1″ × 3″, it is nar-

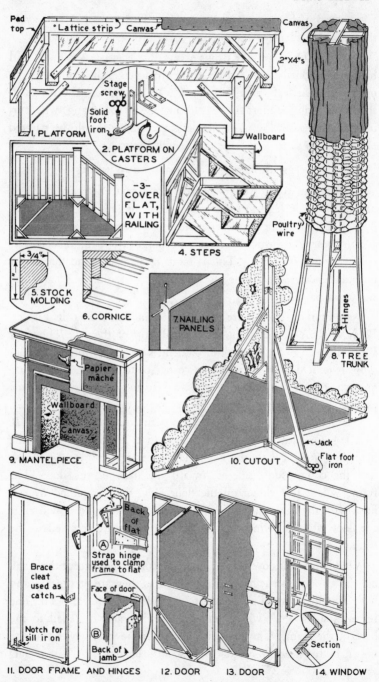

Pad top · Lattice strip · Canvas · Canvas · 2"X4"s
Stage screw · Solid foot iron
1. PLATFORM
2. PLATFORM ON CASTERS
-3- COVER FLAT, WITH RAILING
Wallboard
4. STEPS
Poultry wire
Hinges
8. TREE TRUNK
3/4" · 1"
5. STOCK MOLDING
6. CORNICE
7. NAILING PANELS
Papier mâché
Wallboard
Canvas
9. MANTELPIECE
10. CUTOUT
Jack
Flat foot iron
Brace cleat used as catch
Notch for sill iron
Back of flat
(A) Strap hinge used to clamp frame to flat
Face of door
(B) Back of jamb
11. DOOR FRAME AND HINGES
12. DOOR
13. DOOR
Section
14. WINDOW

row enough to slide in a groove made by nailing pieces ripped from
lattice strips to the inside edges of the frame. 'Muntins' (crosspieces)
are ripped from lattice strip and nailed to the sash. The vertical
strips in the lower sash must be in back of the horizontal one; otherwise the horizontal strip may catch on the upper sash when the
window is opened. Diamond-shaped panes can be outlined with
twilled tape tacked to the back of the sash.

If the window is not practical, you may sometimes dispense with
a backing and merely tack cloth over the back of the window instead. Of course you will use black cloth for night scenes and transparent blue cloth lighted from the rear for daylight scenes. This
device works best when the window is covered with sash curtains.
It cannot be used at all for daytime scenes if there is another opening, such as a door, through which the sky may be seen. In this
case it would be almost impossible to make the two parts of the
sky match.

Arches. The construction of these is shown at *I* and *P,* Fig. 5,
Pl. XXIX, p. 210. The face of the arch is cut from wallboard and
screwed to the face of the opening in the flat. A wooden frame is
built and attached to the back of the opening. This frame supplies
the jambs of the opening and also holds the arch thickness in place.
This thickness is made of wallboard with canvas pasted on both
sides. Canvased wallboard can be bent in a surprisingly small arc
without cracking.

Molding. The appearance of most woodwork is improved by a
trimming of molding. The molding is mitered at the corners and
held in place with 4d finishing nails. A long run can be made up
of several short pieces, as the joints cannot be seen from the audience. Panels are made by joining four pieces of molding at the
corners with 4d finishing nails (Fig. 7, Pl. XXVII, p. 200). Extra
toggle bars or corner braces must usually be placed in back of the
scenery to provide a solid surface to which the panels can be nailed.
Heavy moldings, such as cornices, can be made by combining
one or more pieces of lumber with several pieces of molding (Fig.
6).

Shallow molding, or other details less than ½" in depth, can be
simulated with paint.

Scene Building—D. Steps and Platforms

Professionals use different types of steps and platforms from the ones shown here, but these are far more adaptable and are therefore better suited to amateur use.

Platforms. The top is made of three 2″ × 4″s set on edge with boards nailed across them (Fig. 1, Pl. XXVII, p. 200). A piece of lattice strip is laid flat on top of each edge and nailed in place. The area inside the lattice strip is covered with padding. This is protected by canvas or burlap, which is brought over the sides and ends and fastened with tacks.

The legs are pieces of 2″ × 4″ bolted in place. The central member of the top is supported by transverse 2″ × 4″s bolted to the legs. Diagonal braces are made of any scrap lumber and held in place with 6d common nails.

Platforms over 7′ long require an extra pair of legs and an extra transverse member as well.

Steps. The construction of these is shown in Fig. 4, Pl. XXVII. The 'treads' are 1″ × 10″ and the 'carriages' (the saw-shaped pieces) are cut from 1″ × 12″. Carriages should not be more than 2′6″ apart. Steps must be padded to prevent noise. Several thicknesses of corrugated board covered with canvas will serve this purpose nicely.

Cover Flats. The exposed sides of steps and platforms must be covered either with pieces of wallboard or with special flats made for the purpose (Fig. 3, Pl. XXVII).

Scene Building—E. Irregular Forms

Rocks, tree trunks, etc., are made of light wooden frames and covered with poultry netting which can be pulled into any shape. Canvas, wrinkled in appropriate ways, is sewed over this and painted (Fig. 8, Pl. XXVII).

Scene Building—F. Repairs

A torn flat can be mended by gluing a patch of canvas on the back. Have someone hold a board in front of the tear to provide a smooth surface against which to work.

Bulges in canvas can be removed by spattering them with a little water from the back. This shrinks the material, and stretches it flat again.

SCENE PAINTING

The techniques given here are so simple that one fairly experienced painter can run a crew of six or eight novices and turn out a perfect set.

Mixing Pigments.[1] The tone chart (Fig. 4, Pl. XXVIII, p. 207) will help you choose what pigments to mix. The result of mixing any two pigments will fall somewhere along an imaginary straight line drawn between them on the chart. Thus, chrome yellow and Venetian red will produce an orange tan, lighter than burnt umber but almost as low in intensity. Pale tones are produced by adding whiting. This also decreases the intensity. Black is unsatisfactory for mixing dark tones. Burnt umber is used for this, balanced if necessary with ultramarine.

Start by mixing a little dry color on a piece of clean board. This will tell you whether you have chosen the right pigments and suggest the approximate proportion of each to be used in your paint. Next, mix the required quantity of your pigments dry in a pail or other container, taking care to blend them thoroughly.

To prepare paint, pour into a pail or saucepan as much of this dry pigment as you expect to apply at one time. Add water and mix thoroughly. Test on a strip of bare canvas. Paint should be thick enough to cover but not thick enough to clog the weave. Heat the paint until it is warm to the touch and add melted size in the proportion of two cupfuls to the pail. Rub the paint between forefinger and thumb. If it feels perceptibly slippery, enough size has been added; if not, add a little more. If too little size is used, the paint will rub off. Too much will leave tiny globules of glue on the surface of the work.

[1] The statements made here and in the chapters on lighting and make-up are based on the work of Arthur Pope of Harvard and Stanley McCandless of Yale. They are valuable guides to an understanding of color for practical use but they make no pretense to a scientific explanation of color. In fact, the science of color has many problems both of physics and of psychology to solve before a true theory of color can be devised.

Scene Painting—A. Techniques

An absolutely even area of color is uninteresting, and any imperfections such as patched canvas stand out sharply. By using a variegated color, both these disadvantages can be avoided. If the variations cover small areas, they will produce what appears to be an even tone. Thus, the illustrations in this book contain tones which are accepted as smooth grays but which are actually produced by black dots on a white ground. Any reduction in the contrast between the different tones makes it possible to use larger areas of each and still produce a smooth effect.

If the area of each tone or the contrast between the tones is slightly increased, you will still have an effect of even color, but the surface will seem to have a uniform roughness. This effect is called 'texture.' Natural textures, such as troweled plaster or the grain in wood, may be suggested by arranging the areas of one tone in a definite pattern.

Base Coat. All scene painting begins with a base coat. This is usually of one color, applied with a wall brush. To avoid a pattern when working with scene paint, make the strokes in every direction at random. Occasionally, as when imitating stone work, several colors are applied at once and blended while wet, using a brush in each hand.

Scenery that has already been painted must be covered quickly without unnecessary brushing. Should some of the old paint work through, do not attempt to cover it while wet. Let it dry and apply a second coat.

Usually one base coat is enough. If you are painting over old flats of different colors, the result of the base coat will be far from even, but the irregularities will be hidden by the later coats. Two base coats are required only when the flats have been painted in strong or contrasting colors and the new paint is a pale pastel tone. Some painters always apply an undercoat of whiting. This is not only unnecessary but unwise, as the more layers of paint you use the more likely it is to crack off.

About sixteen quarts of dry color will be needed for a base coat on an ordinary set.

Spatter. This is the usual method of producing a variegated surface and must be thoroughly mastered. The beginner should start
about 6′ from the work and use a fairly dry brush. Later he can
use a wetter brush and work closer. Stand with the left side toward
the work with your hands in the position of Fig. 1, Pl. XXVIII,
p. 207. Strike the brush against the base of your left thumb. A shower
of paint drops will be thrown against the work. Avoid large
splashes. The bristles form a sort of spring pendulum. If your
strokes are in time with the beat of the bristles, the work will go
rapidly and with a minimum of effort.

Spatter lightly over the whole area and build up successive layers
until the desired tone is obtained. This method gives the first layer
time to dry and also enables the painter to fill any thin places in
the early layers. If some places are spattered too heavily, they can
be corrected by spattering with the base coat.

Never spatter with one hand. It causes unsightly patterns.

A high-pressure spray gun may be used for applying a flat coat.
However, it is worthless for spattering, as the spray is too fine.

A 2½-gallon tank sprayer of the type used by gardeners is excellent for spraying scenery, but it requires expert workmanship. The
spraying wand must be kept in constant motion, and some gaps and
blotches are inevitable. However, these can be corrected by hand.
Such a sprayer should be used only for under spatter coats until
you acquire a sufficient skill to use it for the final coat.

Eight quarts of dry color will provide a heavy spatter coat for an
ordinary set.

Scumbling. Wet a rag or a sponge and roll it over the surface
(Fig. 5, Pl. XXVIII). Light paint may be scumbled over dark, or
dark over light. An unlimited number of textures can be produced
to simulate stone, rough plaster, bark, etc. Troweled plaster may
be imitated by a pat-and-smear technique.

Dry Brushing. This is used to imitate the grain of wood (Fig.
3, Pl. XXVIII). The brush should be almost dry. It is held at right
angles to the work and drawn lightly over the surface so that each
bristle makes a fine line.

Lining. Rest one end of a yardstick against the flat and rule a
line on the canvas with an angular liner. The stroke must be made

swiftly or it will wiggle. The yardstick must be held away from the work, for if stick, brush, and canvas come together they will cause a blot (Fig. 6, Pl. XXVIII).

SNAP-LINING. To draw a long straight line, rub a length of cord with chalk or dry scene paint. Have someone hold one end of the cord on one end of the line and hold your end on the other. Pull the cord tight; then draw it away from the canvas and let it snap back so that it leaves a line of chalk or scene paint on the canvas. This line can then be gone over with wet scene paint if desired.

SCENE PAINTING—B. PROCEDURE

The ordinary interior, with walls which will appear to be of a uniform tone, furnishes a typical example of painting procedure.

Walls. Suppose you wish to paint your set the dull blue tone seen in Wedgwood porcelain.

BASE COAT. This should be slightly darker and less intense than the finished set; mix ultramarine, burnt umber, and whiting.

UNDER SPATTER COAT. Use paint of the same value and intensity as that desired but slightly more violet; mix ultramarine, Venetian red, and whiting, with perhaps a little burnt umber. Spatter over the whole surface until the area covered by dots of spatter is about equal to the visible area of the base coat.

TOP SPATTER COAT. Make this almost the tone of the final color but lighter (to compensate for the dark base coat) and more green (to compensate for the violet tinge of the under spatter coat). This top coat should be applied heavily so that the earlier coats are almost imperceptible from a short distance. Carry this top coat full strength up to about 8′ from the floor; then let it thin out so that it vanishes entirely at about 11′.

SHADOW. The top of the set should be darkened. This gives a more natural effect and makes the upper part less interesting and less likely to distract the attention of the audience. The shadow paint may be a darker version of the darkest tone already used— in this case the base coat—or it may be a mixture of burnt umber and ultramarine. Spatter the shadow paint thickly at the top of the set. Then start letting it thin out at the 11′ level and disappear entirely at about 8′. Corners should be shadowed somewhat lower

Plate XXVIII

207

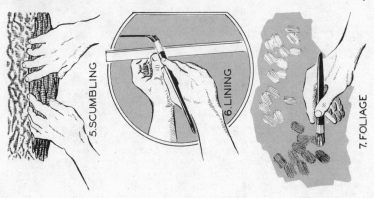

5. SCUMBLING

6. LINING

7. FOLIAGE

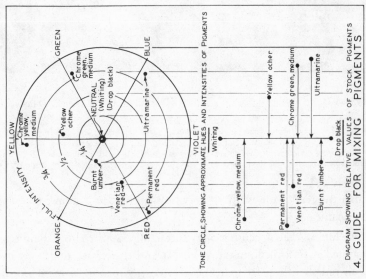

TONE CIRCLE, SHOWING APPROXIMATE HUES AND INTENSITIES OF PIGMENTS

GREEN

BLUE

Chrome green, medium

NEUTRAL (Whiting) (Drop black)

Yellow ocher

Chrome yellow, medium

Ultramarine

YELLOW

FULL INTENSITY

1/2

3/4

1/4

ORANGE

Burnt umber

Venetian red

Permanent red

VIOLET

RED

Whiting

Yellow ocher

Chrome green, medium

Ultramarine

Chrome yellow, medium

Permanent red

Venetian red

Burnt umber

Drop black

DIAGRAM SHOWING RELATIVE VALUES OF STOCK PIGMENTS

4. GUIDE FOR MIXING PIGMENTS

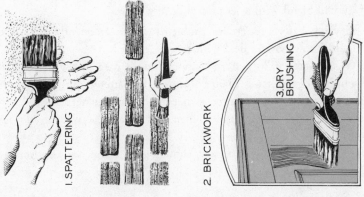

1. SPATTERING

2. BRICKWORK

3. DRY BRUSHING

Yale University Theater

MACHIAVELLI

Setting by Donald Oenslager

This illustration and the one on the following page show a 'unit set.' The main walls of the set are used for all the scenes of the play. Shifts are made by covering or revealing openings, introducing different properties, and changing the light. Shake- spearian plays are often performed in this way. Unit sets are economical, and they permit rapid scene shifts. They also stress the unity of the play, whereas a production with a number of entirely different sets tends to produce a disjointed effect.

than the rest of the walls. Otherwise the effect will seem much too mechanical.

Ceilings. Light ceilings are distracting, so a ceiling should be painted with a medium-tan base coat and spatters of dull blue and dull red slightly paler than the base coat. A ceiling painted in this way will blend with a set of almost any color.

Special Effects. Certain problems recur frequently and you should know how to deal with them.

WALLPAPER. The pattern is applied to the base coat with a stencil, by lining, or freehand. Then the surface is spattered until the pattern is unobtrusive. Less spatter is needed with a patterned wall, and the pattern is more visible when the spatter is wet, so do not overdo it.

WOODWORK. The base coat should be the tone of the finished job. Grain over this with two coats of dry-brush work, one several shades lighter and the other several shades darker than the base. Follow the direction that would be taken by the natural grain of the wood. If rough planks are represented, line the cracks between them after graining. This can be done with a paint mixed of burnt umber and ultramarine, or with charcoal. Highlights, slightly paler than the wood, must be drawn on both sides of every crack, either with paint or with colored chalk. If some of the woodwork consists of actual relief (molding, etc.), the shadows must be darkened just as if the surface were flat and the relief merely painted on. This is necessary to overcome the unnatural shadows which will be cast by the stage lights.

STONE. Make the base coat a blend of several tones. Paint mortar lines over this. Then spatter irregularly with a mixture of ultramarine and burnt umber. Use this same paint to shadow each stone and to draw cracks, if desired.

BRICK. Two methods are used: (1) for smooth brick, use the brick color for a base coat and line in the mortar; (2) for rough brick, use mortar color for the base coat and paint each brick separately with two strokes of the sash tool (Fig. 2, Pl. XXVIII). In

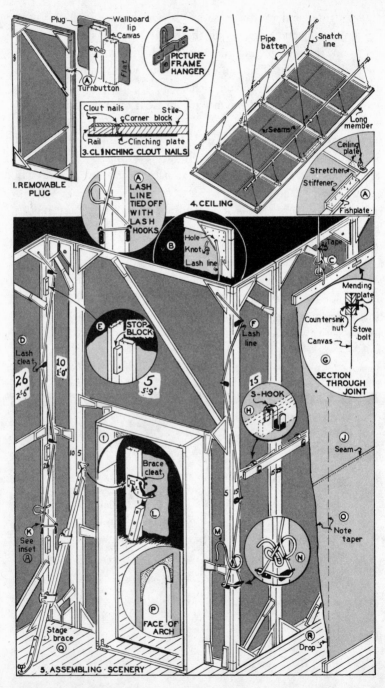

Plug — Wallboard lip — Canvas — Flat
A Turnbutton
1. REMOVABLE PLUG

PICTURE-FRAME HANGER —2—

Clout nails — Stile — Corner block — Clinching plate — Rail
3. CLINCHING CLOUT NAILS

Pipe batten — Snatch line — Seams — Long member
Ceiling plate — Stretcher — Stiffener — A — Fishplate
4. CEILING

A LASH LINE TIED OFF WITH LASH HOOKS
B Hole — Knot — Lash line

Tape C
Mending plate — Countersink nut — Canvas — Stove bolt
G SECTION THROUGH JOINT

E STOP BLOCK
D Lash cleat
10 1'0"
26 2'6"
5 5'9"

F Lash line
15 S-HOOK H
J Seam
O Note taper

I Brace cleat L
M N
K See inset A
10 5
24
5

P FACE OF ARCH
Q Stage brace
R Drop
5. ASSEMBLING SCENERY

either case, spatter the bricks with dark paint to give texture and also shadow each brick to make it stand out slightly.

LEAVES. Blend several similar greens for a base color. Then paint in leaves, making each one with a dab of the sash tool (Fig. 7, Pl. XXVIII). Use two tones, one light and one dark, and work in clusters to avoid an effect of meaningless spots.

WASHING SCENERY

After about six productions, flats must be washed or the paint will flake off. Take the flats outside and stand them up with their faces to the wall. Soak the back of the canvas thoroughly with water from a hose. Then turn them over and scrub off the paint, using a scrubbing brush and the full force of the hose.

ASSEMBLING SCENERY

When two flats are joined at a corner, the one which is most nearly on a transverse axis should overlap the other (Flats 5 and 15 in Fig. 5, Pl. XXIX, opposite). Otherwise, the audience will be able to see through the crack between them.

Lashing. A $\frac{7}{16}''$ hole is drilled through the upper right-hand corner block of the flat to the left of the crack. A piece of $\frac{1}{4}''$ sash cord as long as the flats are high is passed through this hole and knotted on the inner end. This is called a 'lash line' (B and F, Fig. 5, Pl. XXIX). 'Lash cleats' are attached to the stiles as shown at D, Fig. 5. The top cleat is placed on the inner edge of the left stile of the right-hand flat, about 1' from the top. The next cleat is placed about 3' lower on the right stile of the left-hand flat. Continue placing cleats on alternate flats at 3' intervals. If this spacing brings a cleat too near a corner brace or a toggle bar, the cleat must be placed slightly higher or lower. A lash hook is screwed on the inside edge of each stile, 2'6'' from the floor (A and K).

To lash the flats together, the line is first flicked over the top cleat. There is a knack to this which can only be acquired with practice. The main points to remember are: (1) make the throw high; (2) instantly pull the line back with a jerk. Pass the line around the lower cleats, draw it taut and catch it under the lash hooks which automatically grip it. The end of the line is tucked in as shown at A, Fig. 5. Lash cleats may be substituted for lash hooks in an emergency (*M*), but, if they are, the end of the line must be tied off as at *N,* and it is difficult to avoid leaving slack in the line.

When two flats meet as do 26 and 10 in Fig. 5, Pl. XXIX, 'stop blocks' of 1″ × 2″ must be screwed to the stile of the downstage flat. Otherwise the lash line will separate the edges instead of holding them together. Stop blocks are also needed on the tormentors.

Nailing. If the play calls for only one set, lashing can be dispensed with and the walls held together by four 8d finishing nails at each corner. Let the nail heads project ¼″ so they can be withdrawn easily.

Bracing. The corners of the set, plus the weight of the ceiling, supply an amazing amount of rigidity. Nevertheless, additional bracing is always needed in the middle of long walls and on the hinge side (sometimes both sides) of the doors. Bracing is done with stage braces (*Q,* Fig. 5, Pl. XXIX). A brace cleat is fastened to a stile. The brace is turned so that its heel points toward the floor, and one of the hooks at the top end is passed through the hole of the cleat *L.* Then the brace is turned over and the heel is attached to the floor with a stage screw. A 'jack' (Fig. 10, Pl. XXVII, p. 200) may be substituted for a stage brace but is normally less convenient.

Stiffening. If necessary, the walls can be stiffened by putting S-hooks over the toggle bars or over the top of the flats and dropping a piece of 1″ × 3″ in the other half of the hooks (*H,* Fig. 5, Pl. XXIX, p. 200).

Hooks. Ordinary screen-door hooks may often be used to join scenery where a quick release is necessary. Pictures and other light properties are best attached to the set with picture-frame hangers (Fig. 2, Pl. XXIX). When two ropes must be joined or released quickly, a ring should be tied to the end of one rope and a harness snap to the end of the other.

Doors and Windows. These are held in place by strap hinges which are attached to each side of the frame (*A,* Fig. 11, Pl. XXVII, p. 200). The lower leaf is screwed on at a slant with the top slightly offstage. In use, the bottom of the frame is first placed in the opening from the onstage side. Then the free leaves of the hinges are knocked up and the frame is tilted into the flat. The frame is clamped in place by forcing the leaves down so that they wedge against the inner stiles.

SCENE SHIFTING

When a piece of scenery is brought on stage and placed in position, it is said to be 'set.' When it is carried off stage and stored in the wings it is said to be 'struck.' When it is merely shifted into some temporary position it is said to be 'moved.'

Running. The process of shifting scenery by hand is called 'running.' This is not quite so easy as it may seem, for though scenery is light, it is also unwieldy unless it is kept in perfect balance.

Flats are run edgewise to avoid air resistance, and must be kept erect or they will topple over. One man stands behind the flat near the front stile which he grasps with both hands, keeping the heels of his hands inside so his wrists touch the back of the canvas. He then lifts the front end of the flat and moves forward, letting the rear end of the bottom rail drag on the floor. A second man sometimes walks behind, pushing and helping to balance the flat. He does *not* lift the rear of the flat from the floor. A book of several hinged flats can be run in this way provided they are folded first.

Doors and door frames are shifted as a unit, but they must first be removed from the flat. If the doors are opened, the frames will stand by themselves. When shifting, two men carry the frame between them, tilting it so that the door stays closed by its own weight.

Rolling. Heavy or cumbersome scenery is most easily shifted by mounting it on casters. For example, casters may be placed under $2'' \times 4''$s which in turn are fastened between the legs of a platform. Scenery mounted on casters moves easily and must be attached to the floor with foot irons and stage screws (Fig. 2, Pl. XXVII, p. 200).

Casters are made in two types: (1) 'swivel,' which swing in any direction; (2) 'fixed,' which can roll only back and forth. Swivel casters are more generally useful, but the fixed type has a real advantage when the movement is to follow a straight line.

Sometimes whole sets are mounted on platforms, called 'wagons,' which are only 6″ high and may be as large as the playing space. This makes shifting easy and rapid but demands a great deal of storage room.

Flying. On stages equipped with elaborate rigging systems, much scenery can be shifted by lifting it into the flies. On most stages, however, only ceilings, drops, and borders are flown.

DROPS AND BORDERS are hung from the pipe battens with snatch lines. These pass either through holes bored in the upper batten of the drop or border, or through slits cut in the canvas just below the wood (*C,* Fig. 5, Pl. XXIX, p. 210).

CEILINGS are rigged as shown in Fig. 4, Pl. XXIX. Snatch lines run from the ring on each ceiling plate to the corresponding pipe batten. Lengths of 1″ × 3″ should be bolted to the side walls of the set 2′ or 3′ from the tormentors. These should project 6″ above the set and serve as stops to keep the ceiling from sliding too far down-stage when it is lowered into place.

SCENE SHIFTING—ROUTINING A SHIFT

The secret of rapid scene shifting consists in planning and drilling each movement so that no stagehand is left idle or is given a task that cannot be accomplished quickly. Stagehands work best in pairs. The number of pairs required will depend upon the difficulty of the shift, but four pairs may be considered average. The work should be divided into steps and carefully charted in advance. If the set in Fig. 2, Pl. XXV, p. 174, were to be struck and replaced by the set in Fig. 5, Pl. V, p. 18, the chart on the opposite page might be arranged. This procedure is infinitely better than trying to work out a shift by gathering the crew together on stage and then saying, "Well, boys, has anybody got any ideas about what part of this set we should move first?"

The steps for each stagehand should be typed on a 3″ × 5″ card, so that he can refer to it.

When the shift is rehearsed, some of the steps will prove unsatisfactory and must be changed. Every change should be carefully marked, both on the chart and on the cards of the individual stagehands.

Plate XXX   215

STEPS	1ST PAIR	2ND PAIR	3RD PAIR	4TH PAIR
	Joe and Sam	Tom and Lee	Ed and Dick	Dan and Pat
I	Raise ceiling.	Strike 4, 28, & special.	Strike 35 & 62.	Strike 30 & 65.
II	Strike 36 & 60.	Unlash 10 and 12. Strike ladder and 61.	Strike table A and chairs.	Move steps A to platform and strike clock.
III	Strike 23, 1, 2, & 10.	Strike platforms and attached flats.		Strike sofa and bench B.
IV	*Move desk R. and waste-basket.* Strike chairs R.	Strike piano and bench A.		*Set desk C.* Strike table B and chairs.
V	*Move chairs, R.*	*Move door, R.*	*Move door, C.* Strike lamp.	*Move door, L.*
VI	*Set book 6.*	*Set book 5.*	*Move cooler.*	*Set chairs, C.*
VII	*Set flat 4.*	*Set book 3.*	*Set book 2.*	*Move bookcase.*
VIII	*Set backing C.*	*Set backing B.*	*Set backing A.*	*Set book 1.*
IX	*Set desk R.*	*Set door R.*	*Set door, C.*	*Set door L.*
X	Lower ceiling.	*Set chairs, R. and waste-basket.*	*Set cooler.*	*Set bookcase.*

SHIFT CHART

Roman type refers to set in Fig. 2, Pl. XXV.

Italics refer to set in Fig. 5, Pl. V.

Chapter XVIII

STAGE PROPERTIES

The first duty of the property master is to learn what props are required and what qualities they must possess. Printed plays usually contain a list of the props used on Broadway. This is helpful but you cannot rely on it. Your group will almost certainly omit some of the Broadway props and add others.

The director usually mentions and describes the more important props, but the property master cannot depend on this and must attend rehearsals and make up his own list from what he sees. Even this is not infallible. Actors often blur business so badly in rehearsal that the property master may not realize they are using some imagined prop. Also, directors are sometimes forced to add or eliminate props late in the rehearsal period, so there is no way of being sure the prop list is complete until the first dress rehearsal. Nevertheless, the prop crew cannot wait for that and must do their best to get an accurate list as early as possible.

One valuable device is to provide substitute props for some rehearsal soon after the action is completely roughed out. These substitutes may be sticks, boxes, pieces of cardboard, etc., labeled in large letters with the names of the objects they represent. They should resemble the real objects in size and shape, if this can be arranged without much trouble. At this rehearsal the actors are told to interrupt if anything is missing and also to call attention to any qualities which a prop must possess but which the crew may have overlooked. This method provides a valuable prop check without seriously interfering with the rehearsal.

The specific requirements of props are often of basic importance. In one of my own experiences as property master, I built an elaborate, high-backed chair by hand, following the designer's plans.

When it was finished, I discovered that an important scene was played upstage of the chair and that what was really needed was a low stool.

Overstuffed chairs and sofas are too soft for stage use. Actors sink into them and find it impossible to rise gracefully. To overcome this, place boards under the cushions to nullify the effect of the springs.

BORROWED PROPERTIES

Most props for amateur productions are borrowed. Even if honesty does not impel you to take good care of these things, it is necessary to keep the lender's good will so that you may borrow other things in the future. You should not only offer to pay for any accidental damage, but insist upon paying. Fire and theft insurance on borrowed articles is not expensive and is well worth having, not only as protection against loss but also to assure the lender of your reliability and good faith.

If an article is already worn or damaged when it is borrowed, this should be pointed out to the lender and the fact noted in writing. Otherwise the lender may later blame you for the damage. Never borrow objects valued for sentiment, even if the owner suggests lending them himself.

STOCK PROPERTIES

College groups are usually in small towns where the sources from which properties may be borrowed are limited. The best plan here is to acquire a large collection of props of all kinds, either as gifts or by purchasing them secondhand. A carefully kept and up-to-date inventory is essential. The trouble it costs is not one-tenth the trouble it saves.

Knitted slip covers for upholstered furniture are sold at remarkably low prices. You should have several of these in different colors for each piece of furniture you own. In this way you can change its appearance from play to play or even from scene to scene.

Temporary, homemade reupholstering with cheap materials is also possible. I have never done this myself, but most groups include some girl with the necessary ability. As the work need last

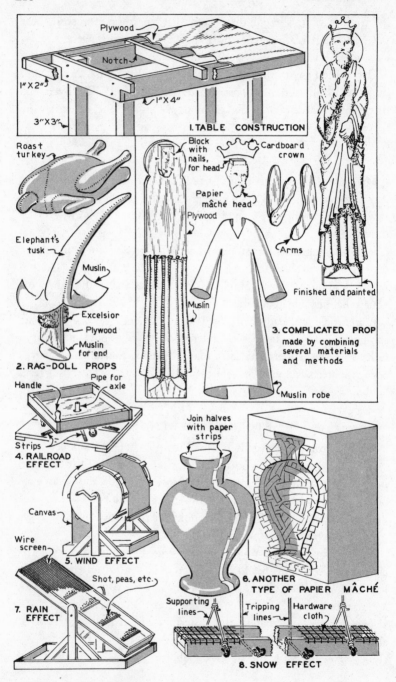

Plywood

Notch

1"X 2"

1"X 4"

3"X 3"

1. TABLE CONSTRUCTION

Roast turkey

Elephant's tusk

Muslin

Excelsior

Plywood

Muslin for end

2. RAG-DOLL PROPS

Block with nails, for head

Cardboard crown

Papier mâché head

Plywood

Muslin

Finished and painted

3. COMPLICATED PROP
made by combining several materials and methods

Muslin robe

Arms

Handle

Pipe for axle

Strips

4. RAILROAD EFFECT

Canvas

Wire screen

5. WIND EFFECT

Join halves with paper strips

6. ANOTHER TYPE OF PAPIER MÂCHÉ

Shot, peas, etc.

7. RAIN EFFECT

Supporting lines

Tripping lines

Hardware cloth

8. SNOW EFFECT

for only a few performances, it can be executed with surprising speed.

If wooden furniture has a waterproof finish, it can easily be redecorated with scene paint or show-card color. When the production is over, the paint can be washed off without difficulty.

Sometimes furniture can be covered with wallboard, either to change its shape or as a basis for nailed-on decoration. I once turned an ordinary piano into an ornate green-and-gold affair by this means. The wallboard was joined to hidden blocks of wood so that the piano itself was not scratched.

MADE PROPERTIES

When you make your own properties, they can fit your specifications exactly. Also, as they belong to you, you can keep them and remodel them later.

Tables. These are made as shown in Fig. 1, Pl. XXXI, p. 218. Use white pine for all parts except the top. Shape the end 1″ × 4″ so that a tongue the width of a 1″ × 2″ projects on each side. Notch the long 1″ × 4″s so that the cross 1″ × 2″s can extend on both sides. These should not be more than 2′ apart. The top should be ¼″ fir plywood.

Oil Paintings. These can be effectively imitated with surprising ease. Join 1″ ×3″s with corner plates to make a frame. Trim it with molding. Paint it with yellow ocher and dab gilt paint on it in a pattern to simulate carving. Tack scene canvas or muslin on the back of the frame. The picture itself should be painted *very* roughly with scene paint, using a wall brush or a sash tool. When the paint is dry, the details can be sketched with five-and-ten-cent store colored chalk and charcoal.

Irregular Shapes. Objects of irregular shape can be carved from balsa wood if you can procure this in large enough sizes. Another method, particularly suited to props with smooth surfaces, is to use the rag-doll technique illustrated in Fig. 2, Pl. XXXI. A third method, and the one most frequently used, employs papier mâché. Tear up paper—newspaper will do—into small pieces and soak it in water overnight. Squeeze out the water and drop the damp paper into prepared paste (see p. 195). Stir until the mixture assumes an even consistency. Build up a rough framework or armature with wood (Fig. 3, Pl. XXXI). Drive nails into this with the heads protruding. Mold the papier mâché over this. Apply only a thin layer at a time; otherwise it may turn moldy before it dries. Modeling done in this way will be rough, but the final decoration of paint should create the desired effect.

Another method of handling papier mâché (Fig. 6, Pl. XXXI) is used when several copies of the same shape are required. The form is modeled in clay or plasticene and a plaster mold made from it. Apply a thin coating of grease or soap to the mold. This will keep the paper from sticking. Layers of wet paper strips are forced into the mold with a brush dipped in paste. The number of layers required depends on the size of the object. After every three layers the paper must be allowed to dry; otherwise it may become moldy. After drying, the paper should be coated with paste before more layers are added. When the paper is dry after the final layer, the object is lifted from the mold, its edges are trimmed, and it is given a coat of shellac. When the shellac dries, the object is ready for painting.

Cloth dipped in hot glue size (see p. 193) and hung on a wooden framework can be used for making imitation statues and bas-reliefs. When the glue cools, the cloth will hold its shape. It should be shellacked before painting. The cloth will give only the rough shape; details must be created in paint (Fig. 3, Pl. XXXI). Small details may usually be omitted entirely.

Food. Stage food which does not have to be eaten may be made of papier mâché, of crepe paper (salads), or like excelsior-stuffed rag dolls (Fig. 2, Pl. XXXI). If the food is to appear steaming hot, a hidden lump of dry ice will provide 'steam.' Real food which is used but not eaten in a production should be heavily salted. Otherwise actors and crew members will eat it before the audience sees it.

Food to be eaten on stage should be: (1) light, so that it requires almost no chewing and may be swallowed quickly; (2) capable of being handled with a minimum of trouble and, if possible, kept without refrigeration. The following suggestions may prove helpful:

MEAT. Cut light gingerbread to shape, or smear white bread with apple butter.

GRAPEFRUIT. Remove pulp and serve only shell. This avoids having an actor swallow a seed or squirt juice in his eye.

FRIED EGGS. Put a half peach or apricot on white bread cut to shape.

FRIED POTATOES. Toast white bread and then cut it into small pieces.

WHISKEY. Use tea, or Coca-Cola and water. Ginger ale makes excellent whiskey-soda. Never serve real alcoholic drinks. An actor needs all the brains he has. I have had several sad experiences where a before-dinner cocktail—which the actor was accustomed to take every evening—proved too much when the extra strain of acting was added, and caused the actor to indulge in imbecilities which ruined important scenes.

WINE. Provide tea for sherry, diluted grape juice for red wine, and pale ginger ale for champagne.

BEER. Use root beer.

Cobwebs. These are made from the ordinary melted glue used in scene painting. Take two small blocks of wood. Put a dab of hot glue on one of them and pat the blocks together and pull them apart until the glue becomes tacky and pulls out in a mass of threads. These may be draped between any two points, such as the arm and back of a chair. Large gaps can be spanned by a thread of gray silk. The web is then draped between the thread and any near-by object.

Snow Effect. A trough like that shown in Fig. 8, Pl. XXXI, p. 218, is filled with white confetti, torn white paper, or the corn-flake 'snow' sold by some novelty stores. The trough is then hung in the flies. When the tripping ropes are jerked, some of the snow is spilled and allowed to float down onto the stage.

Smoke and Fog. Drop dry ice in boiling water. Another and often more convenient method is to burn a little of the white powder known as 'condensed smoke.' This can be purchased from the Arlane Mfg. Co., 4462 Germantown Ave., Philadelphia 44, Pa. It is inexpensive and makes a dense white smoke. Although this product has comparatively little odor, you should use the smallest

LOTTIE GATHERS NO MOSS　　　　　　Setting by Harold Solomon

Realistic interiors like this are usually marked by the deliberate introduction of an abundance of tasteless detail. The dishes shown here are nailed on the flats and fly with the set. They were made from ordinary paper plates, cut to the desired shape, and painted to imitate china.

amount which will create the desired effect. That requires a few experiments before you employ the product in a performance.

SOUND EFFECTS

There is a growing tendency to provide sound effects with records and a loud-speaker. Unfortunately, records are rarely satisfactory. The sounds are almost always accompanied by a 'frying' noise caused by minute scratches in the records. Furthermore, the sounds are difficult to recognize. Before you use a record, play it for a friend and ask him to tell you what it represents. If he does not know, you cannot expect the audience to do better.

A microphone and a loud-speaker permit excellent sound effects. Many magazine articles on radio contain ideas you can use, such as crumpling cellophane for the crackling of flames, crushing a matchbox for breaking wood, etc. Convincing airplane sounds can be produced by bringing the microphone close to an electric fan. Vocal imitations done over the microphone are also effective; auto horns, animal noises, wind, and many other sounds can be satisfactorily produced in this way.

Special Sound Effects. In spite of modern improvements, the old noise makers still hold their own.

THUNDER SHEET. This is a large sheet, some 2'6" × 6', of galvanized iron, hung from a rope so that it does not touch anything solid. It is used for thunder, cannon, and explosions. Shake it, or hit it with a hammer or a padded drumstick.

BELLS. Demountable tire rims are excellent; so are pieces of pipe hung from a rope attached through a hole bored near the top.

RAILROAD EFFECT. Build a platform about 1'4" square (Fig. 4, Pl. XXXI). Mount an 8" piece of ½" pipe in the center with a flange. Attach three or four strips of metal at random angles. Build a shallow box of 1" × 3", joining the corners with corner plates, and screw a piece of ¼" plywood to the bottom. Attach a vertical handle as shown. Bore a ⅞" hole in the center of the plywood and bolt metal casters to the bottom. Put the box over the pipe and load it with bricks. When the box is turned, it will rumble and click like a train. If lattice strips are used instead of metal ones, and rubber-tired casters are substituted, the effect will be that of a wagon on a rough road.

RAIN AND SURF. These may be imitated with the rocking tray shown in Fig. 7, Pl. XXXI. If the bottom is of plywood and the machine is loaded with ½ lb. of rice, it will give an effect of surf when tilted. With a sheet-iron bottom and a load of small shot, the effect will be that of rain on a tin roof.

WIND EFFECT. The canvas in Fig. 5, Pl. XXXI, hangs loosely over the slats on the drum, which rub against it to produce an excellent imitation of the sound of wind. The effect is best when the speed of the drum varies constantly.

HORSE HOOFS. Saw a coconut in half and clean out the nut. Hold a half shell in each hand with the opening down, and knock them against the floor or the top of a table with a rocking motion so that one edge strikes first. With a little practice you can learn to imitate any gait of a horse.

Chapter XIX

COSTUMES

Whether the costumes are designed or selected, they should be appropriate not only to the characters themselves but also to the spirit and style of the play. Cleopatra's costumes in Shakespeare's *Antony and Cleopatra* should differ from those she wears in Dryden's *All For Love,* and both should differ from those for Shaw's *Caesar and Cleopatra.* The costumes should also suit the mood and situation of the scene. In real life a girl may happen to be wearing a gay dress at a moment of tragedy, but this will not do in the theater unless the ironic contrast between the costume and the situation is done deliberately and made plain to the audience.

CONVEYING INFORMATION THROUGH COSTUMING

Even appropriateness is not enough; the costume should actively express the nature of the character, the situation, and the play. Thus, almost any 16th century gentleman's costume in a flashy cut would be appropriate to Petruchio in *The Taming of the Shrew,* but dress him in flame color, fantastically slashed and padded, give him an enormous sword and a huge hat with a broken feather, and the audience is told at once: (1) that the play is a romantic farce; (2) that Petruchio is the male lead; (3) that he is a swashbuckler who will stop at nothing.

Relationships of Characters. The costumes should show the relationships of the characters:

To the play. The costumes do this by indicating the relative importance of the characters. Sometimes this requires great subtlety. In several of Barrie's plays the heroine is superficially a drab little thing, yet the costume must indicate that she is the principal. One way to treat this is to put her in a solid color—say, light blue—and dress each of the other characters in several shades. Two or three contrasting tones make street clothes noticeable, but on stage, where everything is seen at a distance, a single color is more striking, especially if it contrasts with the background. This does not mean that a girl in a red cocktail jacket and a white ball gown would be less emphatic than a maid in an all-gray uniform, but the principle holds good within reason and offers a solution to many difficult problems.

Any unusual feature, such as the man's muff in Fig. 22, Pl. XXXII, p. 231, acts as a costume touch and helps to make the character emphatic. Another useful emphasis idea is to dress your heroine in white for the last act. This sounds arbitrary and certainly will not fit all plays, but every time I have tried it, it has worked well.

To each other. Groups of characters may be put in harmonious costumes to indicate their relationship (see p. 54), or the costumes of the two chief opponents of the play may contrast violently. Sometimes a servant's costume may be a parody of that worn by his master. Costume relationships offer an excellent means of conveying information subtly.

Expressing the Character. The possibilities for expressing the character through his costume are almost endless. Those listed here will not apply to all characters, but they are worth checking every time you design a costume, to make sure you have not neglected an opportunity.

What is his nature? Is he modest or haughty, brutal or kind, shy or boastful, etc.?

What is his age? This is particularly important in costuming older characters in college plays, where both the make-up and the acting of these roles may leave something to be desired.

What are his wealth, social position, taste, etc.? Such things help an audience to place a character at once without puzzling over his status. They can be most easily and quickly expressed through costume. Sometimes the problem is complicated by the fact that the character's condition has changed before the play opened. A penniless White Russian in Paris in 1920 would dress differently from an equally penniless serf who had fled from the Czar and had

Yale University Theater

CHANTICLEER

Setting by Robert Scott

Here we have an example of pure fantasy. This version emphasizes the costumes; the scenery is merely indicated. In the original American pro- duction, the costumes were elaborately realistic affairs made of feathers, and the scenery was worked out in complete detail.

been unable to return to Russia. A rich man may wear old clothes on vacation, but he does not dress like a poor man.

Is he at home or from outside? A hat suggests that he is from outside. Shirt sleeves and slippers indicate that he is at home. More subtle indications are often needed, but you must study the play and the character to find them.

What is his emotional state? Is he cowed or cocky, contented, ambitious, tired, or energetic? Of course the way the clothes are worn is the chief thing here, but the choice of garments and their condition should not be overlooked. A man who dresses just after learning that he has inherited a fortune does not select the same clothes he would if he were contemplating suicide.

COSTUME MATERIALS

If you wish to design costumes, or even talk about them intelligently, you must know the characteristics of materials. Experienced designers often spend many hours playing with two or three yards of material, draping it, moving it through the air, feeling its texture, etc. Actors should also make experiments of this sort in order to learn how to wear costumes (a rare accomplishment) and also in order to discuss their costumes with designers and fitters. If you complain about a costume without being able to state specifically what is wrong, you will merely annoy the costume people and gain their contempt.

Weight. The weight of a material largely determines the way it hangs and the kind of folds it makes. (Compare Figs. 4 and 7, Pl. XXXII, p. 231.) Try to proportion the weights of the material to the emotional weight of the character and the play. Thus in *A Midsummer-Night's Dream* the fairies wear gauzes, the courtiers wear satins and light velvets, and the citizens wear light woolen materials. If any of the characters wore heavy wool, leather, or thick brocade, the play would be damaged.

Fullness. Generally speaking, a costume should be either tight or full; anything in between will merely seem skimpy. Unfortunately, fullness is expensive, but as a partial compensation for this, extra fullness is to some extent a substitute for weight. Six widths of muslin in an 18th century gown would give somewhat the same effect as four widths of velvet.

Stiffness. The stiffness of material is also important. (Compare Figs. 17 and 19.) It determines the way the material folds and the way it moves in air. Stiff materials are usually expensive, so the stiffness is often imitated on stage by lining, with perhaps an inner lining of haircloth, buckram, or tarlatan. Paper may be used for stiffening but it is likely to rattle as the actor moves. Sizing also affects the stiffness of material, and some materials lose their stiffness when washed. Costumes may be stiffened by padding, but its use is largely limited to Renaissance styles (Fig. 13, Pl. XXXII).

Surface. In considering the surface of material you must think not only of color and sheen but also of decoration. Almost any sort of pattern on cloth will increase its apparent richness. There are several sorts of cloth paint on the market, and these may be applied freehand, by stencil and dry brush, or by stencil and spatter. Other processes, such as block printing and batik, are usually more trouble than they are worth.

DYEING. Modern dyes have made dyeing a comparatively simple matter. The dyes sold in drugstores are expensive if large quantities of material are to be dyed. Baco Dyes, made by Bachmeier & Co., Inc., 154 Chambers St., New York, N. Y., are excellent for stage costumes.

DRAPE AND FIT

In all the wide variety of costumes, the material is either 'draped' or 'fitted.' This is the first point to be noticed in studying historical costumes. A draped material usually consists of a rectangular piece of cloth. Thus, most Greek and Roman costumes (Figs. 3 to 6, Pl. XXXII, p. 231) were draped, and attempts to imitate them with fitted costumes are unconvincing. An appearance of fit is given by fastening the material with *fibulae* (the safety pins of antiquity), by lashings of various kinds, or by the way the material is bunched. Fitting involves cutting the cloth to special curved shapes or on the 'bias' (at an angle to the weave) and sewing the pieces together along these cuts (Fig. 15). Of course, a piece may be fitted at one place and draped at another, but in considering the history of costume it is simplest to think that any fitting at all makes a garment 'fitted.'

Drape. When material is draped so that one set of threads is vertical, it is said to hang 'plain' (petticoat in Fig. 23). When the threads are at an angle the material is said to hang 'bias' or 'circular' (veil in Fig. 25). Bias draping is more graceful and feminine and is rarely used in men's clothing.

Fit. Fitted costumes are usually shaped to the body, but the term applies to the way the material is handled rather than to actual fit. The jerkin in Fig. 13 is as truly fitted as the hose.

Fastenings. The methods used to join the materials play an important part both in historical costumes and in modern design.

FIBULAE. (Early safety pins; see shoulders, Fig. 4.) In later Greek costumes, the arrangement of pins became more elaborate—like the sleeves in Fig. 5.

BUTTONS. These were first used like sequins for decoration about 1390 A.D. and used for fastenings from 1400. 'Frogs' (used to fasten the jacket in Fig. 28) are a kind of decorative button with a braid loop rather than a buttonhole. Frogs are effective on ornate military costumes. Hooks and eyes are an unobtrusive substitute for buttons. Hooks and eyes and buttons may be hidden entirely with a flap of cloth called a 'fly.'

LASHINGS.   These are important in some historical costumes (Fig. 4). Belts are a kind of lashing. Lashings may be: (1) purely decorative, like the belt in Fig. 12; (2) used to drape the material (Fig. 5); (3) used to support a garment, as with modern trousers; (4) used to support other objects such as swords, pistols, cartridges, etc. (Fig. 18).

LACING.   This is a particularly decorative fastening (boots in Fig. 3).

SEWING.   Stitches are usually invisible at the distances from which stage costumes are seen. However, sewing is not only a means of joining materials; it may be a form of decoration (e.g., embroidery, usually imitated with paint) and also a means of gathering the material in patterns, called 'smocking.'

ZIPPERS.   When made in bright-colored plastics these are an excellent form of decoration, or they can be hidden with a fly.

Ornament.   Costume ornaments assume an infinite variety of forms—buttons (Fig. 12), braid (Fig. 28), lace (Fig. 19), jewelry (Fig. 15), ribbons (Fig. 22), slashing (Fig. 16), fur (Fig. 14), padding (Fig. 13), etc. In designing ornaments, there are two principles to remember:

(1) Have only one type of ornament on a costume, or if more than one type is used, make one much more emphatic than the other.

(2) Use no ornament that does not *seem* to serve a purpose. The buttons on a man's coat sleeve are excellent examples of this; they seem capable of fastening the cuff so it can be turned back, and in some English-tailored coats this is actually possible. Notice also the cuffs in Fig. 22. The quality in a dress which is spoken of as 'tacky' usually comes from the use of meaningless ornament.

HISTORICAL COSTUMES

Pl. XXXII, p. 231, gives a condensed outline of the history of western costume. A knowledge of costume history is important, not only for period plays but as a source of ideas for both modern and fantastic costumes. Historical designs re-created in modern materials such as oilcloth or cellophane are excellent for musical comedies and reviews.

In studying historical costumes you will, of course, note their materials, construction, and characteristic ornament. However, there is another equally important point which is easily overlooked. Costumes are never invented but are evolved from earlier fashions. Thus, women's gowns in 1640 (Fig. 19) repeat those of the Elizabethan period (Fig. 17) but in softer materials which give an entirely different effect. If you follow the changes from one period to another, you will note that there is a fairly definite distinction between soft, more or less transparent undergarments, and heavy, stiff outergarments. Sometimes the undergarment becomes the whole costume as in women's dresses in ancient Greece (Fig. 4). At other times only the outergarments are visible (Fig. 7). Usually, however, we see some combination of the two. If you will follow the relative prominence of the two types, you will find it easier to understand both the history of costume and the people who produced the different modes. For example, the political revolution in France produced the revolutionary style shown in Fig. 25. This is an attempt to imitate Greek dress (Fig. 4), but whereas the original is a draped undergarment of soft material, the copy is a fitted outergarment of stiff material. A restoration both in style and in politics soon followed (Fig. 28).

BORROWING AND RENTING

Amateurs usually borrow modern costumes. The same considerations apply here that apply to borrowed properties (see p. 217).

Some costumes—particularly uniforms—must be rented, but the results are never satisfactory. You will find difficulties even with the most reputable costumers, and in spite of any effort you can make, rented costumes never fit perfectly. If boots are an important part of the costume, the costumer does not provide real boots but either oilcloth leggings or some substitute (such as light riding boots for heavy German infantry boots). Similar difficulties will be found with swords and other accessories.

Plate XXXII
231

EGYPTIAN 1300 B.C.   GREEK 400 B.C.   ROMAN 50 B.C.   BYZANTINE 540 A.D.

NORMAN 1070   ENGLISH 1370   FRENCH 1470   FRENCH 1520

ENGLISH 1600   FRENCH 1640   ENGLISH 1700   AMERICAN 1775

FRENCH 1800   AMERICAN 1860   ENGLISH 1875   AMERICAN 1895

Worse still, most sets of costumes will contain at least one unpleasant surprise, which may be merely the unexpected shoddiness of a costume or may be the fact that some costume is totally unsuitable or does not arrive at all. As you never discover the difficulty until too late to order a substitute, the situation may easily be serious.

Finally, rented costumes give you no opportunities for artistic design. You must take whatever patterns and tones the costumer happens to have, so you will rarely obtain costumes that are completely suited either to the characters or to the play.

COSTUME MAKING

If a group makes its own costumes, it will build up a wardrobe which can be altered and adapted for future plays. Costume making is easier than ordinary dressmaking because the work does not require so much care, and finish can usually be ignored. If the material is cut with pinking shears or a pinking machine, it either will need no hem at all or can be hemmed with a minimum of trouble. Thread cannot be seen from the audience, so you can either use gray thread for all materials, or use white thread for light materials and black thread for dark ones.

Rich materials can be imitated from cheap ones either by allowing extra fullness or by brushing or spraying dye on the material, much as rough textures are imitated by scene paint (see p. 205). This process requires some experiment, but if you make many costumes it will save a great deal of money.

The patterns sold in department stores cover a wide range. If you cannot find one that exactly suits your needs, you can always solve your difficulty by taking a sleeve from one pattern, a skirt from another, etc.

Alterations. The simplest way to make costumes is to alter everyday clothes. Peasant costumes can be made from worn-out men's suits by cutting the trousers and jackets short and decorating them with bright ribbons. Men's 1890 costumes can be imitated by taking a pleat on the inseam of modern trousers and adding another button at the top of the coat. Imaginary uniforms can be made from those of the U. S. army by wearing the blouse inside the trousers and adding a sash and a different kind of cap.

Chapter XX

Make-Up

Directions for specific make-ups are of little value because faces differ. A make-up which is perfect on Maurice Evans may be ridiculous on you. Lighting conditions must also be taken into account. If the lighting changes greatly from one scene to another, you may have to change your make-up.

PRINCIPLES

The principles given here will solve your simpler problems and guide you in solving your more difficult ones, but a certain amount of experimentation *under the actual lighting used in the scene* is always necessary. If someone else applies your make-up, do not attempt to judge it yourself because you can never see it from the viewpoint of the audience. Do not ask the opinions of your friends because they cannot know what effect is being sought. The director is the only person on whose opinion you can rely; he sees you under ideal conditions, he understands the whole situation, and his interest in your appearance is at least as great as your own.

Do not fight your face with make-up. Study it instead. Note where the bones lie under the skin and where the flesh is padded with fat. Screw your face into knots and observe where the muscles bulge and where the wrinkles come. Also watch for any tendency of the skin to hang in folds along the edge of the jaw. Use these observations as guides in planning your make-up. Put hollows and wrinkles where they would come on you, not where they appear in some picture or on someone else.

Concentrate on the character. Your purpose is to adapt your face to that of the character. Never indulge in make-up for its own sake. Limit yourself to what is necessary, and when in doubt use

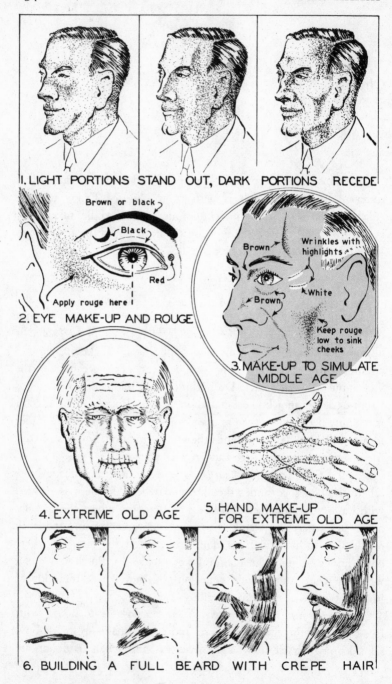

1. LIGHT PORTIONS STAND OUT, DARK PORTIONS RECEDE

2. EYE MAKE-UP AND ROUGE

Brown or black
Black
Red
Apply rouge here

3. MAKE-UP TO SIMULATE MIDDLE AGE

Brown
Wrinkles with highlights
White
Brown
Keep rouge low to sink cheeks

4. EXTREME OLD AGE

5. HAND MAKE-UP FOR EXTREME OLD AGE

6. BUILDING A FULL BEARD WITH CREPE HAIR

too little rather than too much. Make-up is at most a makeshift, something needed when the actor's own appearance does not fit the role. If the make-up is apparent, the effect is always distracting.

Modeling. Within limits, you can model your face with make-up just as you would model clay with your fingers. Simply darken the portions you wish to depress and lighten those you wish to bring out. The faces in Fig. 1, Pl. XXXIII, p. 234 are identical except for the shading. If you use make-up in this way, you will obtain similar results.

In many forms of color work, the warm hues tend to advance and the cool ones to recede. Doubtless this effect also applies to make-up, but it is so slight that it can usually be ignored. For practical purposes you can design your modeling entirely in terms of value. Thus, rouge always darkens the skin, so any rouged area will appear slightly sunken.

In middle-aged make-ups you usually have a choice between modeling and wrinkles. Modeling is better because it is difficult to make a convincing wrinkle, and even the best one may look like a streak of dirt when seen from a distance.

Hue Introduced through Modeling. Hues must often be used subtly. Noticeable rouge and lipstick are undesirable for men. Nevertheless, a handsome juvenile should be a healthy pink. The needed red can be introduced in the modeling, such as the shadows under the brows, nose, and chin. The inner corners of the eyes and the nostrils may also be touched with rouge. A subtle Dracula-like effect can be obtained by using green on these places, and a lavender-and-old-lace lady may shadow her face with violet.

Effect of Distance. Distance blurs the features, so they must usually be emphasized for the benefit of the spectators in the rear of the auditorium. Unfortunately, emphasis which is needed for the rear is often too much for the front. This is particularly noticeable in special effects like scars. I have experimented with almost every known method of simulating scars, but I have never seen one which was visible from the twelfth row that did not look like a smear from the first.

Effects of Lighting. Lighting tends to bleach the tones of the face. This means that most people must make up their eyes and eyebrows, and rouge their cheeks, even when they want their stage appearance to match that of everyday life. This does not apply to those with black hair and dark or ruddy complexions, who can often dispense with make-up.

DIRECTION OF LIGHT. Stage lights rarely cast natural shadows on an actor. This makes it necessary to imitate shadows by slightly darkening the space between the eyebrows and the upper lids and also the lower planes of the nose and chin.

COLOR OF LIGHT. If you paint a piece of cardboard with the different hues of the spectrum, and then illuminate it with light of some strong color such as amber, red, or green, you will observe two effects:

(1) The painted hues will take on some of the quality of the light. Thus if green light is used, the yellow and blue paints will assume a greenish tinge and the red paint (which is the complement of green) will lose its redness. The result is the same as if green pigment had been mixed with the painted samples (see p. 203 and Fig. 4, Pl. XXVIII, p. 207). This effect tends to harmonize the tones of the stage picture, or 'pull them together,' and is usually desirable.

(2) The hues which are similar to the light will appear brighter (i.e., both more intense and higher in value). Those which contrast with the light will be duller and darker. Under green light the green paint will be much brighter, the red will seem almost black, and the other hues will be affected in intermediate degrees. When the light is merely tinted, this effect is not serious. The same thing is true when all the light is of one color, such as the green used for moonlight. However, when two or more strong colors of light—such as blue and amber—are used, the effect is so strong that it creates a major problem. Thus, a make-up which is beautiful under amber light may change to something grotesque or horrible when the actor turns and his face is illuminated by the blue light. To make matters worse, most stage-light colors are impure. That is, they contain color components which are not noticeable in the light itself but which affect the objects illuminated. Blues are particularly troublesome. They contain much red, so that under a blue light the actors' faces often look like ripe tomatoes.

When strong colors are to be used in the lights, the best plan is to limit the make-up to black and various shades of tan. This restriction is not so serious as it may seem, because when the lights supply color you can afford to omit it from the make-up.

MATERIALS AND METHODS

One brand of make-up is as satisfactory as another. They differ chiefly in the tones offered and in the way they feel under the fingers. You can work better with familiar materials, so select one brand and stick to it. In most towns a complete line of material will be stocked by only one shop, and you are therefore limited to the brand it carries. If you are offered a choice of brands, select the cheapest. Price in make-up does not reflect quality but is determined by the manufacturer's policy.

Cold Cream.   This is used both to prepare the face and to take off the make-up afterward. The preparation consists in rubbing on just enough cream to make the face greasy. Do not neglect the ears, the neck (back and front), and the hands. The cream should be rubbed in thoroughly. The more time you spend on this the better. To remove make-up, simply smear cold cream on the face and wipe it off with facial tissues. A special make-up product called Albolene may be substituted for cold cream, and I have also heard vegetable shortening recommended, though I have never tried it. Even if the theater provides the make-up, actors should be required to supply their own cold cream and tissues. If these are furnished free, the first actor to come off stage will use half the supply.

Foundation.   This comes in sticks, tubes, or jars and is often called 'base.' Four bases will take care of most needs—a pale, a medium, and two dark tones. One of the dark tones should be reddish (the color of fresh sunburn) and the other should be a sallow brown of about the same value. Two bases can be mixed on the face to produce intermediate tones.

To apply base paint, dab small spots on various parts of the face, neck, and ears and blend these until a smooth effect is obtained. If your skin is fair or if it nearly matches the base, only a little paint is needed. Making a dark skin paler is more difficult. The base paint can do only part of the job, and the rest must be done with powder.

Base paint can be used for subtle modeling. If your face is round, try using a *slightly* darker base on your cheeks, or if you wish to make your chin more prominent, paint it with a lighter base than the rest of your face.

Liners. These are similar to base paints but of a stiffer consistency. They are usually bought in richer tones. Black, dark brown, light brown, violet, blue, green, yellow, and white are all useful. Liners are applied with a toothpick or a small 'stump' of twisted paper. Stroke the pick or stump on the paint and then draw your line with the side as if you were trying to cut the line with the edge of a knife. Liner colors are also used for shadows and are then applied with a sidewise movement of the stump or with the tip of the finger. Some liner colors are sold in pencil form. These are much more convenient but also more expensive.

EYEBROWS. Unless your eyebrows are naturally black, they should normally be darkened with a brown or black liner. Make the outlines clean-cut. A certain amount of shaping is usually desirable if it can be done by thickening or lengthening the brow. 'Blocking out' the natural brow, so that the new one can be painted any shape desired, can be done by smearing soap or base paint over the brow. This will not work well if the brow is too dark, but it is usually possible to block out straggling hairs and so make the brow thinner and give it a sharper outline. For white eyebrows, dab white liner on the brows and at the same time rub them the wrong way to make them shaggy.

EYELASHES. These should usually be darkened. This can be done by blackening the hairs with 'mascara.' Another method is to draw a line in black or brown liner along the upper lid from the inside corner to a little past the outer corner (Fig. 2, Pl. XXXIII, p. 234). Another line should be drawn on the lower lid, starting directly below the pupil and meeting the upper line at the outer corner. Girls can make their lashes seem longer by painting a black crescent on the skin between the brow and the lid (Fig. 2). The special artificial eyelashes made for stage use are effective but also expensive.

EYESHADOW. The flesh below the brow should normally be shadowed, although this is not shown in Fig. 2. The area to be painted varies with the face and with the character, and can only be de-

Community Theater, Harrisburg, Pennsylvania

THE MIKADO

Setting by Julia Comstock Smith

Comic opera and musical comedy are nearly always done in a fantastic style. This example is almost pure fantasy, but often there are strong romantic tendencies, and some modern musicals call for an element of expressionism. The 'sky' in this set is simply the back wall of the stage house, plastered and painted a pale blue-gray. The scenery, costumes, and make-up are in precisely the same style.

termined by experiment. The hue will also vary. Blue or violet is often used, but green, red, or brown may be required in special cases even for straight make-up. The red dot at the inner corner of the eye (Fig. 2) gives an appearance of health and vitality to youthful make-ups.

WRINKLES. Draw the lines where your own wrinkles come when you grimace. Use brown or maroon liner (never black). Each wrinkle should be highlighted on both sides with a line of white, yellow, or pale flesh-colored paint (Fig. 3).

Rouge. The so-called 'moist' rouge is really a red grease liner. It comes in light, medium, and dark tones. Use it for lips and cheeks, and for shadowing and modeling when a red tone is desired.

CHEEKS. A rouged area always appears sunken, so do not place the rouge low on the cheeks unless your face is too full or the role demands a haggard appearance. The proper area for the normal face lies on the upper edge of the cheek bone and extends from a point immediately below the pupil to the temple, where it sometimes extends above the eyebrow (Fig. 2). How far the rouge should be worked into the eye socket, both above and below the outer corner of the eye, depends on the face. If the eyes look red, as if you had been crying, the rouge is too close. If you look as if you had been sunburned while wearing dark glasses, the rouge is too far away. Apply the rouge by placing a tiny spot in the middle of the area and blending it outward with a clean finger. Rouge must blend so perfectly that you cannot tell where it ends. Cheek rouge applied in this way not only will tint the face but will frame the eyes and make them seem brighter.

Dry rouge is used over powder, either to correct a make-up which is too pale, or for a between-act repair job. The tone universally known as 'No. 18' will blend with most make-ups.

Lips. Shape the lips as you will, using your finger, a stump, or a brush. The outline should normally be knife-sharp. Sometimes a dark-brown line drawn around the red is helpful. Avoid using excess rouge on the lips if the make-up must be worn in a kissing scene. In most cases, men should leave their lips bare, without make-up of any kind. If the lips seem too pale, draw a brown line around them or rub on a little rouge and then wipe it off with a cleansing tissue.

Powder. Make-up is greasy, and the painted surface must be dulled with powder. Theatrical powder is much better than the kind sold for street make-up. Simply pat the powder on lightly with a puff and dust off the excess with a 'complexion brush.' The powder should normally match the base paint, but it may be used for corrections; e.g., if the make-up is too dark, a paler powder can be used. A wide range of powders is desirable. White; pale, medium, and dark pink; and pale, medium, and dark tan will be enough to meet most needs. Intermediate tones can be blended by mixing two or more powders in the lid of a can.

Hair. Natural-hair wigs are the only kind worth considering for serious plays. They are usually rented, as they are too expensive to be bought. The dressing of the wig with 'brilliantine' or lacquer is of the utmost importance and should be entrusted to someone with hairdressing experience. No wig can simulate the close-cropped effect at the back of the neck which men's modern styles demand. However, toupees which cover the front and top of the head work perfectly. If the hair at the sides and back does not blend with the toupee, it can be lightly colored.

Most men's wigs and some toupees have a flesh-colored forehead piece called a 'blender.' This can be adjusted to fit the forehead by pleating the wig at the sides under the hair and holding each pleat in place with a few stitches. After the wig is on your head, cover the edge of the blender with a strip of 1″ adhesive tape (the plastic type is best because it is thinnest). Apply base paint over this so that the blender, the tape, and the skin are all the same tone. The edges of the tape may need to be still further hidden by painted wrinkles, as in Fig. 4, Pl. XXXIII, p. 234, where the edges of the tape are shown by dotted lines.

ARRANGING. Actresses' coiffures should be designed by someone familiar with the play and the character. They can be kept in place with brilliantine or lacquer. The possibilities of arranging an actor's hair with brilliantine or lacquer, and perhaps a curling iron, should not be overlooked. A fresh haircut leaves a pale patch at the back of a man's neck which can be corrected only by working make-up into the short hair. To avoid this, men should have their hair cut a few days before the first dress rehearsal.

COLORING. Blond or brown hair can be darkened or reddened with 'rinse,' which can be washed out after the play is over. Mascara will serve the same purpose. It works much better on some people than on others. There is a blond mascara, but I have had no experience with it. The metallic powders used for radiator paint produce realistic and glamorous effects, but they cannot safely be left in the hair overnight. Also, they should not be employed when the costumes are borrowed; some particles are sure to fall on the clothing, and they can never be completely removed. Dry powdered scene paint (yellow ocher, Venetian red, and burnt umber) color the hair realistically but lack the sheen of metallic powders.

Hair is often grayed with white theatrical powder or dry cornstarch, but the result is rarely convincing. Aluminum powder or white mascara will give better results. Gray temples or streaks can be produced with either white mascara or a white liner.

MOUSTACHES AND BEARDS. These are made of crepe hair, which comes in all colors. It is sold in the form of a braided rope. Unbraid as much as you expect to use, dampen it, lay it between two towels, and press it dry with a flatiron. This will straighten it. If you wish

to curl it again, dampen it and wrap it around a pencil. To make
a moustache, first draw the moustache on your face with black or
brown liner. Avoid excess grease. Then cover the drawn moustache
with 'spirit gum.' When the gum has dried slightly, add a second
coat and apply the crepe hair. Use only a little hair and make sure
that the strands run in the direction which natural hairs would
take. Press the hair firmly in place until the gum is dry. Trim the
moustache with scissors. To make it keep its shape, you may use
another coat of gum on top of the moustache. If such a moustache
should fall off, the paint may keep the accident from being noticed.

Beards are more complicated but no more difficult. Gum the first
wisp under the chin so that it stands straight out (Fig. 6, Pl.
XXXIII, p. 234). This both covers the bottom of the chin and provides a support for the rest of the beard. Cut the next wisp square,
fan the cut end, and stick it *end on* against the face. Add other
layers, starting at the bottom and working upward. When the beard
is in place, trim it with scissors. Then, with a lining color that
matches the beard, draw lines at the top edge of the beard to hide
the artificial appearance which the edge will otherwise show. If
properly drawn, these lines will seem to be separate hairs growing
out of the skin.

UNSHAVEN EFFECT. Cheap pipe-tobacco held in place with spirit
gum gives an excellent imitation of a week's growth of whiskers.
Finely chopped crepe hair can also be used.

Shaping the Face. Nose putty is the most common material for
actually changing the shape of the face. Have the part free from
make-up and grease. Apply spirit gum. While the gum is drying,
break off a piece of putty and knead it in the fingers until it is soft.
Press the putty on the face over the gum and force it down until
it adheres thoroughly. Grease the fingers with cold cream and mold
the putty to the desired shape. Cover the putty with base paint to
make it blend with the rest of the face.

The face may also be shaped with absorbent cotton stuck on with
spirit gum and covered with a shell of collodion. Cover the collodion
with base paint until it matches the face.

The cheeks may be made plumper by pads of tissue paper. Chew
the paper until it becomes a sort of papier mâché. Place a wad of it

on each side between the teeth and the cheeks. Press on the outside of the cheeks until the pads are molded to the shape of the teeth. After a little practice these pads cause no difficulty in talking, but if they are left in place too long they will make the gums tender. To avoid this, the actor should remove them when he comes off stage and put them back just before his next entrance.

Missing Teeth. These can be simulated by a make-up preparation called 'black tooth-wax.' It is placed between the teeth rather than over them, unless several teeth in a row are to be blacked out.

AGING THE ACTOR

Almost every college play requires at least one actor to increase his apparent age through make-up.

Maturity. Ages from thirty-five to forty-five are simulated chiefly through modeling. Use a rather sallow base and dark rouge. Keep the rouge low on the cheeks to make them seem hollow. If the men need lip make-up, use brown rather than red, or outline the lips in brown. Women should use as little lip rouge as possible. Hollow the temples as in Fig. 3, Pl. XXXIII, by drawing a vertical line in brown above the outer corner of the eyebrow. Leave the front of the line sharp but blend the back so that it fades away toward the hair. Put brown shadows at the root of the nose in the corner between the nose and the eye socket (Fig. 3). Slight pouches under the eyes and wrinkles at the outer corners of the eyes may also be used.

Middle Age. For characters from forty-five to fifty-five use the above make-up with a paler base. Whiten the hair at the temples and add a few streaks of gray. Hollows where the muscles of the face have begun to sag (Fig. 3) may be simulated with brown paint or dark rouge.

Old Age. Here the hair and eyebrows should be white. For men, bushy eyebrows may be added with crepe hair and spirit gum. Rouge should be kept low and be either very light or dark but not medium. Use no lip rouge. Paint over the edges of the lips to make them thinner. For extreme old age, paint out the lips entirely. Wrinkles should be made with maroon, highlighted with white.

Illumination
Style
Mood
SPstage picture
I information
Emphasis
Interest

Chapter XXI

STAGE LIGHTING

Good stage lighting will serve a number of functions simultaneously. It should:

Provide the desired illumination. Normally the maximum visibility is desirable. However, there are cases where the lighting should hide or obscure something rather than reveal it; hastily constructed scenery may serve if it is placed in shadow, and a murder will seem less brutal under a dim light.

Assist in setting the style. Stage lighting rarely succeeds in duplicating nature. The chief difference between lighting for realism and for theatricalized realism is that the former demands windows or light fixtures to provide an apparent source for the illumination which is actually supplied by the stage-lighting instruments, whereas the latter is usually content to illuminate the stage without explaining the source from which the light is supposed to come. The more extreme styles often call for arbitrary shafts of light and strong colors never seen in real life.

Assist in controlling the mood. Lights have a profound effect on mood. Often a mood can be shifted from somber to gay simply by bringing on more light, or by changing the tint of the light from cool to warm.

Contribute to the stage picture. Light has such a strong influence on the values and hues of the stage picture that an entire scene change may be effected simply by changing the lights or by special lighting effects.

Convey information. Lighting can indicate such things as the time of day, the weather, whether or not an offstage room is occupied, and whether or not a fire is lighted (also, by inference, the season of the year).

Distribute emphasis. Bright light emphasizes an object; dim light subordinates it.

Build or conserve interest. Increasing light produces a powerful effect of build. Diminishing light may be used as a means of conservation.

THE QUALITIES OF LIGHT

In order to think in terms of light you must understand its qualities. Unfortunately these will not fit satisfactorily into the same pattern as those of pigment, although the resemblance is close. The difference is not a mere matter of nomenclature but is somehow fundamental, though no one seems to have discovered its exact nature (see footnote, p. 203).

Distribution. Light occupies space and is more concentrated at some points than at others. The form of light is called its 'distribution.' Unless light shines directly into the eye, it is invisible except when it strikes some object. When there is smoke or dust in the air, the distribution of light can be seen plainly. Otherwise we see only those objects, such as scenery, properties, actors, etc., which form the boundaries of the light.

DIRECTION. Unless it is reflected or refracted, each individual ray of light travels in a straight line and in one direction. A coin held in a ray of light will be brightly lit on one side and completely dark on the other. Direction is the most important factor in stage lighting, so the intelligent control of direction occupies much of our attention.

Most stage-lighting instruments produce cones of rays. If the cone is clear-cut, the light is said to be 'sharp edged.' If the edges of the cone are blurred, so that they cannot be definitely located, the light is 'soft edged.' Light that escapes from the cone entirely, either because the instrument is defective or because the light has struck something and been reflected, is called 'spill light.' Spill light is often valuable; in fact it provides the chief illumination on the walls of most sets. At other times it is extremely undesirable, but it may be difficult or even impossible to eliminate.

Color. In lighting we can rarely control hue and intensity separately, so it is convenient to treat them together under the term 'color.'

Brightness. This quality in light corresponds roughly to value in pigment. However, value is intimately connected with hue and intensity, whereas 'brightness' is largely independent of them, both in theory and in practice.

Movement. This includes all changes in distribution, brightness, and/or color. 'Movements' from one degree of brightness to another are far more common than movements which change the distribution.

THE QUALITIES OF LIGHT—SOURCE AND CONTROL

Nearly all the light used on stage has its source in incandescent electric 'lamps.' These lamps are housed in metal and glass 'lighting instruments' which control the light output by focusing the rays in the desired direction. Each instrument is connected to the 'control board' by an electric 'cable.' The control board contains 'switches' for turning the light on and off, and 'dimmers' which regulate the current supplied to each instrument and thus govern the brightness of the emitted light.

Types of Instruments. A small number of instrument types will meet all ordinary stage needs.

FLOODLIGHTS. A 'floodlight' or 'flood' (Fig. 3, Pl. XXXIV, p. 250 and Fig. 5, Pl. XXXV, p. 260) consists principally of a reflector which surrounds the lamp except in the front. Floodlights throw a wide, soft-edged cone of light with a good deal of spill. They are efficient in the sense that comparatively little light is wasted, but they permit almost no control of the distribution. Both the types illustrated serve the same purpose.

SPOTLIGHTS. These are equipped with lenses which make the beam narrower, sharper, and brighter than that of a floodlight, and also give control of the distribution within fairly wide limits. Three types are on the market:

(1) Spotlight with spherical reflector and bi-convex or plano-convex lens. This type is inefficient, bulky, and unsatisfactory. It should be obsolete.

(2) Stepped-lens spotlight (Fig. 3, Pl. XXXV). This has a spherical reflector and an almost flat lens grooved in concentric rings. It is small and efficient, and gives an extremely soft edge. When the

lamp is moved toward the lens, the beam is widened ('flood focus'). When it is moved away from the lens, the beam is narrowed ('sharp focus'). If the soft-edged effect permits too much spill, this can be partially corrected by the use of a funnel (Fig. 3, Pl. XXXV). If the funnel is omitted and the lens is removed, the instrument is converted into a floodlight.

(3) Ellipsoidal-reflector spotlight. In this type (Fig. 4, Pl. XXXV) the reflector surrounds the lamp except in front. These efficient instruments are ideal for long 'throws' (i.e., when the light is far from the object). One adjustment gives the beam any shape (cross section) desired. Another sharpens or softens the edges. Although these instruments usually have two plano-convex lenses, a few of them are fitted with stepped lenses. Nevertheless, their characteristic shape makes it easy to distinguish them from the ordinary stepped-lens type. Occasionally it is desirable to convert these instruments into a sort of semiflood by removing the lenses.

STRIPLIGHTS.   These consist of a row of small floodlights mounted in a single housing (Figs. 4 and 5, Pl. XXXIV). The lamps should be wired in three circuits with Nos. 1, 4, 7, etc. on the first circuit, Nos. 2, 5, 8, etc. on the second, and Nos. 3, 6, 9, etc. on the third. This arrangement permits three colors of light, and an infinite number of mixtures, to be produced by the same instrument. Striplights cast almost no shadow.

EFFECT MACHINES.   Much ingenuity has been expended on lighting devices which can imitate anything from a snowstorm to an eruption of Vesuvius. Unfortunately most of them are expensive and unreliable, and the effects they produce are rarely convincing.

Control of Distribution.   Light distribution is governed by the number of instruments used, their types, and the way they are arranged. The scenery, the costumes, and the groupings also play a vital part in distribution, although we would hardly think of them as lighting instruments.

Control of Color.   Light is colored by placing a transparent material, such as glass or gelatine, over the face of the instrument. Sheets of gelatine and similar substances are called 'mediums.' They are so flimsy that they must be supported by metal 'color frames,' and most varieties fade rapidly with use. They are sold in some seventy different tints, as well as in a clear 'frost,' which diffuses the light, and several mottled patterns. Colored glass is used chiefly for strip-lights which are equipped to hold lenslike disks called 'roundels.' Roundels are permanent but expensive, and their range of colors is limited.

THREE-COLOR SYSTEM. As everyone knows, all the pigment hues can be mixed from the three primary hues. The same thing is true of light, except that the light primaries are different. The light primaries are conventionally spoken of as 'red,' 'blue,' and 'green,' but on the chart (Fig. 4, Pl. XXVIII, p. 207) the so-called 'red' would be nearer red-orange, the 'blue' would be blue-violet, and the 'green' would be yellow-green. As the chart indicates, the various shades of violet light are produced by mixing 'red' and 'blue.' Mixtures of 'blue' and 'green' give the greenish blues. 'Red' and 'green' give the orange and yellow tints, which in light we call 'amber' and 'straw.' All three primary colors combine to form white light.

Control of Brightness. This is governed by:

DISTANCE BETWEEN INSTRUMENT AND OBJECT LIT. If an object is placed close to an instrument and then moved away, the brightness falls off rapidly at first and then more and more slowly as the distance increases. The basic principle here is the law of physics that the brightness of the light is inversely proportional to the square of the distance. However, other factors affect the situation, so that in practice it would often be more accurate to say that brightness varies inversely as the distance; e.g., an object 10′ away is 1/10 as bright as an object 1′ away. The effect is very marked for the first 8′ or 10′, so a light should not ordinarily be placed where an actor will move back and forth within this range. This is the reason why it is undesirable to place lights behind the tormentors, a practice that could otherwise be recommended.

SIZE OF APERTURE. Floodlights and stepped-lens spotlights can be dimmed by covering part of the face of the instrument with cardboard. This has some effect on the distribution but much less than you might expect. The trick is of little or no value with strip-lights and will not work at all with ellipsoidal-reflector spots.

CHANGING FOCUS OF STEPPED-LENS SPOTLIGHT. The beam of a stepped-lens spot is much brighter on sharp focus than on flood focus. This effect cannot be attained with any other instruments.

EFFECT OF COLOR MEDIUMS. Color mediums are extremely in-efficient. A pale gelatine like No. 54 'Light Straw' wastes 15% of the light, and a No. 36 'Dark Blue' gelatine will absorb 97%. Normally this is a serious disadvantage, but occasionally an over-bright instrument may be dimmed by using a neutral gelatine like No. 75 'Gray.'

AMOUNT OF ELECTRICAL CURRENT. This is the chief means of controlling the brightness of an instrument. Of course, the greater the current the brighter the light. As the current decreases, the light grows more orange—an effect which is sometimes of con-siderable importance.

TYPE, NUMBER, AND ARRANGEMENT OF INSTRUMENTS. The effect of these factors is obvious. Light from a spot is brighter than that from a flood. Several instruments will give more light than one, and a beam of light is brighter in the center than at the edges. This last effect is more noticeable when the beam is soft-edged.

Control of Movement. If any of the control devices mentioned above is changed, the result will, of course, be movement. How-ever, in normal practice, we use only the electrical controls, operated from the control board.

THE LIGHTING LAYOUT

The method of lighting given here is based on that devised by Stanley McCandless of Yale. It is flexible enough to fit every type of play, and its principles are so simple that even the most complicated layout can be planned with ease. The normal positions for all the standard instruments are shown in Fig. 1, Pl. XXXIV, p. 250. See also Fig. 2, Pl. XXIV, p. 170.

Area Lighting. Lighting the acting areas obviously calls for the maximum of control, so our principal instrument must be the spot-light. As a spotlight will illuminate a space equivalent to one acting area (p. 17), the electrician can work in terms of the same areas as those used by the director and actors.

SPOTLIGHTING. If you will sit in the auditorium, with an actor on stage, and have someone shine a spotlight on him from various angles, you will soon learn that light from directly in front elimi-

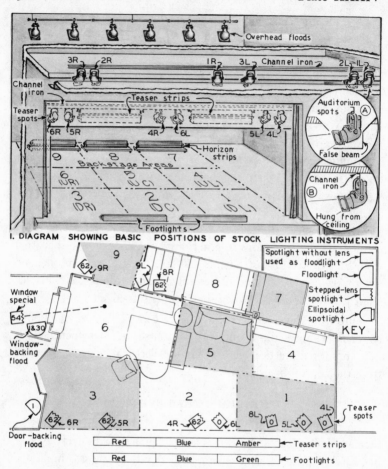

1. DIAGRAM SHOWING BASIC POSITIONS OF STOCK LIGHTING INSTRUMENTS

Spotlight without lens used as floodlight
Floodlight
Stepped-lens spotlight
Ellipsoidal spotlight
KEY

| Red | Blue | Amber | ← Teaser strips |
| Red | Blue | Green | ← Footlights |

2. LIGHTING LAYOUT — SHOWING ADAPTATION OF THE SYSTEM TO A SET

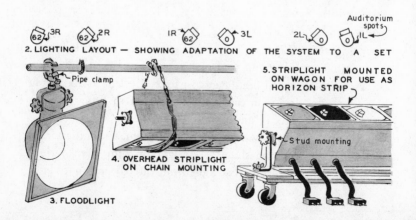

3. FLOODLIGHT

4. OVERHEAD STRIPLIGHT ON CHAIN MOUNTING

5. STRIPLIGHT MOUNTED ON WAGON FOR USE AS HORIZON STRIP

nates shadows on the actor and makes him look like a flat, cardboard cutout. When you experiment by having the light moved to one side, you will find that the best effect is produced when the beam shines along the 45° axis. You will also learn that a light placed on a level with the actor is never satisfactory, because it casts distracting shadows on the set. When you experiment with raising the light, you will find that here, too, an angle of about 45° is best.

This means that in order to locate the ideal position for an area spotlight, you should stand in the center of the area with one arm pointing straight in front of you. Swing 45° to one side and then raise your arm about 45°. You will now be pointing along the diagonal of an imaginary cube, one corner of which is at your head and shoulders, and the sides of which are on the stage axes. Your finger will be pointing at the far corner of the cube, which is the desired instrument location. In practice it is not always possible to mount a spotlight in the ideal position, but if the position selected is reasonably close to the ideal, the results will be satisfactory.

Now, if you go back to your actor standing on the stage and lit by a single spotlight shining along the diagonal of a cube, you will find that when he turns in profile away from the light, a large portion of his face and the whole front of his body will be in darkness. This effect is obviously undesirable and must be counteracted by mounting another spotlight to shine from the other side. This light should also be directed along the diagonal of a cube.

If both lights are equally bright, the actor will appear flat, much as he did when the light was in the center. This can be corrected by making one light definitely brighter than the other. The strong light will cast enough shadows to model the actor, and the weak light will illuminate the dark portions sufficiently to make detail visible. Unfortunately, the balance here is delicate. When the actor walks across stage, he moves nearer one light and farther from the other. This changes the relative brightness of the two lights and destroys the balance. To avoid this difficulty, we use what is known as 'warm and cool' lighting. This employs different colors in the two spotlights, and one of the colors is relatively warmer than the other. The warmer color should always be placed in the stronger light.

The difference in warmth need not be great. It is sufficient to use a pale pink or straw on the strong, warmer side and plain white light on the weak, cooler side. This difference in color makes it possible to use light of almost equal brightness and still get a modeled effect. The eye recognizes the warmer areas on the actor's face as high-lights and the cooler areas as shadows. Moreover, the balance is less critical, so the movements of the actor do not noticeably affect it. This is an important virtue.

The three downstage areas can be lit adequately only from positions near the ceiling of the auditorium (Fig. 1, Pl. XXXIV, p. 250). *A* shows how the lights can be concealed in a false beam. At *B* the lights are hung below the ceiling in full view of the audience. This is far from ideal, but *anything* is better than not being able to light the faces of your downstage actors. The ellipsoidal-reflector spotlight is the only type which is satisfactory for auditorium use.

BLENDING LIGHTS. As each area requires two spotlights, twelve will be needed for the six areas. It is impossible to focus these lights to give an even effect over the entire stage. There will be bright places called 'hot spots' and dark places called 'holes.' These irregularities can be smoothed out by striplights mounted behind the teaser. The light from the 'teaser strips' should be bright enough to blend the irregularities but not bright enough to cancel the directional effect of the spotlights.

Background Lighting. Most of the light on the set proper is spill from the acting areas, and for many scenes no other illumination is needed.

TONING. If more light is required, or if you wish to control the hue of the set, you will use 'footlights,' which are striplights placed in a 'trough' along the front of the stage. Of course you cannot change the set from red to blue by changing the color of the footlights, but you can change it from red-violet to blue-violet, and this is enough to have a decided effect on the mood of the play. Also, if you use the same flats in two different scenes, the hue can be disguised somewhat by changing the color of the footlights.

The footlight color has little effect on the actors or their costumes because it is overwhelmed by the stronger light from the area spots. However, light from below is valuable because it kills the shadows on the underplanes of the actors' faces. In fact, many designers use footlights for this purpose alone.

BACKINGS. These are most easily illuminated by floodlights. Sometimes the flood is fitted with a frosted medium and turned directly toward the backing (see the UR. backing, Fig. 2, Pl. XXXIV, p. 250). However, if actors use the offstage area, this method will usually cast distracting shadows. These can be avoided by turning the light on the rear of the set (DR., Fig. 2) and letting the reflected light illuminate the backing. As the reflection comes from a large area, there will be almost no shadow.

SKY. The upper part of the sky is usually lit by floodlights. Even a small area of sky will require two floods, and four to six may be considered minimum for a sky of any size. If the sky must change color, you will need two or three sets of floods. Real skies are normally lighter at the bottom. This effect can be produced by placing a row of striplights called 'horizon strips' about 3' or 4' from the lower edge of the sky. Horizon strips are also used for sunset effects.

Lighting for Composition. Normally the instruments used for illumination will also provide the composition. However, some scenes need special instruments for this purpose.

Lights for Conveying Information. Special instruments may also be used to convey information. A spot may throw a shaft of sunlight in a window to announce that the weather is fine, or a floor lamp may glow to supply a motivation for light which really comes from the stage instruments.

Naming Instruments. Each instrument must have a specific name so that it can be referred to by the workers. Mr. McCandless' system of naming instruments is one of the most valuable parts of his lighting method. The acting areas are numbered from '1' to '6' starting at the DL. corner (Figs. 1 and 2, Pl. XXXIV, p. 250). You will also find it convenient to call the backstage areas '7,' '8,' and '9.' If an area is not lighted, its number is omitted, but the numbers of the other areas remain the same. Thus, if there are no instruments for Area 4, there is no number 4, but the UC. area is still called '5.' The spotlight striking the area from L. is called 'L' plus the area number (L1, L2, etc.). The spotlight from R. is called 'R' plus the number (R1, R2, etc.). If, for any reason, both spotlights should be on the same side, the light farthest R. is called 'R' and the one farthest L. is 'L.' If there are more than two spotlights on an area, the others are called 'specials' and may be designated by the number of the area or by some name chosen by the light designer. Thus, the spotlight in the UR. corner of Fig. 2 might be called the '6 special,' the 'window special,' or the 'sunlight special.' Such names should be descriptive, so they will be easy to remember. Flood-lights may be designated by area (the '9 flood') or by name (the 'window-backing flood'). If special striplights are used, they are given names.

The Lighting Layout—Designing a Layout

The work of designing a lighting layout for a particular production is done on tracing paper placed over the ground plan of the set (Fig. 2, Pl. XXXIV). The instruments are represented by easily drawn symbols. The designation of each instrument is placed beside it. This usually suffices to indicate the area on which the instrument is focused. In the case of special instruments like the 'window special' in Fig. 2, a black dot may be placed on the plan where the center of the beam will fall, and a broken line drawn to connect this dot with the instrument. The same method may be used with floodlights, although this is rarely necessary. Every medium has a number in the manufacturer's sample book. The number of the medium to be used with each instrument is written inside the symbol for that instrument. If two mediums are called for, both numbers are written. A 'o' indicates that no medium will be needed. Striplights are indicated by narrow rectangles divided into as many compartments as there are color circuits in the strip. Teaser strips and footlights are really made up of two individual striplights (called 'sections'). This is standard practice and does not need to be shown on the diagram. However, if an unusual number of sections is to be used, this can be indicated by a note.

In exterior and other complicated sets, it may be necessary to work out the sightlines of the lights and also the lines of the light beams themselves. The method of doing this is shown in Fig. 2, Pl. XXIV, p. 170. Note that the beams from the teaser spots must cross the beams from the auditorium spots at a point above the heads of the actors (*F*, Fig. 2).

Design Procedure. Begin by noting the areas to be spotlighted. If one side of the set is very shallow, the upstage area can be omitted. (See the small sketch, Pl. IV, p. 17.) Next locate the standard spotlights for these areas. If special spotlights will be required, these should also be located and placed on the drawing. Give each special a name. Then decide on the number and location of the floods used to light each backing. If a sky is involved, plan the number of overhead floods to be used. Locate their up- and down-stage position and their height above the stage floor. Normally, they should hang as low and as far downstage as the scenery and sightlines permit. The number of sections to be used in the horizon strips should then be determined. They should be placed as far downstage as possible. Teaser strips and footlights are usually added as a matter of course.

Selecting Colors. The footlights will work on the three-color system, so one circuit should be fitted with 'red' roundels, one with 'blue,' and one with 'green.' The teaser strips may use the same arrangement, but 'light amber' or 'straw' roundels are often substituted for the 'green.' Green is not often needed overhead; the amber is more useful and gives a stronger light. Amber and blue give an almost white light. If green light should be required, the amber roundels can be removed and replaced with a green gelatine.

AREA SPOTLIGHTS. For daylight exteriors, and interiors lit either by daylight or electric light, the combination of No. 62 'Light Scarlet' (actually a pale pinkish amber) on the strong side, and nothing or No. 1 'Frost' on the weak side will prove ideal. For sunset or firelight effects, try one of the following on the strong side: No. 56 'Dark Straw,' No. 57 'Light Amber,' No. 58 'Medium Amber,' No. 60 'Dark Amber,' or No. 61 'Orange.' If a more colorful effect is desired, No. 26 'Light Sky Blue' may be used on the weak side. For moonlight effects, blue mediums should not be used, as they bring out the red in faces and costumes and produce an effect utterly unlike moonlight. Try No. 43 'Light Blue Green' for the strong side, and either omit the weak side altogether or use No. 46 'Dark Blue Green.'

If none of these suggestions work, or if you have some special problem, such as a fantasy, it will pay you to experiment with the following colors, which are listed with the warmest first and the coolest last: No. 2 'Light Flesh Pink,' No. 9 'Dubarry Pink,' No. 54 'Light Straw,' No. 53 'Very Light Straw,' No. 17 'Special Lavender.'

BACKINGS. These are normally lit with the same mediums that are used on the acting areas.

SKIES. For late evening or night skies use No. 36 'Nonfade Blue' or No. 38 'Dark Navy Blue.' Most gelatines are either too vivid or too purple for a daylight sky. Try taking a sheet of No. 30 'Light Blue Special,' or No. 40 'Light Green Blue,' and snipping a number of small holes in it with a pair of scissors. Place a No. 1 'Frost' over this and place it in an overhead flood. The frost will diffuse the light so that an even blue will result. If the color suits you, you can equip the other overhead floods in the same way.

EQUIPMENT AND METHODS

A knowledge of lighting equipment is vital, but the technical methods of using it are extremely simple.

EQUIPMENT AND METHODS—A. WIRING

If your stage is not permanently wired, the instruments may be connected with the control board by No. 14 twin-conductor cable. The cable may be the type known as 'stage' cable. Rubber-covered cable is decidedly better but also more expensive. Short cables are called 'jumpers.' In permanent installations, pairs of wires are run from the control board to various points around the stage where instruments are likely to be located. These wires are run in metal conduits of the type used for residence wiring.

Connectors. Cables are connected with the board on one end and with the instrument on the other by means of 15-ampere 'connectors,' like the one shown in Fig. 3, Pl. XXXV, p. 260. The 'load' half of the connector has two projecting pins of brass. The 'line' side has two holes into which the pins fit. The pins are slotted. If they do not fit snugly, they can be enlarged by driving a knifeblade into the slots. A knot like that shown in Fig. 3 keeps the connector from being pulled apart. As all wiring must be instantly interchangeable, this connector is the *only* type that should be used. Every cable and jumper should have its length in feet marked in white paint on the half-connector at each end. When wire runs in conduit, each circuit terminates in a 'pigtail,' which is a 1'6" length of rubber-covered cable fitted with a line connector.

EQUIPMENT AND METHODS—B. INSTRUMENT MOUNTINGS

By far the most convenient way to mount instruments is on a channel iron or an angle iron bored with ⅝" holes as shown in Fig. 4, Pl. XXXV. Square-headed ½" bolts are best, although bolts with hexagonal heads will do. The leather washer gives a joint which holds firmly and yet allows the instrument to be adjusted. A spot or floodlight hung in this way should have a 'yoke' mounting like that shown in Fig. 4. If the instrument is equipped with a 'flange' mounting (Fig. 5), an iron 'knuckle' will be needed. This is a piece of strap iron 2" wide by ³⁄₁₆" thick, bent at a right angle and bored with ⅝" holes at both ends. If striplights are equipped with stud mountings (Figs. 4 and 5, Pl. XXXIV, p. 250), they may be hung from channel or angle irons by means of knuckles (Fig. 5).

Pipe Mountings. When a spot or flood must be supported on a pipe batten or other pipe, a 'pipe clamp' (Fig. 3, Pl. XXXIV) is used. Similar clamps are sold to support striplights. When striplights are hung in the flies, a 'chain' mounting (Fig. 4) is better. An instrument hung in this way will swing back into position if it is knocked out of focus by a piece of moving scenery.

Stands. Backing lights are generally mounted on stands (Fig. 3, Pl. XXXV). A tall stand is called a 'giraffe.'

Wagons. Horizon strips are often mounted on wagons (Fig. 5, Pl. XXXIV). Similar wagons can be made for lights on stands. The stand should be attached to the wagon with stage screws, and the wagon should be weighted to minimize the danger of an upset.

EQUIPMENT AND METHODS—C. INSTRUMENT SPECIFICATIONS

Manufacturers' list prices are subject to discounts. When you order, be sure to mention your status as "school," "college," or "civic theater" and ask for the appropriate discounts. Instruments are

DIVINE COMEDY

Yale University Theater

Setting by **Peggy Clark**

Expressionistic settings like this depend on changes in the lighting for interest and variety. They should not be attempted without adequate electrical equipment and ample time for light rehearsals.

usually priced with accessories. As these are rarely the ones you want, you must state that your specifications cover only the instruments, and that you are listing accessories separately.

Lamp catalogs quote a 'rated life' for each lamp. However, as stage lamps are burned in closed housings without adequate ventilation, they cannot be expected to last for the full period.

If you are unable to afford the equipment described here, do not waste money buying cheap substitutes. You can easily make your own spotlights and floods. Use 'reflector lamps,' which are sold in 'spot' (#R/SP) and 'flood' (#R/FL) types. Both types come in 75-, 150-, and 300-watt sizes. They can be mounted in adjustable porcelain sockets. With a little ingenuity, you can bend coat-hanger wire to make holders that will attach to the socket and extend in front of the lamp to hold a color frame.

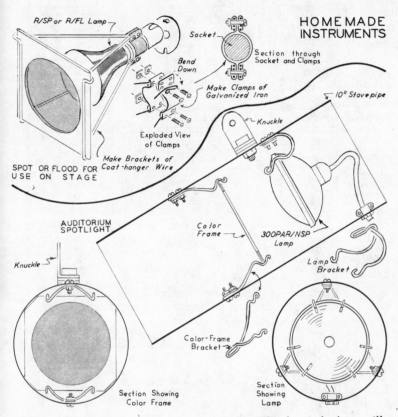

R/SP or R/FL Lamp

Socket

Bend
Down

Section through
Socket and Clamps

Make Clamps of
Galvanized Iron

Exploded View
of Clamps

Make Brackets of
Coat-hanger Wire

SPOT OR FLOOD FOR
USE ON STAGE

HOME MADE
INSTRUMENTS

10" Stovepipe

Knuckle

Color
Frame

300PAR/NSP
Lamp

Lamp
Bracket

AUDITORIUM
SPOTLIGHT

Knuckle

Color-Frame
Bracket

Section Showing
Color Frame

Section
Showing
Lamp

Spots and floods made in this way cannot be focused, they spill a good deal of light, and they are easily broken. On the other hand, they are both inexpensive and highly efficient.

Spotlights. You will need at least six ellipsoidal-reflector spotlights for auditorium spots and six of the stepped-lens type for teaser spots. Both types should be equipped with yoke mounting, 18″ asbestos-covered leads fitted with 15-ampere half-connector, vertical color-frame holder, and two color frames. If possible, add a few extra instruments of each type for use as specials.

Ellipsoidal-reflector type (Fig. 4, Pl. XXXV) with push-type framing shutters and 500-watt lamp (#500 T12/9 or #500 T12/8; the former gives 20% more light, but the latter will last about four times as long). Some companies make these with either a stepped-

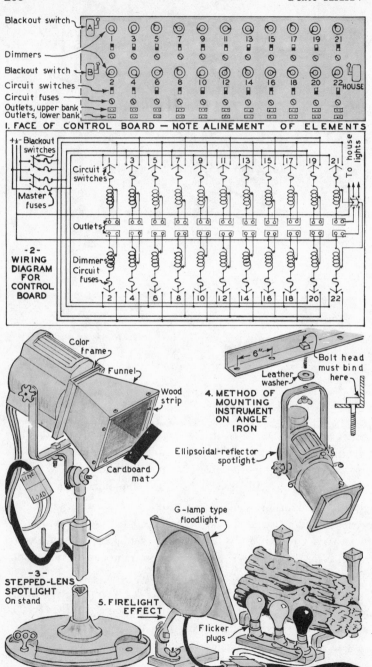

Blackout switch
Dimmers
Blackout switch
Circuit switches
Circuit fuses
Outlets, upper bank
Outlets, lower bank

I. FACE OF CONTROL BOARD — NOTE ALINEMENT OF ELEMENTS

+±- Blackout switches
Circuit switches
Master fuses
Outlets
Dimmers
Circuit fuses
To house lights

-2- WIRING DIAGRAM FOR CONTROL BOARD

Color frame
Funnel
Wood strip
Cardboard mat
LINE LOAD

-3- STEPPED-LENS SPOTLIGHT On stand

6"
Bolt head must bind here
Leather washer
4. METHOD OF MOUNTING INSTRUMENT ON ANGLE IRON
Ellipsoidal-reflector spotlight

G-lamp type floodlight
5. FIRELIGHT EFFECT
Flicker plugs

lens or two plano-convex lenses. The plano-convex type costs more, but it spills less light—which is highly desirable for instruments used in the auditorium. Specify the lens size according to the distance from the instrument to the face of an actor standing in a downstage area. All sizes have about the same efficiency. The 6″-lens size fits average conditions.

For throws under 20′ — 4½″ lens.

For throws between 20′ and 35′ — 6″ lens.

For throws over 35′ — 8″ lens.

If you make your own auditorium spots, use 300-watt 'projector' lamp (300 PAR56/NSP). This fits a special heat-resistant 'mogul, end-prong socket.' Mount the lamp and color frame in a length of 10″ stovepipe. Leave pipe open at both ends and arrange color frame and lamp so that air can circulate freely. Otherwise, the lamp may crack from its own heat.

Stepped-lens type (Fig. 3, Pl. XXXV), 9″ x 9″ x 8½″, with spherical reflector and 50-watt lamp (#500 T20/64).

Floodlights. Both types listed serve the same purpose. The chimney type is better but more expensive. Both should be equipped with yoke mounting, 18″ asbestos-covered leads with 15-ampere half-connector, vertical color-frame holder, and two color frames.

Chimney type (Fig. 3, Pl. XXXIV), 500-watt (#500) or 1000-watt lamp (#1000), ellipsoidal reflector, and ventilating chimney.

G-lamp type (Fig. 5, Pl. XXXV). 400-watt lamp (#400 G/FL) and ellipsoidal reflector.

Striplights. The type listed will fit all striplight needs (see Figs. 4 and 5, Pl. XXXIV). Section 7′6″ long, with 15 individual spun-metal reflectors 6″ on centers, wired for 3 circuits of 500 watts each; 100-watt lamps (#100A); every circuit to have a 3′ rubber-covered lead at each end of the instrument (6 leads in all), so that two sections can be connected together; leads to be fitted with 15-ampere half-connectors, load connectors on one end, line connectors on the other; both stud and chain mountings; combination color frames for roundels and gelatines; set of roundels, 5 'red,' 5 'medium blue,' 5 'straw.'

Firelight Effect. As Fig. 5, Pl. XXXV shows, this consists of 3 ordinary sockets, 3 flicker devices of the type used in store windows and for Christmas trees, and 3 low-wattage lamps of different colors. A spot or flood, equipped with an amber gelatine, provides the principal light, while the small lamps come on and off at irregular intervals to provide a flickering glow on the edge of the fireplace.

CONTROL BOARD

A control board is simply a convenient arrangement for governing the amount of electrical current supplied to each lighting circuit.

Elements. The elements used in the board are:

Switches. These turn the lights on and off. They may also be used to change the route by which the current travels.

Fuses. These are safety devices. They prevent fires and also protect your equipment from overloads. Never swear at a fuse when it blows. It sacrificed itself in the line of duty and may have saved you a twenty-dollar repair job or a twenty-thousand-dollar fire loss.

Circuit breakers that screw into regular fuse sockets are now available. As they can be reset by pushing a button, they are extremely convenient and never wear out.

Dimmers. These regulate the amount of current in each circuit and therefore the brightness of the light. There are three types:

(1) Resistance dimmers are necessary with direct current, but they are obsolete for alternating current. The load must match the dimmer. If a 1000-watt lamp is used with a 500-watt dimmer, the dimmer may burn out; if a 250-watt lamp is used, the lamp will still be shining when the dimmer is on its lowest point.

(2) Variable transformers handle any load from a single watt to their rated capacity. The only sizes you need are the 500-watt and the 1500-watt. If your dealer does not carry these, get the next larger sizes, which may be 750-watt and 1700-watt.

(3) Remote-control dimmers permit a board so small and portable that it can be operated from any part of the auditorium or stage. They are undoubtedly the dimmers of the future, but at present they are too elaborate and costly for ordinary use.

Connectors. Old-fashioned boards were 'wired-solid,' so that one dimmer always controlled one circuit. If the circuit did not happen to be in use, the dimmer was wasted, however much it

Plate XXXVI   263

1. ARRANGED BY R. AND L. SIDES

Teaser strip

1L 2L 3L 1R 2R 3R Red Blue Amber Specials

1   3   5   7   9   11 13 15 17 19 21

Footlights

4L 5L 6L 4R 5R 6R Red Blue Green Specials

2   4   6   8 10 12 14 16 18 20 22

2. GROUPED BY SIDES

Teaser strip

1L 1R
2L 2R Red Blue Amber
3L 3R   Specials

1   3   5   7   9   11 13 15 17 19 21

Footlights

4L 4R
5L 5R Red Blue Green
6L 6R   Specials

2   4   6   8 10   12 14 16 18 20 22

3. ARRANGED BY AREAS

Teaser strip

1L 1R 2L 2R 3L 3R Red Blue Amber Specials

1   3   5   7   9   11 13 15 17 19 21

Footlights

4L 4R 5L 5R 6L 6R Red Blue Green Specials

2   4   6   8 10 12 14 16 18 20 22

4. GROUPED BY AREAS

Teaser strip

1L 2L 3L
1R 2R 3R Red Blue Amber   Specials

1   3   5   7   9 11   13 15 17 19 21

Footlights

4L 5L 6L
4R 5R 6R Red Blue Green   Specials

2   4   6   8 10 12   14 16 18 20 22

METHODS OF SETTING UP CONTROL BOARD

might be needed elsewhere. In modern boards each circuit ends in a regular, 15-ampere line connector. A stage cable can be simply plugged into any of these. Circuits that run in conduit are equipped with a pigtail and load connector at the board end, so they can be plugged into any dimmer circuit desired.

Mastering. Light cues often require many changes to be made at once. This can be done mechanically by mounting a whole row of switch- or dimmer-handles on a single shaft and providing each handle with a locking device which either couples it to the shaft or permits it to operate independently. Such an interlocking system is expensive and almost worthless, though out-of-date manufacturers still recommend these dimmers highly.

Electrical mastering is both better and simpler. The board shown in Pl. XXXV, p. 260, has two master circuits, of the type known as 'blackout' circuits, each with its own switch. With this arrangement, a situation where the stage lights go on or off without affecting the moonlight outside becomes extremely easy; without such an arrangement, such a partial blackout becomes both complicated and noisy. Master dimmers may also be provided, so that several circuits can be handled either independently on their own dimmers or as a group by the master. This is extremely valuable, but it would probably not be worth while on a board as small as the one shown here.

Principles of Board Design. This subject is too complicated to be treated in detail, but much may be learned from a study of the diagrams in Pl. XXXV. Three principles are particularly important.

SIZE OF BOARD FACE. The operating face of the control board should be as small as possible so that all the equipment can be within easy reach of a single operator. A board over 4′ wide will require two or more operators, which not only is a nuisance but makes co-ordination difficult.

ALINEMENT. The operator should be able to find any handle instantly. This is possible only if the parts are alined so that the different elements—switches, dimmer handles, etc.—are in horizontal rows, and the elements belonging to each circuit are in vertical columns.

BALANCE. Ordinary electric wiring provides a 'neutral' and two 'hot' lines which are alternately positive and negative. The load on the two hot lines should be approximately equal, or the electrical system may suffer serious damage. The wiring diagram shown in Fig. 2, Pl. XXXV, runs both hot wires through both blackout switches. This looks a little complicated, but it is really simple and it balances the load automatically.

BOARD SETUP. The instrument circuits should be plugged into the board in a systematic arrangement, so that you may easily remember what dimmer controls what instrument. One of the plans shown in Pl. XXXVI, p. 263, should normally be followed.

Chapter XXII

PROCESS OF PRODUCTION

Work on the production starts when the script is first read. The preliminary interpretation must be done at this point, for it is foolish to select a play without making sure you can understand it. When the play has been chosen, the interpretive work is intensified. How far it is carried at this time depends on the policy of the director, but as a minimum the principal values, theme, and treatment (including spirit and style) and the rough characterizations must be determined. If any speeches seem inconsistent with the elements chosen, satisfactory explanations must be found.

PRELIMINARIES

The more you can get done before rehearsals start, the less trouble you will have and the better your production will be.

Production Plan. The general plan of production should be fixed as soon as possible. It should answer the following questions:

(1) How elaborate will the production be? Will you skimp or splurge? If money and effort are to be spent on certain items but not on others, which items are to be favored?

(2) Will the cast be large or small? Will you decrease it by cutting unnecessary characters? Or will you add more?

(3) How many sets will be used? How will the shifts, if any, be handled?

(4) Will the scenery be of new construction, or built by reassembling stock units, or will a stock set or a drapery cyclorama be used?

(5) Will many properties have to be made, or can they be taken from storage or borrowed?

(6) Will costumes be borrowed, altered, made, or rented?

(7) How important is the lighting? Will it be conventional or specialized?

Designs. The designs for scenery, costumes, etc. are generally worked out simultaneously with the production plan because the plan and the designs affect each other mutually. Ordinarily the working drawings for the scenery and the lighting-instrument lay-out are not made until the designs are completed.

Scripts. If printed scripts are used, they should be ordered as soon as the number required is definitely determined. If scripts are to be typewritten, they will have to wait until the director finishes any cutting he plans to do on the original.

Casting. When the rough characterizations have been decided upon, a meeting of the casting committee is called. (See p. 78.) This should be several days before the preliminary tryouts, which are scheduled for a week or ten days before the first rehearsal. If tryouts are held earlier, interest will sag. If they are held later, there will be no time to fill roles which are not assigned during the regular tryouts. As soon as an actor is cast, he should be given his script so that he can start familiarizing himself with the play.

Staff. Crew heads should be appointed as soon as possible, given a rough idea of the task ahead, and told to recruit their crews.

STAFF MEETING. This should be held as soon as active work on the production is ready to start, which is usually about a week before the first rehearsal. All designers, crew heads, and assistant heads should attend. The director gives the crew heads their scripts. He then shows whatever plans, sketches, working drawings, models, etc. have been prepared, or he may display pictures in books or magazines to illustrate points on costume or furniture style, or on methods of interior decoration.

The production plan is then stated briefly, and the task of each crew outlined. Any special difficulties are pointed out so that work may be started on them at once. Decisions as to whether doubtful items will be considered scenery, lights, props, or costumes are made at this time. The prop master should be warned that the prop list in the printed script will be changed by both omissions and additions. Everyone is encouraged to ask questions, as this is the best way to avoid difficulties and misunderstandings later.

The staff meeting is valuable not merely because it permits necessary instructions to be given briefly, but also because it makes the crew heads realize that they are part of an organization working toward a common goal.

REHEARSALS

There are two distinct ways of arranging rehearsals. One is to schedule the various scenes in an arbitrary order, so that all those involving the same group of actors can be rehearsed together. This plan is supposed to save time, because actors need not attend except when their scenes are being rehearsed, and also because troublesome scenes can be rehearsed more often than those which flow smoothly. However, in order that the actors may learn the continuity of the play, special rehearsals are required in which the scenes are run through in their natural order; so in the end the method may lose more time than it gains. I have never used it myself and therefore am not able to judge it fairly.

In the other method, the play is rehearsed an act at a time until it has been memorized. From then on the whole play is gone through at every rehearsal. Little time is really wasted by this system. Actors are not called unless they appear in the act being rehearsed, and those with small roles are allowed to be absent from several of the other rehearsals. Easy scenes are run through without interruption. More time is spent on difficult scenes, and special rehearsals may be called for them if they need it. This system not only stresses continuity but permits the entire schedule of regular rehearsals to be published in advance, which makes it possible for the actors to plan ahead. If the acts do not prove convenient divisions, some other apportionment of the play can be made.

Length and Number of Rehearsals. Regular rehearsals should each last three hours, if possible. Shorter periods are inefficient. During the early rehearsals, when the action is being worked out and the acts are being rehearsed separately, each act (or each third of the play) will require about three hours. With a shorter rehearsal period or an inexperienced cast, the play must be divided into more than three sections. Later, when the whole play is to be run through at each rehearsal, the play itself will take about two hours, and at least an hour is required for correction and comment. If the rehearsal lasts too long, actors grow weary and lose interest. Amateurs rarely learn much after working three hours, so this period is both a practical minimum and a practical maximum. From eighteen to thirty regular three-hour rehearsals will be needed, depending on the complexity of the play and the experience of the cast.

Dress rehearsals should last five hours, from the time the actors are told to arrive at the theater until the time they are dismissed. If they are kept longer, they are not likely to sparkle the following evening. At least two dress rehearsals are necessary, three are better, and four or even five may be desirable if the production presents difficulties in scenery or lighting.

Preliminary Rehearsals. Before putting the actors on the stage and giving them movements, groupings, etc., some directors like to spend one or more rehearsals reading the play and discussing it. I once conducted a careful experiment by producing the same play with two casts and the same number of rehearsals. One began work on stage immediately. The other took part in an elaborate preliminary discussion in which the meaning of every line was analyzed. Some of the actors in the second cast were highly intelligent, but during the subsequent rehearsals none of them gave any evidence of remembering these preliminary discussions. Since that experience, I have always started stage work immediately.

Foundation Rehearsals. During the first nine rehearsals the foundations of the action should be laid. This means: (1) that the groupings and movements are worked out and made to fit with the essential business; (2) that all motivations are supplied; (3) that both lines and action are learned. In other words, by the tenth rehearsal the cast should be able to give a scratch performance, which would certainly lack artistry but which would at least flow smoothly.

Details should not be stressed during this foundation period. If an actor has a complicated piece of business such as setting a table, he should be allowed to go through the motions vaguely without worrying about the exact location of each fork or the exact cue for placing it. The director who insists on too much detail at the start confuses the actor. On the other hand, the actor should not be

Yale University Theater

THE MURDERERS   Setting by Mary Lou Williams

This is a realistic melodrama, and the setting is done in complete detail. However, both the mood and composition depend chiefly on the somber lighting. The contrast between deep pools of shadow and broken areas of light is characteristic of modern melodramas of action.

permitted to make simple mistakes. If the character uses a New York telephone, the actor should be told at once to dial seven figures instead of the four or five which are required in his home town.

FIRST REHEARSAL. The director supervises the placement of rehearsal furniture before the actors arrive (Fig. 3, Pl. XXV, p. 174). He begins the rehearsal itself with a detailed explanation of the set, showing sketches and ground plans, and identifying each piece of furniture and each door and window.

Next, the actors who open the play are grouped and told to start reading. From then on they read the lines and follow any directions given them by the director. Actors are encouraged to make small movements which come naturally, but they should not sit, rise, or make large movements without explicit instructions. Such actions are almost certain to conflict with the director's plans. For the same reason actors should ignore any movements called for by the stage directions. Business inherent in the lines—such as holding out a cigarette case on the line "Cigarette?"—can normally be inserted by the actor without waiting for directions.

Whenever a scene is reached for which the director has designed a definite grouping, the actors are placed in the proper positions. Simple floor patterns may also be explained at this first rehearsal, but complicated ones are merely roughed in and the details left until later.

No matter how carefully the director has planned in advance, difficulties are certain to arise. There may be an overwhelming reason why an actor should be DL. and another, equally overwhelming reason why he should be UC. at the same moment. Some essential act may be impossible without destroying an important grouping, or perhaps the act is possible but demands a movement which is too awkward to be satisfactory. If the director cannot solve such difficulties at once, he does not waste time on them. Instead, he points out the nature of the difficulty, promises to correct it in the future, and goes on with the rehearsal.

Finish the act in a little over two-thirds of the rehearsal period. During the remaining time, the act is run through again rapidly. The actors are not interrupted unless they forget something or unless the director sees a way to clear up some difficulty in a few words. This repetition of the act at the end of the rehearsal is vital. It fixes in the actor's memory what has been learned. Without the repetition, half of what has been done will be forgotten by the next rehearsal. Furthermore, you will find that on the repeat, many difficulties disappear as if by magic. For these reasons the director should always leave time for a repeat, even if he does not complete the act. During the repeat, the director notes and lists the principal remaining problems. He solves as many of these as he can before the next rehearsal.

SECOND REHEARSAL. The act is worked through again. When a trouble spot is reached, the director interrupts. If he has solved the difficulty, he makes the necessary explanations and corrections. If not, he may experiment with possible solutions or he may ask the actors for suggestions. If results are not forthcoming almost immediately, the director drops the problem and goes on with the re-

hearsal. The last forty-five minutes of the rehearsal are used to repeat the act.

THIRD REHEARSAL. This is devoted to memory training. The actors are not permitted to use their scripts, even if they have to be
prompted word for word. Scripts interfere with the business and
inhibit the emotions, so the actors must dispense with them at all
costs. The act should be run through as often as time permits.
The director interrupts to correct mistakes and to clear up easily
solved difficulties, but he should not introduce anything new or
make extensive corrections. Also, the director can accomplish a
good deal in whispered conferences with offstage actors.

FOURTH TO NINTH REHEARSALS. During the fourth and fifth rehearsals Act II is treated exactly as Act I was in the first and second. In the sixth rehearsal Act I is run through once to keep it fresh
in the actors' minds and then Act II is run through as often as
possible in the remaining time. Scripts must not be used. Act III is
roughed out in the seventh and eighth rehearsals, and in the ninth
rehearsal the whole play is run through for memory without scripts.

Pick-up Rehearsals. The play should now be in a state where
the actors can go through it without undue prompting and without
breaks in the action. If they have not reached that stage, one or two
more rehearsals on fundamentals may be needed.

Speed Rehearsal. In this rehearsal the play is raced through at
top speed, like a film run too fast. Actions may be blurred and
words may stumble over each other, but nothing, however small,
should be omitted. Devote an hour to each act and try to get through
it three times. Such a speed rehearsal is a great strain on everyone.
The prompter must be prepared to cut in if an actor delays his cue
by a single beat, and the director must constantly call for more
speed, or the actors will slow down. However, the results are worth
the effort. Nothing else gives the actors such a firm command of
their lines. The great concentration required does much to destroy
self-consciousness. Finally, the ability to play at high speed has been
demonstrated, so that there is no excuse for dragging during the
later rehearsals or in performance.

Pointing Rehearsals. During the next three or four rehearsals:
(1) Details are added in business and movement. (2) Groupings

and poses are refined. (3) Dull scenes are enlivened by adding touches. (4) Unsatisfactory matters are corrected; there will usually be a number of these—groupings which do not distribute emphasis correctly, movements which show false relationships, etc.

The best plan is to start with the beginning of Act I and make each correction as you come to it. Continue in this way until there is about one page of script left for each remaining minute of rehearsal. Then stop making corrections and run through the rest of the play by the end of rehearsal. At the next rehearsal run through the play until you come to the spot where you stopped work the time before. Then proceed slowly, making corrections and adding details until there is just time to run through the rest of the play before the rehearsal ends. Continue in this way at each rehearsal until the whole play has been worked over.

Technical Rehearsals. If the play presents many scene shifts or other difficult technical problems, special technical rehearsals must be called, at which only the crews involved are present and at which the whole time is devoted to their problems. Whether or not such special technical rehearsals are necessary, part of the time of the later rehearsals must be spent on minor technical problems such as costumes, make-up, light and sound cues, accustoming actors to complicated props, etc. Sometimes all these matters can be taken up at one rehearsal, which is then given over entirely to them. The actors run through the play and each technical detail is worked out as it is reached. More often, such matters are dealt with in regular rehearsals. An actor may use an offstage period to put on a costume or make-up. He then wears this during his next appearance so that the director, designers, and crew heads may check it. Work on sound and light cues is interpolated in the same fashion.

Rehearsals for Pacing and Build. One or two rehearsals near the end should be reserved for work on pacing and build. The director must have noted those scenes which demand this treatment and be prepared for them. Scenes rarely need to be slowed down, but some will call for a faster tempo and others will require a steadily increasing pace which is really a part of build. Probably the technical aspects of the builds, such as increasing numbers of actors, greater movement, etc. will have already been worked out, but builds in emotional tension can hardly be treated effectively until the play is complete and running smoothly. It is this type of build which should be stressed in these rehearsals.

Polishing Rehearsals. The last two or three rehearsals are run through without breaks except at the intermissions. The assistant stage manager sits beside the director in the auditorium so that she can take his notes, and the actors are told to get along as well as they can without a prompter. Between acts the cast is called to the footlights. The director's notes are read and supplemented with any necessary explanations. Such rehearsals give the play its final polish and are an important element in assuring smooth performances.

Special Rehearsals. If the play involves important crowd scenes, they should be worked out at special crowd rehearsals. These are scheduled between regular rehearsals until the crowd knows its movements and cues. If any principals work directly with the crowd, as Mark Antony does in *Julius Caesar,* they must attend these rehearsals. When the crowd has a fair idea of its functions, it should be called for every second or third regular rehearsal. In the other rehearsals any crowd lines are read by the assistant stage manager. This procedure permits the members of the crowd to gain a feeling of the continuity as a whole, but does not demand an undue amount of rehearsal from them. It also provides a number of rehearsals in which the principals can work without the distractions which are inevitable when a large number of actors are present.

Scenes requiring much detailed business, such as fights and love scenes, must also be worked out at special rehearsals. These should last about an hour each and be scheduled to suit the convenience of the actors involved. Work on such scenes is hopeless until the lines have been mastered, but should be started as soon thereafter as possible. The number of special rehearsals will depend on the difficulty of the individual scenes and also on the time the actors and director can devote to this work.

Coaching. Coaching differs from directing in that it deals with the individual actor and aims primarily at increasing his general acting ability rather than merely fitting him for the current play. Even the best coaching cannot turn a bad production into a good one, but it can elevate a fair production to a fine one. In amateur

Yale University Theater

HAMLET

Setting by Mary Elizabeth Plehn

Shakespeare is undoubtedly effective when produced in a replica of an Elizabethan theater. However, unless the direction is extremely skillful, such a production can easily turn into a stilted museum piece. Also, I question whether a play staged in this manner ever reaches either the dramatic intensity or the poetic beauty which can be attained by the more modern methods of staging.

work, coaching does more than anything else to raise the standard of the acting.

The director should spend at least one one-hour coaching period with each actor, from the lead to the most insignificant bit player. With a large cast this consumes much time, but it also pays big dividends both in the current play and in any future work with the same actors.

An actor should not be called for a coaching period until he is ready for it. Readiness involves subtle psychological matters which directors can learn only by experience, but the following general principles can be laid down. If an actor badly misinterprets his role, or displays any serious technical deficiencies, e.g., bad posture,

Yale University Theater

HENRY IV, PART I

Setting by Frank Bevan

Here we have a modern adaptation of an Elizabethan stage. It has most of the advantages and
none of the faults of a reproduction like the one
shown on the opposite page. A simplified setting of
this type provides an excellent solution to the problem of producing Shakespeare on either a limited
stage or a limited budget. Elaborate lighting effects are out of key and should be avoided.

inhibited movements, or a tendency to mouth his words, his coaching on these points should begin as soon as rehearsals start. Such
actors will probably require additional coaching later. With other
actors, coaching is wasted until the foundation rehearsals of the play
are over and the actor has learned his lines.

Each actor presents special coaching problems. Until the director
learns to recognize these he will do well to treat matters in the following order:

(1) Bring out the interpretation of the play by asking the actor
to state what he expects the audience to get from the performance
in return for the time and money they will spend. Is the play a
comedy to make them laugh? A melodrama to thrill them? A
drama to stir their emotions? In other words, the director should
have the actor outline the principal values in his own language.
Next, ask him to name the principal character (see p. 42). I find
that specifying the principal gives an actor a perspective on the
structure of the play which he may otherwise lack. This is true
even where the identity of the principal is obvious, but, of course,

it is especially important if the principal does not have the largest or most prominent role. Then, if the actor does not play the principal part himself, the director should ask him to describe the function of his own character and show how it contributes to the play. Even an intelligent actor will find these questions difficult, and the director may have to supply broad hints. Nevertheless, directing the actor's attention to these points will work wonders with his understanding of the play, particularly if he is made to realize that *his job is to do everything that will add to, and nothing that will detract from, the contribution of his part to the purpose of the play as a whole.*

(2) Correct any technical weaknesses that the actor may have displayed in speech, posture, footwork, etc.

(3) Work out small details of his business. This really amounts to a brief private rehearsal, but it is usually most conveniently handled during a coaching period.

(4) Ask the actor what problems of interpretation or technique have troubled him, and help him to solve them.

(5) Finally, show him how to interpret lines (see p. 46) and how to work out a silent script (see p. 134). Either his first scene or his most difficult scene may be used for an example. Even if there is only time to cover half a page, this work will produce gratifying results.

Dress Rehearsals. The purpose of dress rehearsals is to weld the acting and technical work into a single whole. *The director should never change movements or business after dress rehearsals begin* unless he is compelled to do so by some unforeseen technical difficulty.

The first dress rehearsal is devoted to fitting the technical matters, such as scenery, costumes, lights, etc., into the play, to accustoming the actors to these things, and to working out the problems they raise. The actors should run through their lines and business without attempting to get into character.

The last dress rehearsal should be run off in all details as nearly as possible like a performance, even to the point of raising the curtain at the usual time.

If there are more than two dress rehearsals, the treatment of those between the first and last depends on the technical condition of the play. If the scene shifts, light cues, etc. are ragged, it may be necessary to devote a good deal of time to them and even to interrupt the rehearsal at frequent intervals to repeat a missed cue or correct an unsatisfactory effect. When technical matters are well in hand, it is best to run through each act from curtain to curtain without interruptions, and to save corrections and comments for the intermissions.

Curtain Calls. Both audiences and actors like curtain calls. After serious plays, however, they break the spell. The spell is also broken if a 'dead' character takes a bow. If the 'corpse' remains on stage at the end of the last act, this difficulty can be avoided by taking one 'action' call, i.e., having the actors stay in character and enact a brief pantomime, such as gathering sadly around the body. In ordinary plays, curtain calls are highly desirable and they should be carefully rehearsed. Usually the actors stand in pairs and bow first to the audience, then to each other, and then to the audience again, while the curtains open and close.

With a small auditorium, it is difficult to get more than three calls. The first call usually consists of four to six leads. The second call is taken by the principal supporting players without the leads or the minor actors. The last call is taken by the whole company. A cast of any size usually presents a traffic problem in getting one group on and another off through a limited number of doorways. This problem must be given due consideration during dress rehearsals.

PERFORMANCES

The performance is the proof of the production. Surprises are always to be expected. Plays that promise to be sure-fire hits will fail dismally, but next time an apparent failure may blossom into a success.

Actors should arrive at least an hour and a half before curtain time. The stage manager must make a record of their presence, so he will know when the cast is complete. If they show any tendency to dawdle, he should insist that they get made up and dressed at once.

The director should reach the theater at least an hour before the first performance and half an hour before subsequent performances. He rarely has much to do, but his presence inspires confidence. Also, if emergencies arise, he must be there to deal with them.

Five minutes before curtain time the stage manager gathers the cast and available staff members on stage so that the director can start them off with a little talk. The main purpose of this is to give the actors something to think about and thus check any tendency to stage fright. However, the director can use his talk to remind the actors to speak with extra volume and clarity for the first five minutes while the audience is settling down. Other important points which the actors have shown a tendency to forget may also be mentioned. The talk should end with a few compliments and the director's best wishes.

If the production has been well prepared, the director does not stay backstage but sits in the last row of the auditorium. The production itself is left in charge of the stage manager.

Curtain. An audience is almost never on time, and it is hardly wise to start the performance while people are still pouring down the aisle. A method should be arranged so that the house manager can signal the stage manager. This signal is given at the first lull in the stream of late-comers. The stage manager glances around the stage to see that everything is ready and that the actors are in their places. He then signals the electrician to take the house lights down and bring up the footlights. This is done slowly to permit stragglers in the auditorium to scurry to their seats. If a warning chime is used, it should be struck as the house lights dim. When the electrician reports that the house lights are out, the stage manager gives the signal for the curtain and the play begins.

Intermissions. When the curtain closes at the end of the act, the stage manager cries "Strike!" in a loud, clear voice. This is the signal for the crews to shift the set if necessary and for the actors to change their costumes. Presumably there will be enough applause to keep the audience from hearing the cry. When the applause begins to die, the stage manager signals the electrician to bring up the house lights slowly and dim the footlights. After the house lights are up, they should aways be checked by the stage manager, because even the most reliable electricians have been known to make mistakes which left the audience in darkness.

The length of the intermissions depends partly on the time required for costume and scene changes, and partly on local custom. If coffee is served in the lobby, one intermission must last ten or twelve minutes. If there is no coffee, one intermission of five minutes and one of eight minutes is a satisfactory arrangement. The shorter intermission should come first, unless there is a difficult scene or costume change between the first two acts, in which case the long intermission will be needed for the change. The length of the intermissions should be printed in the program, so spectators can choose the best time for a cup of coffee or a smoke.

A minute before the end of the intermission, the lobby lights are flicked off and on as a warning that the curtain is about to rise.

The director should always go backstage during the first intermission to encourage the actors with any compliments that they may have deserved. He should not upset actors with criticisms or corrections at this time. However, if they have set too slow a pace or spoken too softly, he may tell them to "Pick it up" or "Make it louder."

Assistant Stage Manager.   During the performance, the assistant stage manager sits in the wings and prompts. She should be placed as far downstage as possible so that her voice may be directed at an upstage angle. This will make her more audible to the actors than to the audience. She must follow every word of the play, for if she lets her attention wander for an instant, some actor is sure to forget his lines.

In addition to her work as prompter, the assistant stage manager usually signals cues to actors who cannot see the stage. She also handles minor sound effects such as doorbells. She should mark in the script the times when the curtains open and close on each scene and also any audible audience reactions such as laughter, applause, etc.

Actors.   When an actor is not acting he should never be seen or heard. This means:

(1) No one should peep at the audience through the curtain or some convenient door.

(2) Actors should never appear in the auditorium or on the street in make-up. Friends who want to see them after the play should go backstage.

(3) Actors should never go into the auditorium during the performance, not even to watch the last scene from the obscurity of the back row. If one spectator notices that a character in the play has suddenly turned into little Willie Jones, the illusion of the play is spoiled for that spectator.

Afterward. The play is over when the last curtain falls on the last performance, but the production is not complete until the last borrowed garment and prop have been returned, and all scenery and equipment is dismantled and stored. Crew heads should supervise this work personally and check each item to make sure nothing has been overlooked. When everything has been completed, the crew head reports to the director so that he will know the facts in case any complaint or criticism should arise later.

Chapter XXIII

FINANCIAL MANAGEMENT

The commercial theater has been called with justice "the worst run business in America," and most amateur groups are no better than the professionals in this regard. There is no excuse for this. Even the most idealistic theater owes a due attention to business. Business means more money with which to pay for better equipment or a larger staff. Business means more tickets sold—and therefore a larger audience. Above all, good business methods mean financial self-respect.

FINANCIAL RECORDS

The financial records are generally kept by the treasurer, but the business manager, the director, and the technical director all play a part in designing the system and in providing the information on which the records are based.

Bookkeeping. Good business begins with accurate bookkeeping. As the number of entries will not be large, every organization can find some member who has had accounting experience and who is willing to undertake the small amount of work involved. The accounts will vary with the organization, but the following may be considered basic.

INCOME ACCOUNTS	EXPENSE ACCOUNTS	ASSETS & LIABILITIES
Season Tickets	Production Expense	Cash—General
Single Admissions	Salaries and Wages	Cash—Petty
Sales and Rentals	Rent	Stock
Program Income	Office Expense	Equipment
Miscellaneous Income	Promotion Expense	Accounts Payable
	Tickets	Accounts Receivable
	Advertising	Capital
	Program Expense	
	Miscellaneous Expense	

'Production Expense' should be handled with a separate account for each production. Anything bought for a particular production is charged to that production. The same rule applies to items like royalties and costume rentals. Materials such as lumber, hardware, canvas, and paint, which are bought for general use, are charged to 'Stock.' A rough inventory is taken at the end of each production and the materials used are then charged to the production.

Inventory. This need not be accurate and can be taken in half an hour. Items such as paint and canvas are estimated. When items, such as screws, come in boxes, only whole boxes are included in the inventory; broken boxes are charged to the production. The same rule applies to lumber: whole pieces are counted as 'Stock'; cut pieces are charged to the production.

As an example of this method, suppose the inventory taken before 'Production #80' shows one box of $\frac{7}{8}'' \times 9$ screws at 70¢ a box. During the production four more boxes are bought at 75¢ a box and charged to 'Stock.' The total cost of the five boxes is therefore $3.70 or 74¢ a box. When inventory is taken after the production, you find three unopened boxes and one from which only a few screws have been removed. You count only the unopened boxes in your new inventory, so you must charge two boxes to 'Production #80' at $1.48 and credit the same amount to 'Stock.'

EQUIPMENT. Items such as spotlights should be charged to 'Equipment.' Each year 10% can be marked off to depreciation, but any lighting instrument or other comparable piece of equipment is worth at least $3.00 if it is worth keeping at all, and it should not be inventoried below this figure. The only satisfactory way to inventory scenery is to decide arbitrarily that each unit (flat, ceiling, border, door, door frame, etc.) is worth $3.00. If a piece of stock scenery is built during a production, the materials used in it are charged to the production. The production is then credited with $3.00 and the same sum is charged to 'Equipment.' When a stock unit is destroyed during a production, either by accident or through alterations which make it worthless for other plays, the production is charged $3.00, and $3.00 is credited to 'Equipment.'

Budget. No expenditure is ever justified in itself but only in relation to: (1) available or estimated funds, (2) the other demands on your resources. The intelligent way to control your finances is through a budget in which your various items of income and expenditure can all be considered at one time and weighed against each other.

Before the season begins, list your sources of income. These should correspond to your income accounts. Opposite each one write the amount you can conservatively expect to receive. The total will be your gross income for the season. Next list your fixed expenses such as rent, salaries, etc. Subtract these from your income and the result is the amount you can allot to production expenses, equipment, and other items you can control. Now distribute this among the various expense accounts. Royalties are usually fixed in advance and can be set down at once against the production to which they apply. Other items may be more difficult to estimate unless you have a set of well kept books for the previous season. If you have such books, you should be able to determine your probable expenses with fair accuracy. Otherwise you may be reduced to guessing, but a considered guess will give you a basis by which your actual expenditures can be measured. If after one or two productions you find that certain guesses have been too high or too low, you can revise the budget for the rest of the season with this in mind.

The items listed in the budget should correspond to the titles of the accounts in your books. It does not help the director to be told that he can spend $300 on his first production if the books are kept in such a way that 'Lumber' is handled as an expense account. Such a method would provide no way to distinguish the cost of the lumber used in the production from lumber bought and kept in stock, which is not an expense but an asset.

PROMOTION

If you present a definite season, with the number of productions fixed in advance and a more or less stable audience, a 'membership' or 'season ticket' campaign is advisable, because: (1) your income, or at least your minimum income, is fixed in advance and you can prepare your budget with assurance; (2) campaign methods will sell many more tickets than ordinary publicity; (3) you can count on a larger attendance and are less at the mercy of weather, competing events, etc. Campaigning methods are set out in detail in a pamphlet called *Building an Amateur Audience* (see Bibliography, p. 289).

Publicity. You will need publicity for two purposes: (1) to inform prospective spectators of the nature of your plays and the dates of your performances, and, if possible, to induce them to attend; (2) to inform prospective participants of the nature and dates of your activities, such as tryouts, and, if possible, to induce them to attend.

Publicity should be reasonably dignified, appropriate to the play, and not too expensive. It should aim at increasing the attendance rather than at flattering the vanity or furthering the interests of any individual or inner group. Within these limitations it can be said in general that the more publicity you obtain, and the more striking it is, the better.

NEWSPAPERS. These provide your most convenient means of publicity, but the road to newspaper publicity is paved with many annoyances and disappointments. The following suggestions may help you to avoid some of these.

(1) Newspaper people have their own ideas of what constitutes news. One paper will accept almost any girl's picture but will not print a man's picture unless he has been convicted of murder or been elected President of the United States. Other papers feel that women represent sex, which is obscene and should be avoided. There are endless taboos and blind spots of this sort. No argument will change them. All you can do is to learn what 'policies' a particular paper has and then try to take advantage of the useful ones and avoid hopeless conflicts with the unpleasant ones.

(2) Competitive spirit is strong between the staffs of different papers, even when the papers themselves are under the same ownership. Never give two papers exactly the same story. If the main point must be the same, as when a new play is announced, vary the story by giving one paper a brief synopsis of the play, another some anecdotes of its Broadway run, etc. Stories should be divided fairly among the various papers. The smaller papers will not expect as many 'breaks' as the larger papers but they must receive their share.

(3) Do not put more than one real point in a story, or use more than one such point in an interview. If you do, you will help neither yourself nor the paper. Most people read only the first paragraph, and the rest of the story is wasted except in so far as a long article is more impressive than a short one. Try to have as many different stories as possible with a point for each. Thus, if you announce the whole cast at once, you have only one story, but if you announce the leads first, then supply an article on some cast member who happens to be locally prominent, and finally release the names of the whole cast, you will have three stories. Moreover they will actually be more interesting because they will not be overcrowded.

(4) In towns under a hundred thousand population the social page is often your best outlet, even though you may feel that your stories belong on the dramatic page.

(5) Newspaper reporting is grossly inaccurate. If the stories printed about your work contain fewer than one major mistake of fact to every two inches of type, you may consider yourself lucky.

(6) Reviews are an essential part of your publicity. Try to have your work treated seriously rather than in an all-the-home-talent-were-wonderful spirit, but never complain of an unfair review. It does no good and puts you in a bad light. Console yourself with the thought that, in the long run, you will receive far more undeserved praise than undeserved criticism. If reviews irritate you, stop reading them. They will rarely teach you anything. Few papers can afford reviewers who know as much about the theater as you do yourself.

(7) Photographs are the best possible newspaper publicity, but most papers insist on taking their own pictures and most press photographers are interested in nothing but crowding as many faces as possible in front of the camera. Plan your pictures in advance. Choose situations where a number of actors can be grouped close together with their faces showing and yet doing something both interesting and dramatic.

(8) You may be forced to buy newspaper advertising to obtain publicity, but avoid it if possible. It will not sell enough tickets to pay one-tenth of its cost.

POSTERS. Silk-screen posters displayed in store windows or other public places are excellent publicity. Your local library can recommend a book on the subject, and your art store will give you other helpful information. If some member of your group does the work, the cost is extremely low.

WINDOW DISPLAYS. Often some store will decorate a window for you or let you decorate it. The shop that provides the gowns for the actresses may display them beforehand with a poster announcing the play.

MISCELLANEOUS. Unusual publicity stunts are particularly effective. One theater organized a half-mile street parade to announce an old-fashioned melodrama. Another gave a cup each year to the citizen who had made the greatest contribution to the life of the city. The more ideas of this sort you can devise, the better known your theater will be.

HANDLING TICKETS

Seats should always be reserved. This involves keeping the box office open for several days before the run of the play begins, but it is not difficult to obtain volunteers for this service. Many groups have ticket agencies at some central location, such as a student union or a downtown shop.

Tickets. When seats are reserved, the row and seat number must be on each individual ticket. These can be written in by hand, if only one performance is contemplated. However, if you plan a number of performances, either of one or of several productions, it is cheaper and more satisfactory to buy your tickets from some company like the Globe Ticket Co., 625 Eighth Ave., New York, N. Y., which furnishes sets of tickets with the seat numbers individually printed. As you can rarely be sure of the dates in advance, the sets of tickets should be numbered rather than dated. The numbers will then correspond to particular performances. It is well to distinguish the sets of tickets by having them printed on stocks of different colors.

Passes. You will have to provide each newspaper with two passes for the opening performance of every production, and if a paper demands more than two passes you are not in a position to

VENICE PRESERVED   Setting by Donald Oenslager

Elaborate productions like this are impossible without a sound financial organization. Without effective publicity, there will be no audience to see the play. A theater which thinks wholly of the box office has little value, but a theater which ignores the box office cannot exist at all.

refuse. Merchants who lend articles or contribute services should be given passes. This is not merely a matter of common decency but is necessary to build up good will. No other passes should be given, even at the risk of your being considered stingy. People who enter free usually adopt a critical attitude and will exert a chilling influence on the legitimate spectators around them. Once you start giving passes you will be unable to stop. It may seem mean to refuse a pass to Bill, who has worked hard building scenery and is too poor to afford a ticket, but if you give him one, Mary will insist that she has also worked hard rehearsing her part and that if she is not given a pass her mother will not be able to see her act. Some one else will then advance a claim, and soon all your best customers will be occupying free seats.

Length of Run. A full house is much easier to play to than a half-empty one. Try to fit the number of your performances to your probable attendance. It is better to turn a few people away than to add an extra performance. Those who are turned away will complain, but they will come early next time.

If your audience does not fill the auditorium, the balcony should be shut off. Another device, called 'dressing the house,' consists of leaving one or two empty seats in each row. If skillfully done, this will make the audience seem much larger than it really is.

PROGRAMS

People feel angry or hurt when their names are misspelled, misapplied, or omitted. To avoid this, the program must be edited with great care. The fact that program preparation is always a last-minute task makes mistakes fatally easy and is an added reason for taking pains. Before the copy goes to the printer it should be brought to rehearsal, and every staff member and actor should be asked to read it through carefully and call attention to mistakes. This process should be repeated with the printer's proof.

Costumes, properties, or services supplied gratis by business houses should be adequately acknowledged in the program.

If your program is to be printed, the work will take several days. This may make it necessary to have final additions and changes multigraphed on separate sheets and inserted by the ushers.

CURTAIN

BIBLIOGRAPHY

Organization

Dean, Alexander. *Little Theatre Organization and Management.* New York: D. Appleton-Century Co., 1926.
  Invaluable.

Nelms, Henning. *Building an Amateur Audience.* New York: Samuel French, 1936.
  Out of print but contains complete instructions for conducting a subscription campaign.

Organizing a Community Theatre. Cleveland, Ohio: National Theatre Conference, c/o Western Reserve University, 1945.
  Paper-bound pamphlet with each chapter written by a different director.

Directing and Acting

Dean, Alexander. *Fundamentals of Play Directing.* Revised edition, with revisions and a chapter on central staging by Lawrence Carra. New York: Holt, Rinehart and Winston, Inc., 1965.
  This book was left unfinished at Mr. Dean's death, so it contains only half of his enormous contributions to the technique of directing. It includes much material on acting and many exercises that may be used in connection with this volume.

Dolman, John, Jr. *The Art of Play Production,* 2nd ed. New York: Harper and Bros., 1947.
  The chapters on practical art theory are essential for any real understanding of the theater.

Speech

Avery, Elizabeth, Jane Dorsey, and Vera A. Sickles. *First Principles of Speech Training.* New York, London: D. Appleton & Co., 1928.
  Contains valuable exercises for correcting common speech defects.

Kenyon, John S., and Thomas A. Knott. *A Pronouncing Dictionary of American English,* 2nd ed. Springfield, Mass.: G. & C. Merriam Co., 1953.
  A satisfactory guide to pronunciation for theater work.

Design

None of these books deals directly with design for the theater, but all of them are stimulating and all contain valuable material.

Bragdon, Claude. *The Frozen Fountain.* New York: Alfred A. Knopf, 1932.
  An exciting introduction to the principles and methods of design.

Graves, Maitland. *The Art of Color and Design,* 2nd ed. New York: McGraw-Hill Book Co., 1951.
  This book is more complete than the others listed, but is less applicable to theatrical needs.

Pope, Arthur Upham. *The Language of Drawing and Painting.* Cambridge, Mass.: Harvard University Press, 1949.
This book contains the clearest and most useful discussion of pigment mixing and color design. Anyone working in color will find it invaluable.

Ramsey, Charles G., and Harold Reeve Sleeper. *Architectural Graphic Standards,* 5th ed. New York: John Wiley & Sons, Inc., 1956.
A compendium of data useful to scene designers.

Watkins, Charles Law. *Language of Design.* Washington, D. C.: Phillips Memorial Gallery, 1946.
Expensive and flimsily bound, but extremely valuable because it discusses at length the meaning of the various abstract art elements (see p. 61 of this volume).

Scenery and Properties

Burris-Meyer, Harold, and Edward C. Cole. *Scenery for the Theatre.* Boston: Little, Brown & Co., 1938.
An encyclopedic work describing the methods used in the commercial theater.

Nelms, Henning. *A Primer of Stagecraft.* New York: Dramatists Play Service, 1941.
A handbook covering in detail the simplified methods used by amateurs for the construction, painting, and shifting of scenery.

Lighting

New developments in equipment have made the older books on lighting out of date.

Costumes

Costumes of All Nations. London: H. Grevel and Co., 1907. Reprint of *Zur Geschichte der Kostume,* Munich.
No text, but the best general collection of costume plates ever published.
A number of excellent works on special periods also exist. Consult your local library.

Exmouth, Charles Ernest Pellew. *Dyes and Dyeing.* New York: Robert M. McBride and Co., 1928.
Highly readable and the standard work on dyeing.

Pepin, Harriet. *Modern Pattern Design.* New York: Funk & Wagnalls, 1942.
This was written to guide the designer of modern dress patterns, but it is full of valuable ideas for the costume designer and wardrobe mistress.

Make-up

Corson, Richard. *Stage Make-up,* 3rd ed. New York: Appleton-Century-Crofts, Inc., 1960.
An excellent book containing much new material.

Liszt, Rudolph G. *The Last Word in Make-up,* 2nd ed. New York: Dramatists Play Service, 1949.
Contains splendid photographs and a chapter on television make-up.

Theaters

Burris-Meyer, Harold, and Edward C. Cole. *Theatres and Auditoriums.* 2nd ed. New York: Reinhold, 1964.
A valuable contribution to a sadly neglected subject.

INDEX

References printed in boldface type indicate photographic illustrations, drawings, diagrams, charts, or their accompanying captions. When there is more than one text reference to a topic, the principal references are indicated by italics. A few technical terms not covered in the main text are listed, with their definitions.

Index